WE ALL
HEAR VOICES

WHICH ONE ARE YOU FOLLOWING?

ERNIE FOUGERE

D1096830

WE ALL HEAR VOICES
WHICH ONE ARE YOU FOLLOWING?

Table of Contents

FOREWORD

The book We All Hear Voices" is the personal testimony of Ernie Fougere and his journey with the Holy Spirit, through one-on-one encounters. You will catch the heart and spirit of the man, throughout the different chapters of his life. His honesty in sharing his need of salvation and how God built his character and integrity gives you insight into the reality of his journey. There is drama, danger, humour, excitement and truth in each phase.

I have been privileged to know Ernie and his wife Joane over the past thirty-two years. Ernie and I became close brothers in the Lord like a David and Jonathan relationship. It was a joy to watch the Holy Spirit transform his life and marriage and take their family on many exciting adventures.

This book will thrill you, captivate you and enlighten you spiritually. It will produce a hunger in you to get to know the living God on a daily basis for yourself. Your challenge will be, "Will you follow the voice of the Holy Spirit?"

Thank you, Ernie Fougere, for this book and your example. Ernie, my friend.

Alex Florence

ONE

A Shocking Awakening

I was born in a small village in Nova Scotia, Canada, where most of the people were either farmers or fishermen. We owned one of the bigger farms. Work was hard and plentiful year-round for we didn't have the luxury of tractors and combines. We used real "horse power." We woke up early in the morning to milk the cows before eating breakfast and going to school, only to do it all over again after coming home. Gardening and harvesting were backbreaking work as well. From a very young age, we all learned hard work.

My parents came from a very religious Catholic background, having brothers and sisters who were priests and nuns. After supper every evening we would all kneel on the kitchen floor in front of a statue with a lit candle and recite the rosary. It seemed to take forever and if we sat on our legs instead of kneeling properly, we were quickly reprimanded.

One day when I was a young teenager, I was told that a rich relative, an uncle from Montréal, had agreed to pay for me to finish my education at a seminary in New Brunswick. Another uncle named Ernest, a priest himself, told my parents he knew I was chosen and the one in the family that was called to become a priest. His proof was that I was given his name at birth. He had been a priest and told my parents he felt I was the chosen one in the family to follow in his religious footsteps. In our community, every family felt honoured if it had a priest in the family.

I accepted the news fairly well for two reasons. First, my father had a serious problem with alcohol. He was a gentle man, but when he drank, which was becoming most of the time, he turned into a violent person, similar to Dr. Jekyll and Mr. Hyde. It got to the point where I seldom saw him sober. I was concerned what I would do to him if he continued to treat the family the way he did under the influence of alcohol. I could imagine myself doing things that I knew I would regret forever. So I felt it would be good to leave before anything bad happened. The other reason was that all the hard work I had to do on the farm would finally come to an end.

However, I had never ventured more than ten miles from my natal village, so the thought of going to another province scared me for weeks, right up to the day of my departure.

I arrived at my new dwelling at the seminary in New Brunswick and spent many lonely nights crying myself to sleep. How I missed my family and friends back home. Then I remembered that it was really not my decision; I was more or less forced to go. My family had decided what my future would hold for me. They wanted someone from the family to become a priest and I was the chosen one. I really had no say in the matter.

As time progressed during my two years at the seminary, I began to witness things I had never seen before. Strange occurrences were happening between the priests and the brothers and a lot of the students. I tried to figure out what was going on night after night. We students all slept in the same dormitory, which had several adjoining rooms that were occupied by priests and brothers. These supervisors made sure everyone was in bed at a certain time and no one was allowed to make any noise after the lights went out. What was puzzling to me was that there were always students going in and out of the brothers' rooms after lights-out, staying for hours on end. I witnessed this every night. I was awake for hours on end anyway because of my loneliness for my friends at home.

One day, a good friend of mine said he wanted to tell me something. He started sharing how one night in the dormitory he was approached by one of the brothers who asked him to come to his room. He went on to describe things that happened in that room. If he had not been a close friend of mine, I would never have believed what he said. Before being sent back to the dormitory, he was warned never to say a word about this to anyone or there would be grave consequences. In the following days, I began to hear the same horror stories from other students who were also close friends of mine. I couldn't understand how such disgusting things could be going on without anyone in authority doing something about it.

If I'd had any doubts about what my friends said, those stories were soon confirmed. One night I saw a brother heading toward my bed. Whether he was coming for me or not, I didn't know, but I wasn't going to wait and find out. I quickly and quietly slid my pillow under my blankets and hid under my bed. I was there for about five minutes and was glad to discover he did not see where I was hiding. When I crawled back into bed, I noticed an empty bed about four beds away from mine. That boy was the chosen one that night.

The following night, I did the same thing and put my pillow under my blankets. This time, instead of hiding under my bed, I decided to go out for a walk on the beach, which was only a few blocks away. I knew if I was caught, there would be serious consequences but I was coming to the point where I didn't really care. As I walked the beach, I felt such peace. I had time to reflect about what was going on in the dormitory and what I should do. I sure didn't want to sleep there anymore but what choice did I have? No moon was out that night and I walked carefully along the beach in complete darkness. Suddenly, I tripped over what I thought was a large piece of driftwood. A voice said, "Watch where you're walking." I looked toward the sound of the voice and to my utter surprise, I saw one of my teachers, a priest, lying on a blanket, curled up with the secretary of the seminary.

I froze in my tracks, not knowing what to say or do. He looked at me and said, "What are you doing here?"

Without thinking I replied, "What are you doing here?"

He replied, "I'll deal with you in the morning. Make sure you come and see me before you go to class."

As I stumbled back to the dormitory, I wondered who would deal with that priest. Things seemed to be getting worse and worse, leaving me in confusion. What should I do now? I knew pretty well what would happen at his office the next morning.

But that meeting never happened. When I got back to the dormitory, my hands trembling with fear, I packed up all my clothes into my backpack and quietly exited the building.

I knew there was a town about thirty miles away so I headed down the road in that direction. As I was leaving the grounds, I said to myself, "If this is what God is like and he's allowing all of this to happen to me, doing nothing about it, I don't want to know anything more about God." At that moment I rejected him —forever, as far as I was concerned. Anger filled my whole being. I had no idea what was in store for me or my future. This experience had completely devastated me. My hope was shattered.

TWO

Caught Up in the Mob

I walked down the road in a daze until I could walk no more. Suddenly, behind me I heard a semi-truck approaching. I flagged it down to see if it would stop. To my surprise it did. I climbed into the cab, putting my backpack of clothes next to me on the floor. The truck driver immediately started to ask me questions. "What are you doing on the highway at this time of night?"

I didn't want to tell him the truth, so I lied and told him I was going to the city to look for a job and that I had been traveling all day from Nova Scotia. When we arrived just outside the city, he stopped at a truck stop. I got out and thanked him for the lift. I continued walking down the highway towards the city. In about fifteen minutes I saw a park and decided to rest for a while on a bench there. I fell sound asleep and did not wake up until late the next morning.

The realization hit me that I had very little money and would have to find work as soon as possible in order to survive. I could see the city only a short distance away. I walked to the outskirts and noticed a warehouse along the railroad track, "N.B. Wire Fence Co." On a large double door there was a sign that read, "Are you looking for work?"

I was excited to see the sign and immediately went into the warehouse. Walking up to the first person I saw, I told him I was available to work. He said he was just an employee, and pointed

5

to the foreman with whom I should speak. When I approached him, he asked, "Are you available to work right away?"

In one day I had landed my first job in the big city. I thought, *That was easy!* What I didn't know was that the work consisted of unloading 300-pound spools of wire used to make chain link fences. Luckily I knew what hard work was all about. I was used to it, having grown up on the farm. Before I left that day, I explained my financial situation to my foreman and asked if I could get paid cash for the next few days. He answered, "No problem" without hesitation.

He told me he was impressed with the amount of work I had done that day and paid me thirty-two dollars. I felt like a rich man. I walked back to the park and once again slept on the bench. Within a week I was able to rent a small one-room apartment. Now I had some shelter and food to eat. I continued to work at the wire and fence company for months. I knew that my job was secure because most of the employees usually didn't last more than a week. I do have to admit—it was backbreaking work.

Getting an education was of utmost importance for me, so in the months that followed, I worked day shift for a month and went to school at night. The next four weeks I would work night shift and go to school during the day. This made for very long days and one day I decided to let my foreman know that I would be looking for a less strenuous job. When I worked up enough courage to tell him of my decision, he surprisingly offered me a much easier job. It consisted of simply lowering chain-link fences into a vat of green paint and taking them out, hanging them out to dry. All of this was done on a track with a pulley system. It seemed like a picnic and I could hardly wait to go to work every day. Not only was the job much easier but I also received a 20% pay hike. I was finally able to buy a few luxury items such as a toaster and an electric frying pan.

After I'd been a few months in the big city, I thought it would be a good idea to let my mother know what I was doing. I was reluctant to tell her, though, because I didn't know how she would react. I knew she wouldn't be happy that I hadn't let her know before this. No one, including my mother, knew what had happened to me or where I was. One evening, I worked up enough courage to call her. I was amazed to discover that no one at the seminary had told her anything about me. Two weeks after my departure from the seminary, she had called to see how I was doing. She was a little worried about me and wondered why I hadn't contacted the family. I used to keep in touch with them at least once a week because I was so lonely there. They told her I had run away. I briefly explained to her that I had left the seminary for personal reasons but I didn't want to talk about them at this time. I told her where I was, and how I had found a good job and she was happy for me, but curious to know why I had left and couldn't understand why I wouldn't tell her.

I gave her my phone number and asked if she could call me once in a while. I couldn't afford long distance calls on my meagre budget. She understood that and reluctantly accepted my decision to leave the seminary without knowing the details.

Not long after, I received a phone call from my rich uncle in Montréal. My mother had given him my phone number. He told me that she had called him and explained what I was doing. He said he admired me for wanting to continue my education at any cost. My determination to get an education while working every day really impressed him. He then made me an offer I couldn't refuse. He offered to pay all of my living expenses and schooling so I wouldn't have to work another day. He would pay for me to go to college in the city where I was living and after I finished, he asked if I would come and live with him in Montréal and go to university. He wanted to pay for my university education! My uncle and aunt were not able to have children and I believe they thought of me as their son. After I finished college, I moved to Montréal with them and our relationship grew stronger and closer as the years went by. My uncle became the dad I never really had.

Since I was running from God, I was happy that my uncle and aunt were not as strictly religious as my parents were. The only time we went to church was on Easter and then my uncle took us to either a Chinese or Korean Church where the whole service was done in their native language, which even he didn't understand. I often wondered what had happened for them not to be following God or going to church any more, but never had the courage to ask. I wondered if their experience had been as bad as mine. My circumstances had turned around now, like night and day, but God was not involved at all—or so I thought. It was as though he had never been there.

Not long afterwards, my life suddenly took a turn for the worse. After I had left university, I was able to get a very good job with a large oil company called PetroFina. I was working on the eighteenth floor of a high-rise building in the centre of downtown Montréal. As I looked out at the skyline of the city, I felt I was finally on top of the world and my new life could go nowhere but up and up to higher heights. At this new company, I became close to one of my co-workers who worked in an office right next to mine. Often we would talk about our future and our dreams. I could tell that he wanted different things than I did. I wanted to be married to a loving wife, have children and a house of my own, with both of us owning our own cars. He saw himself living in a mansion, surrounded by women and driving expensive automobiles. He thought life should be a continuous party.

After a few months, he began coming to work in tailor-made silk suits. He also started driving an expensive sports car. I knew his salary was the same as mine and wondered how he could afford such luxuries. I thought he must have a rich uncle like I did, but his uncle was obviously a lot richer than mine. As our friendship progressed and his material possessions increased, my curiosity got the best of me. One day I finally asked him, "How can you afford all these things on a salary like ours?"

His answer floored me. He said, "I make more money on weekends working for my uncle than I make here in a whole month."

Soon I worked up enough courage to ask him what his uncle did. He told me his uncle was second in command in the Italian underground world—in other words, the Mafia! In the same breath, as if this were normal, he asked me if I wanted to get involved with him on the weekends for some quick cash.

"I could use some help," he said. "The business is really growing. Our friendship has grown over the months, and I believe you can be trusted. What do you say?"

Without a further thought, I said, "Sure, when can I start?"

He said, "This weekend would be great," then added, "The only reason I'm telling you all this is because for some reason I really believe you can be trusted. You will work directly with me. We will be a team, and split the profits fifty/fifty, right down the middle." He continued, "You have to commit to do this every weekend and I will need to introduce you to my uncle, which we could do tomorrow night at one of his bars. Is it a deal?"

"Let's do it." I had a lot of questions to ask his rich uncle. My friend called him and scheduled a meeting the next day. I was very excited about the whole thing since it seemed that my dreams for my future were about to start. Money would no longer be an issue for me to fulfil my plans.

The meeting the following night proved to be very exciting as far as the money aspect was concerned, but the way it would have to be acquired struck me with fear. I would definitely have to become involved with the underground world in order to make that kind of money. Thoughts raced through my mind: *What if I got caught? What if I got shot? What if my family found out?* But these thoughts vanished when my mind shifted to the money I'd be making.

When his uncle told me that the job we were doing that weekend would be with the help of the police I was baffled. *What are the police doing working with the Mafia?* I had much to learn about the underground world. In the months that followed, I quickly discovered that in order to make a lot of money, you had to learn a brand-new way of living. It was easier with the police on our side. I found out that money talks and makes people do things they would not normally do. The love of money *had* become the root of so much evil in the lives of these people—now including myself—but I wouldn't admit it.

Without going into too many details, in the years that followed one thing led to another and gradually I was in way over my head with no chance of escape. I knew more than I ever wanted about the underground world and fear haunted me every day. Situations were so bad that it became a matter of survival. It was either them or you. The desire to live could make a person do things he would normally not do. These things began to weigh heavily on my conscience to the extent that I knew I would have to do something. I realized that with the amount of information I had acquired over the years, it would be impossible for me to leave with their approval. I knew far too much.

"Shootouts" were a common occurrence between the various gangs. The control of bars and the collection of protection money became more and more dangerous, to the point where we had to "shoot or get shot." I was living in a very different world, completely controlled by greed for money, coupled with the desire to try to stay alive to spend it. On many occasions we had to dodge bullets in nightclub shootouts, not knowing whether we were going to come out alive or if this would be our last collection.

On at least four occasions my life was miraculously spared. Twice my friend was wounded, but not seriously enough to stop working with me on weekends. What was I to do? I knew the names of all the people involved in the Mafia and the names of most of the policemen that worked for them. I knew everything about their operation because of my affiliation with my friend's uncle.

I reached the point where my whole being was taken over by intense fear. It was hell on earth. I was even frightened I might go crazy. I reflected back to my time on the farm and at the seminary and believe me, those times were tame compared to the predicament I was now in. I knew of no way of escape because I risked the chance of being eradicated if I ever dared to leave this wild lifestyle.

After spending sleepless nights for weeks, wondering if there was anything I could do to get out, I felt I had to do something soon or I would regret it for the rest of my life. I didn't even know how long that life would be—a day, a week, a month, a year? I just sensed I needed to do something quickly before it was too late...if it wasn't already too late.

THREE

Running For My Life

In my past years, I had listened to an inner voice that would sometimes speak to me, and things always turned out well when I did what it instructed. Maybe it was time to pay attention to my heart again and act quickly. I had come to a decision. I had to act quickly so I wouldn't be suspected of anything. This would be the boldest act of my life but hopefully it would save my life.

I told my uncle and aunt I would be leaving within a day or so to visit other parts of our vast country of Canada. I said I wanted to take a break from work for a while. I didn't know where I was going but would keep in touch with them. I called the oil company I was working for before I boarded the train and told them I had quit because something had happened beyond my control and asked them to deposit my last pay cheque in my bank account as usual. I bought a one-way train ticket from Montréal to Vancouver. It took me three days to arrive at my destination.

I had lots of cash, so I knew I wouldn't need to find a job for a while. I had a sleeping berth on the train which kept me very private and chose to stay in my berth almost the entire trip. I was afraid if I went to another part of the train, someone might recognize me from my underground night job in Montréal and I wouldn't make it to Vancouver alive. Paranoid, I stayed in my berth all the time, only going to the dining room for food once a day, even though all my meals were included in my train fare.

We had a delay in Winnipeg, where they had to de-ice the brake line because it was -40° C outside. When the train arrived in Vancouver, it was nice and warm compared to the weather in Montréal and the prairies. The first thing I had to do was find a place to live. I didn't want to sign a one-year lease, in case I had to make a sudden departure. I was convinced I was being followed and knew the mob was out to get me.

I ended up living in Vancouver for almost two years on a month-to-month basis. It cost me more for rent because I didn't have a yearly lease but at least I knew I could make a quick getaway if I needed to. I lived all of that time in Vancouver in perpetual fear. It harassed me every day, every minute of the day.

I started to let my hair and beard grow. I thought this might stop "them" (whoever "they" were) from recognizing me, but even that didn't get rid of the fear that haunted me. About six months after arriving in Vancouver, I decided to look for a job I could do at night, preferably in the early morning hours. Most people would be in bed and my chances of being found would be greatly reduced. I secured a job and because of my previous accounting experience with the oil company in Montréal, I was hired immediately. At my previous job I had been "bonded" and this job required I be bonded as well. That was ironic, considering my past underground work. I would be carrying thousands of dollars in cash on a regular basis. An even greater fear set in a few days into the job. Vivid memories that I wanted to forget continually haunted me.

I had to go to the office after working hours and pick up large amounts of cash in different briefcases. These were in a vault to which I had access and each case would have to be delivered to various ships' captains so that they could pay their crewmembers as they arrived at different ports along the Pacific coast in British Columbia. Two of the biggest ship lines were from Japan and I was kept busy a minimum of four days a week, travelling to the various ports and meeting the ships' captains with the cash as the ships arrived. All my work was done at night and into the wee hours of the morning. I saw a lot of sunsets and sunrises in my travels in those days.

I had secured the perfect job for my situation and the pay was very good. But one day I heard that the previous guy who had my job suddenly disappeared. The money he was carrying was never found, but his body was discovered five months later in Idaho. That didn't help my paranoia one bit. I thought, *Maybe that was why I was hired right away. No one else wanted the job.* This resurrected my previous death-defying experiences with the underground world. I began to think the best thing for me to do was to leave and go somewhere else before it was too late. I decided to pack up my clothes once again, buy a car and a tent trailer and start travelling. If I kept on the move it would be harder for me to be found. So I did.

I crossed the border into the U.S.A. where the population was ten times larger than Canada's, thinking it would be easier to hide among all those people. I had never been in the States before so it was kind of exciting. I travelled throughout the western states for about a month, constantly questioning whether I was doing the right thing. I knew I couldn't keep running the rest of my life but I justified my decision by remembering what had happened to others who had tried to leave the underground organization without their permission. In my case, I had been working for the number two boss and knew far too much about their operation to be allowed to leave. The others who tried to leave knew much less than I did and I saw firsthand what happened to them. So I felt my actions were justified. Maybe things would change in the future. I longed for those changes to happen, but in the meantime I would just keep running.

While in Arizona, I recalled that a lot of people from the underground world from New Jersey, New York and Chicago vacationed there and I could possibly have the misfortune of running into them. My fear intensified and I decided to go into Mexico. I was sure no one there would have heard of or seen me before. It sounded like the best place to hide. I had been told that the cost of living was much cheaper and convinced myself it was the right decision. My money would eventually run out but Mexico would allow me to stay longer than anywhere else in North America. So Mexico would become my new home as long as my money held out.

FOUR

Fleeing to Mexico

As I crossed the border into Mexico I noticed something unusual. I waited in one of the three lines to Customs and Immigration and noticed cars leaving the line and going ahead of all the others. They had been approximately fifteen cars behind me in my line, so I thought I would find out what was going on. When I saw another car in front of me trying to manoeuvre out of the line, I got out of the car and went up to him and asked him why people were getting out of the line and going up to the front. He said to me, "If you don't want to stay in line all day in this heat, you just have to pay the customs guy five dollars and he will push you through the line into Mexico."

I realized corruption must be everywhere, including Mexico. Money talks and money can open doors for you, no matter where you live. This episode prepared me for what was in store for me as I travelled in Mexico. I got out of the line, drove up to the front, paid my five dollars and within ten minutes I was across the border.

All around me I saw such poverty that I was shocked, especially in the first small town I drove through. What was I getting into? It had to get better as I drove farther. My gas gauge was nearly on empty so I pulled into the first gas station I saw and started to fill up my car. In Canada and the States it took about $30.00 to fill up my 1963 Valiant convertible, but I knew it would cost me less here in Mexico because everything was cheaper in Mexico, right? As I filled my tank, the price began going over

$40.00 and I started to become concerned. *The difference must be in their currency*, I thought, so continued to fill my car.

The price was soon over $60.00. I stopped and went in to find out why it was so high. But the gas attendant didn't speak English and our communication was not going anywhere. So I took out some American money and showed it to him and he started taking what I owed him for the gas. He took $63.00 and smiled at me. It was no use to try and explain to him that he was ripping me off, because I couldn't explain that my car was usually full at $30.00. I bit my tongue, said nothing and left. I thought, *If I am going to live here, I'll have to learn their language; otherwise I'll lose all the money I have.*

As I approached my car, three small kids were trying to clean my windshield with old dirty newspapers. I also noticed my hubcaps were missing. I got into the car to leave and two of the kids placed themselves in front of it and would not let me move. I glanced in my rear view mirror in order to back up, and there stood another kid with his hand out wanting to get paid for the mess they had made of my windshield. I thought to myself, *These kids must belong to the owner of the gas station who just ripped me off. Like father, like son.* I reached into my pocket and gave them a handful of change. The kids in front of the car came and joined their other friend for a cut of the money and I was able to leave. I was thankful, then looked down and noticed my gas tank was only half full—after paying $63.00! My first day in Mexico was not a very good experience. Things would definitely need to get better.

I continued my journey through villages, towns and cities, bumping into some people who spoke English and was able to get a crash course on what to pay for services and how much they were worth, which saved me a lot of money.

Mazatlán and Puerto Vallarta had many tourists so I spent more time at those places. It was good to be able to communicate with people in English. I even found a tourist who spoke French, which was a real a bonus for me, since it was my native tongue. I had my own accommodations, a tent trailer, and eating was very cheap. However, I knew I couldn't hang around at these tourist locations too long, since underground people could show up there for vacation and someone might recognize me. That would be the end of my time in Mexico. So I travelled on to small towns and villages where tourists never vacationed or visited. I felt safer there.

Even though I was now farther away from Montréal than I had ever been before, the tormenting fear persisted. I realized you can't run away from fear because it follows you everywhere. I constantly ran into situations that reminded me of my past, triggering that awful dread all over again, even though I was thousands of miles away.

I met many tourists on my travels. One in particular insisted I should visit Guadalajara, one of the oldest cities in Mexico. It supposedly held a lot of the history of that country, so I decided to make it part of my trip. I bought a map to see where it was located. Until then I hadn't used a map and just travelled wherever the highway took me. It was the first time I had taken advice from someone. It didn't feel right for some reason but I decided to go anyway. It turned out to be one of the worst experiences of my entire trip.

As I entered the city I was impressed by the many statues and sculptures at seemingly every street corner. I parked my car and trailer along a side street to go see them up closer. As I walked and admired these works of art, I realized I was not familiar with any of the names inscribed on them, so after a dozen or so sculptures and statues, my interest waned and I walked back to the car. Again I noticed the extreme poverty and decided to head towards the downtown area. Downtown had even more sculptures. They seemed to be everywhere. I had been strongly advised not to leave my car and trailer unattended for more than a few minutes, keeping it in my sight at all times. My experience with the hubcaps at the service station at the Mexican border reinforced that advice, so I looked around for a young teenager who had nothing better to do than watch my car. There were many to choose from. It seemed like these young men were all just loafing around. I wondered why none of them were in school.

I went over to one boy who seemed to be less childish than the others and in my broken Spanish asked him if he could watch my car for a few hours. He amazingly understood what I asked and immediately stationed himself on my hood with his back against the windshield. I didn't know how much to pay him because I didn't know how long I would be gone. I took out a few American coins from my pocket and showed them to him and in my again broken Spanish asked him how much he would charge. He pointed to a quarter and smiled. I told him I would pay him after I got back and he seemed OK with that so, in more broken Spanish, I told him if he took good care of my car I would give him three quarters. His face lit up like a light bulb. I then felt confident enough to leave and knew he would take good care of my car.

The next four hours spent in downtown Guadalajara traumatized my life for the next forty years. After that, six months hardly went by without me reliving my terrible experience there. I had nightmares and relived the drama over and over again.

First, I was in shock to see young girls at every street corner, as young as ten years old, prostituting themselves for a few pesos. In some buildings you could see the services they offered in plain view through windows which had their curtains wide open. It was heart-wrenching and I quickly moved on. This continued for blocks and blocks. It was the most degrading sight I had encountered in my whole life.

But what I experienced next was even worse. I noticed three women standing along a busy intersection. They were about forty to fifty feet apart and all had babies strapped to their backs. As I approached the first woman, she stretched out an old rusty tin can to me, begging. I knew if I gave her some money, the other two women would come after me for money as well, so I waved her off. Since I was close to where she was standing I noticed a putrid smell coming from her and tried to go around her. She then turned her back to me to expose her child's head coming out of the cloth that was wrapped around her. To my horror, I saw that the baby had been dead for days and was starting to decompose. This was the tactic these women used in order to get people to give them money.

I couldn't eat for days afterwards and felt sick to my stomach as this scene played through my mind over and over. After this drama, I walked around for hours, oblivious to my surroundings, until I recognized the street where I had parked my car and headed in that direction, hoping it would still be there. I approached my vehicle and noticed that the young teenager was still there and was amazed to find everything looking fine. I gave him a one-dollar bill and he was delighted, smiling from ear to ear as he left.

Now I was very anxious to get out of this place that seemed like hell on earth. I drove for many hours and couldn't get away fast enough. I pondered whether it had been a good idea to come to Mexico in the first place. My emotions were running wild on me.

FIVE

Narrow Escapes

Eventually I found myself in the Durango Mountains of Mexico, a place where the Aztec Indians lived. I was told they were the first people to settle in Mexico. I learned they used to offer human sacrifices to their gods, one of them being the sun god. These sacrifices were performed on specially-constructed altars. My curiosity got the best of me and I wanted to see these people. As I entered their area I noticed a lot of dead animals along the roadway. They all looked bloated as though someone had pumped air into them. I thought they must have been hit by trucks that travelled those back roads on a daily basis. Thick vegetation grew on both sides of the narrow road. The roads didn't seem to have any ditches so it was easy for me to pull off to the side when I saw trucks approaching me at breakneck speeds. I also noticed a lot of wild dogs feeding on the dead carcasses.

The area seemed like a deserted no-man's-land and I wondered if I had done the right thing by going there. What if there were no gas stations and I became stranded? What if these Aztec people were not civilized and didn't want me there? I hadn't brought much food with me because of the heat. What if I ran out of it? What about my water supply? All these questions flashed across my mind. After pondering my situation I decided I would go on for an hour or so to see what was ahead, making sure I at least had enough gas to turn around and go back if this situation worsened.

Within fifteen minutes I noticed some civilization. I saw some Aztec Indians butchering an animal by the side of the road. There must have been a dozen of them and they were all taking a portion of the meat back into the bush in mesh-like bags. Blood dripped everywhere. I couldn't tell what kind of animal it was they had killed since it had already been skinned and cut up into pieces, small enough for each individual to carry home. I watched them from afar, nervous at the thought what they might do if I approached them. I stayed parked along the road for thirty minutes and in that length of time, they all disappeared into the bush. The carcass was then taken over by wild dogs and vultures. This was my strange initiation to the Aztec people.

The sun was starting to set and as I rounded a turn I noticed a small black and white road sign that announced a village up ahead. I don't remember the name, only that it started with the letter "X." I could see it was a small village with only a few buildings along the highway. People were walking along the road carrying firewood and various other things on their heads. Suddenly several wild dogs attacked and started biting the tires on my car and tent trailer. I thought they must be mad and infected with some kind of disease. Not wanting to deal with a flat tire, I accelerated, running over one of them in my hurry. I looked out my rear view mirror and saw it lying motionless on the road. I thought, *That will be one less wild dog they will have to contend with.*

What happened next completely horrified me. The minute the people saw that I had killed a wild dog, they blocked the road in front of me, while others hurried away, coming back with machetes, knives, clubs and anything else they could find. These weapons were handed out to various people on the road. They started coming towards me waving their weaponry in the air. I was only about 150 feet from this horde and they were closing in on me. I didn't know what to do. They were all screaming as they approached my car. Since it was a narrow road and I was pulling a

22

tent trailer there was no way I could turn around fast enough to high-tail it out of there. What was I to do? Their actions told me they meant business and it was an ugly scene. The first thing that came to mind was to accelerate and make believe I was going to run them down. As I approached them they did not budge and by now they were right in front of my car, so what could I do? The answer came quickly as a knife blade pierced through my rag top, right next to my left ear. Others banged their weapons all over my car and tent trailer. Instinctively I accelerated to get out. My life was in grave danger. It was them or me.

Within seconds no one was left in front of the car and as I sped down the road, I could see in my rear view mirror that I had seriously wounded or maybe even killed a few of them as they lay on the road. People were still running after me with their weapons in hand. Finally they were out of sight. Then I started to panic. What if they reported me to the police and had gotten my license plate number? I would make headlines in the news and my whereabouts would be made known to the world, including the Mafia mob that I was convinced were still looking for me.

What if I was put in jail? I had heard of horror stories of people being put in Mexican jails for years and years, forever asking bribe money from relatives to get them out, but never being released because the jailors kept wanting more money. My time in Mexico was getting worse by the day. I was now convinced I had made a terrible decision in going there. After this horrifying experience, I drove until I came to a gas station. It was late at night and I parked there, waiting for it to open in the morning. I couldn't go any farther anyway; I was almost completely out of gas. It gave me time to think about my situation and try to figure out the next best thing to do. After filling up the car with gas the following morning, I decided I would go to the nearest police station and ask them some questions about these Aztec people and their behaviour. I knew enough Spanish now to make myself understood.

I drove around until I found a police station. In order for the police not to misunderstand what had happened, I decided to ask them if there was someone who spoke English or at least understood it well enough for me to explain my situation. The person on duty did not know any English at all. I made him understand enough to ask if there was an officer on their staff who did speak and understand English well. There was, but he was on call in another village. I was told he would be back at the office around noon. It was now nine o'clock, which meant I would have a three-hour wait. That didn't matter. I just wanted to get this thing settled once and for all. It had tormented me all night and stopped me from getting any sleep so I was very tired. For the next three hours I tried to figure out how I was going to explain the whole mess to them. It crossed my mind many times that maybe I should just leave and forget the whole thing. But what if they found me, locked me up in jail and threw away the key? No one would ever hear about me or know where I was. Negative thoughts bombarded me. How could anything positive come out of this? Nevertheless, I opted to stay and soon the policeman arrived back in his cruiser, half an hour early. Reality clicked in and I was extremely fearful. I gave him enough time for the other policeman to explain my situation about not being able to communicate properly in Spanish. Soon he was at the door signalling me to come in. The moment of truth had arrived. There was no backing down now. I was sweating profusely as I entered the building but it wasn't because of the heat. I was very nervous about what I had done.

I explained the whole episode to him in detail and when I finished talking, he said, "This is not the first time this has happened. This problem has existed for years. They worship wild dogs as their gods. They are called *dingos*, and if anyone kills them they believe that person must die. You were very lucky to escape alive. Many Mexicans have not been as lucky as you. This small group of people has caused us problems for years. We don't get involved in their affairs, but thank God they are not all like that. Other Aztec Indians across Mexico are, for the most part, peaceful people. I wouldn't be too concerned about the whole thing, but I strongly suggest you don't return that way. They are known to take the law into their own hands and settle scores their way."

When he said that, it was as if a huge boulder had been lifted off of my back. I was a free man. I left the police station thinking, *This is the best day of my life.* Joy enveloped me. I realized I had done the right thing; otherwise this episode would have been just another memory to plague me and play havoc with my mind. My plate was already full and overflowing. I had to stay focused on why I was here in Mexico. I picked up some canned food and water and started back on the road again.

With this awful experience behind me, I drove until I came upon a huge waterfall. I could see it from the road and found a small path-like road and turned onto it. It brought me right to the base of the waterfall. No one was around. It was the most beautiful place I had ever seen. Birds were singing and fruit and berries were available for the picking. I stayed there for six days and never saw a single person. I wanted to stay there forever but my food was running out. You can only eat so many berries. So I packed up my things, closed up my tent trailer and once again was back on the road. I'd had a good time of rest and relaxation. The peace I felt at the waterfall was refreshing to my soul and I hoped I would spend many more hours in the Durango Mountains. But soon I came to a busy highway. A sign ahead of me said I was heading to Mexico City. It would take days to get there but the thought of visiting the largest city in Mexico was exciting. Time was on my side. Time was one thing I had a lot of. Money was quite another thing. It was slowly disappearing on food and gas. Who knew what was waiting for me around the next corner? The peace I had experienced at the waterfall was still on me, and I felt as if I had no worries in the world. I knew that wasn't reality, but decided to enjoy it while it lasted.

I finally arrived in Mexico City and headed into the downtown area. I noticed that traffic lights didn't mean anything to the drivers, especially the taxis. They went through intersections regardless whether the light was green, yellow or red. Within the first few minutes I came very close to running into several cars. It didn't take me too long to understand their driving habits. I decided, *If you can't beat them, then join them.* That way I would at least stay alive longer. It was complete chaos but I somehow survived without getting into an accident.

As I approached a large hotel, a thought suddenly came to me from nowhere that someone must be protecting me from these wild, maniac drivers. I pulled into the parking lot of the hotel and noticed there weren't many cars, so it was easy for me to find a double parking stall for my car and trailer. It looked like an expensive place so I was sure they would have real American and Canadian food available. What a treat that would be—real food for a change. Several people stared at me as I walked in. I had a long beard and long hair and was dressed in a dirty T-shirt and cut-off jeans. I wanted to get to the food as soon as possible, but instead of directing me to the dining room area, they asked me to sit at the bar. It didn't matter to me, as long as I was served the food I was craving. Glancing at the menu, I instantly saw exactly what I wanted and had longed for, a juicy steak with baked potatoes and a cold beer. It was my dream come true. As I was enjoying my steak and beer, I was interrupted by a well-dressed lady who came up to me and asked if I would mind her sitting next to me. Plenty of seats were available around the bar. My shabby clothes and hair completely clashed with her appearance. I noticed she had a French accent, from Quebec, not from France. Why was she interested in me? I soon found out.

She said, "I noticed the license plate on your car as you pulled up in the parking lot. You're from Canada, are you not?"

Of course I couldn't deny it, and answered, "Yes, from Western Canada." Was she hired by someone to find me? Fear gripped me as I thought of where she might be from. Was she part of the underground world I came out of in Montréal? I asked her what part of Quebec she was from and her answer appeased my fear. She said she had been living in Mexico City for years but visited Canada once in a while for business.

"Are you going back to Canada soon and are you by any chance able to go through Quebec on your way back?" she asked.

I answered, "I don't know when I will be returning to Canada. I might keep going to South America, now that I am in Mexico."

Immediately she replied, "They are not letting anyone through Panama into South America at this time."

I didn't know why that was the case and I didn't care if I knew right then; I just wanted to get her out of my space at the bar.

However, she said something that caught my attention. "If you decide to go back to Canada within the next month or so and you are willing to go through Quebec I have a good business proposition for you that could make you a sizeable amount of cash. Here is my card. You can get in touch with me at any time here at the hotel. I live here. I have a sister in Quebec and I need someone to take her a package. I can't trust the postal system and need to make sure the package is delivered to her personally by hand. Think about it and let me know if you are interested. We can talk about it further, once I know you are willing to help me with this delivery."

Since my money supply was running low, I didn't dismiss the idea and told her I would think about it and get back to her. She agreed and left. When I finally finished my meal and asked the bartender for the bill, he told me some lady had taken care of it. I didn't have to guess who that person was and was glad the bill was taken care of—a bill, I might add, that was really beyond my means. As I left, I pondered the conversation I'd had with her. I needed to think about it before making a decision. I was sorry I hadn't asked her what she was willing to pay me but I had her card and if I decided to go ahead with it, she would surely tell me. She probably wouldn't tell me, though, until she received my commitment to do it for her.

After three days contemplating whether I would take her up on her offer or not, for some strange reason, I began to have a desire and a longing to go back to Canada, specifically Montréal. It certainly didn't make sense. I would be going back to the same place I had been running from for more than two years. It seemed ludicrous, yet that desire grew stronger and stronger during the next three days. Now I was confused.

Then out of the blue came a thought: *They would never look for you in Montréal. They know you were smart enough to get out of town, never to return.* For some reason it made some sense to me and the desire became even stronger. What was going on? I decided to look for a phone booth to call this lady. Within half an hour I had scheduled an appointment with her at the same place we had met before. We would meet at noon the next day and maybe she would even buy me a nice lunch again, the kind I couldn't afford.

That night as I lay on my bed, I realized I couldn't keep running all my life. I also really needed money since my reserves were quickly drying up. All these circumstances were combining to make my decision to go back to Montréal easier to accept, regardless of what could happen after I returned. I had a peace about it and felt deep inside that everything would be all right. Montréal was a huge city and I rationalized that if I lived on the other side of town I would be safe from the underground world. All the action and crime were concentrated on the east side of town and downtown. I would make sure I lived far from those places to avoid bumping into any old acquaintances. I would stay inside at night wherever I chose to live and not chance bumping into anyone I knew at night when all the underground business took place. Feeling good about it, I finally fell asleep. The next morning when I woke up, I still had a great peace about it all and prepared to go see this lady. My curiosity was getting the best of me.

I arrived at the hotel ten minutes early. She was already sitting at the bar waiting for me. She had a menu in one hand and a drink in the other. I recognized her right away because she was wearing exactly the same clothes as the previous time I had met her. I wondered if she had done this on purpose to make it easier for me to recognize her. I didn't ask. She offered to buy me lunch, which was great, and again I chose something I couldn't afford. Next to her purse on the bar I noticed a round cylinder about two feet long and four inches in diameter. She immediately came to the point with regards to our rendezvous. It looked like there might be some prints in this cylinder that she wanted to sell. She asked me what my decision was and when I told her I would be going back to Montréal she smiled from ear to ear. I continued my conversation with her about not leaving for another couple of weeks, since I still wanted to visit a few other cities before I left Mexico. At that, her smile disappeared. She seemed eager to speak so I let her talk.

She said, "Here's the deal. I want you to bring this cylinder to my sister who lives on a small island near Montréal, called Nuns' Island. I will pay you $1000.00 for your troubles, $250.00 when you leave and my sister will pay you the balance when she has the package in her hands. Is this a deal?"

The sum of money made me say yes immediately, without thinking about anything else that should have been of importance for me to consider.

She said, "Very well, give me a call when you get back here and I'll give you the package and the $250.00. You know where I live. I'm not planning to go anywhere in the next thirty days."

As I travelled over the many miles, I kept wondering where this bizarre idea of returning to Montréal had come from. I couldn't figure it out so tried to dismiss it out of my mind.

However, the closer I got to the date of my departure, that strong fear started to come back. I started to drink heavily, thinking this would cause me to forget what was about to happen. The only thing I could afford was cheap Tequila. One evening I met up with some Mexicans in the camp ground where I was staying. They had guitars and lots of Tequila and invited me to a party they were having that night. We started drinking early that afternoon and the next morning I found myself in a pool of blood on the floor of my tent trailer. My recollection of that evening was completely gone. The only thing I remembered was being attacked by some wild dogs on the way back to my tent trailer. I tried to fight them off but to no avail. Somehow I must have been able to reach the trailer on my own. I couldn't believe the amount of blood I had lost and the wounds I had on my face and neck. It frightened me but somehow I managed to leave the campground and drive myself to the hospital. On the way there, I had to stop several times, since I felt so dizzy I thought I would pass out. Blood covered my face and clothes and when I arrived at the hospital it didn't take them long to find me a doctor. They must have thought I would die at any moment. I remember them giving me a tetanus shot and starting to clean my wounds. I must have passed out, because I woke up all clean and wearing a gown. When I finally left the hospital I decided that cheap Tequila would no longer touch my lips. That stuff was dangerous. I could have died that night. I had learned my lesson.

Sad to say, my drinking continued, but this time I told myself I would control the quantity I drank. That way I wouldn't experience a disaster like I had the last time, ending up in the hospital. The constant fear of returning to Montréal was what was causing me to drink heavily. Not only was I drinking daily now, but people also introduced me to marijuana, which was plentiful everywhere in Mexico for a very cheap price. It was called Acapulco Gold and I started liking the effect it had on me. It would completely take away any fear I had and cause me to be hilariously happy. With the combination of marijuana and Tequila I often did not remember the next morning what had transpired the night before. This concerned me but my concern was overruled and this behaviour went on day after day. I thought I had finally found a way to eliminate the fears that had plagued me all these years. The only problem was that they would return the next morning after the effects wore off. I then began to smoke it during the day, but found it would cause me to be careless when driving.

Another thing that concerned me was what would happen if I was caught by the police while driving. In all the months I had been in Mexico, I had never been stopped by the police. That concern was drowned by my drinking and smoking as I drove from village to village. I was enjoying my freedom from fear so this way of life continued until I was ready to call the lady and pick up her package at the hotel for delivery in Montréal. I didn't want her to see me drunk or high when I did the pickup so I stayed sober that day. We arranged a time to meet, the exchange would be done and I would be on my way.

I realized my finances were quite low because of all of my drinking and smoking in the weeks I was gone travelling. The $250.00 she was about to pay me would help me continue this lifestyle and make me forget my fears on my way to Montréal. I arrived fifteen minutes early and sat in the lobby to wait for her. When the time came for her arrival, she was nowhere to be seen. I walked throughout the lobby and into the bar area but she was not there. While waiting, I began wondering what was actually in the package. It must be something valuable for her to pay me that kind of money. My curiosity now made me decide that when she arrived I would ask her the contents before agreeing to leave with it. This thought had barely been on my mind a few seconds when she walked into the lobby from the elevator. It had completely slipped my mind to ask the reception her room number when she was not showing up. But it didn't matter now. Here she was, cylinder in hand, walking towards me. She greeted me as she glanced at me sitting there, and said, "Follow me"—not even a "Forgive me for being late."

I went with her and when we arrived in the parking lot she asked me where I was parked. I pointed in the direction of my car and she followed me. When she got to my car she seemed to be nervous about something, continually glancing around the parking lot. I asked her if she had the money and she said yes. My next question seemed to make her very frustrated and angry. I asked her what was in the package and she became very defensive towards me.

She said, "What's in the package is none of your concern; your only concern is to deliver it to my sister for the amount of money we agreed upon. I have already lost several weeks in the delivery of this package because of your travelling around."

I could see fear on her and easily recognized it, because I had lived with it myself for so long. As she handed the package over to me and gave me the money in an envelope, an inner feeling of caution suddenly came all over me. I didn't understand, but I instinctively knew I was not to take the package and she would have to find someone else.

I didn't want to tell her this, but before I knew it, it was coming out of my mouth and I couldn't stop it, even though I wanted to. Something strange was going on that I didn't understand. What happened next was downright bizarre.

She went completely crazy on me, grabbed the package and the envelope of money out of my hands and started hitting me with her handbag. She dropped the package and the money on the ground and started kicking and scratching me like a wild cat. As this was happening, she was swearing at me in French and I was sure I heard every swear word that existed in the French language. Although this only went on for a few minutes, it seemed like an eternity. People were coming toward us to see what all the commotion was about and when she saw them, she stopped, picked up her package and ran back into the hotel, still swearing for all to hear.

I'd had many strange experiences in my travels, but this one was sure different. What I asked hit a nerve and she completely lost control. As I stood next to my car in the parking lot, bleeding from the facial scratches I had received, I also noticed there were more scratches on my arms and I was bruised on my shins. She had viciously attacked me. I glanced down at my feet and saw she had forgotten about the envelope of money on the ground. I guessed that everything that had just happened to me was not all bad! I still had the money and quickly left before she realized her mistake and came out once again. As I sped away from the parking lot, I was glad I had received a tetanus shot at the hospital the previous month. I wouldn't need another one now. I replayed in my mind what had just happened, not knowing which attack was worse, the wild dogs' or hers and chuckled to myself as I tried to find my way out of the city. Now the pain of my bruises was really starting to hurt and I knew I would have to find a drugstore to buy antiseptic to apply to my wounds. I opened the envelope as I was driving. Sure enough, there in the envelope were five crisp $50.00 bills. Somehow that eased my pain.

SIX

Rescued By That Voice

For the next few days, what had happened to me in the parking lot troubled me. *Why did I say to her that I didn't want to deliver the package and that she would have to find someone else? Why was I not able to stop myself from saying it?* It was as if something took over my tongue and made me say something I had no intention of saying. It was very disturbing. In order to get it out of my mind, I convinced myself it must be all the booze and drugs I had been taking over the last weeks that were getting to my brain and making me say things. So, for the next few days I eased up on my drug intake, in case it was the culprit.

Because drugs, especially marijuana, were so cheap in Mexico, I decided I would stock up before I left. It would bring me a very hefty profit in Montréal and support me as I looked for a job and an apartment. Finding the drugs was a piece of cake, since you could buy it anywhere you went, especially on the beaches and in all the bars. I wanted a large quantity so was able to purchase it at a premium price. Now I was ready to head for the border. On my travels there, people were inviting me to eat with them at various campgrounds along the way. This had never happened to me before but I was very glad about it since it was saving me a lot of money on food and water. Things seem to be getting better the closer I got to the border, but I forced myself not to get too excited about it, because my past experiences had shown me that things can quickly change without any apparent reason.

For the next few weeks I travelled slowly toward the U.S. border. I tried to follow the coast as much as possible and camp along the ocean. The sunsets and sunrises were spectacular. I decided to cross at the Brownsville, Texas border entrance. When I was about two miles from the border, the same strange feeling that had happened to me in the parking lot with the woman in Mexico came all over me again. Only this time it seemed to me much stronger than the last time. An inner voice, for a lack of a better explanation, strongly commanded me to get rid of the drugs I had bought before crossing the border. I sensed that if I didn't, something disastrous would happen to me. It was so real, I pulled over to the side of the road to figure it out. Something was happening to me that I didn't understand. Again I rationalized that it must be all the drugs I was smoking that were starting to affect my mind, but that didn't make sense since I had not smoked any dope for days.

I had hardly brought the car to a halt alongside the road when I felt a huge urgency to get rid of the drugs. It was so strong that I got out of the car, opened my trunk, took out my stash and flung it into the field next to the road as far as I could throw it. *I must be going crazy*, I thought. I immediately wanted to cross the fence, go back and pick it up but knew it would not be the right thing to do, so got into my car and left quickly before I could change my mind. As I drove away, for some reason, deep inside I knew I had done the right thing and a peace came over me even though I had just thrown away a lot of potential cash that I would desperately need once I got back to Canada.

My thoughts started drifting back to other incidences I had encountered on my travels so I pulled over to the side of the road once again because it was starting to affect my driving. I couldn't keep my mind on what I was doing. I remembered the episode with the wild dogs and the Aztec Indians and how I just knew I had to go to the police about it. Did that make sense? I remembered how I survived the drunken night without dying in my tent, waking up in a pool of blood. Somehow I knew all this was related to what was going on in my mind now, but it still didn't make sense. Nothing was making sense anymore. What was happening to me? As I pondered these things, I entered the road once again and was finally ready to cross the border.

I was in for the shock of my life.

As I approached the line-up to enter into the States, a sheriff came up to my window and told me to get out of the line and park my vehicle along a wall. I had hardly stopped when about half a dozen sheriffs pulled up beside me with two German Shepherd dogs, their guns out of their holsters pointing directly at me. They didn't think I was obeying their command to get out of the car fast enough so they yanked me out and shoved me over to stand facing against a wall. When I tried to turn around to see what was going on, they shouted at me, swearing and telling me not to do that again. I knew they must be searching my car and suddenly realized what a great idea it had been to get rid of the drugs a few minutes before.

I could hear some of their conversation and at one point heard one of them say, "We will finally catch that woman with this evidence and lock her up once and for all."

I thought, *What woman? I am by myself.* Then I remembered the woman with the package in Mexico City. How could I forget? Maybe the police in Mexico had seen me with her and now were looking for her package in my car. The police were dressed in different uniforms so I knew I was being searched by both Mexican and U.S. law officers.

It started to rain heavily but they would not let me take shelter or turn around. Other bits of their conversation came to my ears. "Take out the back seat, check the tires, strip the tent trailer, check his suitcase." They had me stand there for at least an hour, by which time I was completely drenched. Finally they all approached me and asked me what I had done with the package I had been given. I explained to them what had happened and how I had refused to take the package.

What I heard next was music to my ears. "OK, you're free to go." As they all departed I overheard them say, "We'll catch that b-- yet. She must be getting desperate and running out of money to have these gems delivered. It's obvious she'll try and use anybody to make the delivery." It sounded like they were surprised that she would use the likes of me.

I turned around to leave and could hardly believe my eyes. My car was totally torn apart. Tires were off the rims, seats were on the ground, my clothes were all over the ground covered in mud; my tent trailer camping equipment was scattered everywhere. A closer look also revealed that parts of the motor were on the ground. Under the front of the car was my air filter and cover. When it had started raining they didn't even have the decency to close my ragtop, so the car floor inside was completely soaked along with everything else.

When I saw this mess, I went inside to complain about the devastation. It looked like a hurricane had hit my car. The answer I was given was that the border sheriffs had all left and I would have to deal with it the best way I could. I told them I couldn't move the car and they handed me a business card of a towing company in Brownsville, Texas that I could call. I asked them if they could call for me. They handed me a phone to make my call.

Half an hour later a flatbed tow truck arrived. I'd had enough time to pick up my muddy clothes, camping equipment and all the other pieces lying all over the ground. I threw everything into the tent trailer and closed it up. I was quite concerned that I wouldn't have the money to pay the tow truck company, but figured I would deal with that when the time came. I was told the vehicle would not be ready until the next morning, so I unhitched my tent trailer from the car and stayed in the parking lot of the towing company.

I tried to sleep that night but everything in my tent trailer was wet and so were my clothes. Somehow I managed to get a few hours' sleep. I couldn't believe the way I had been treated and was thinking of reporting them. Then I wondered whom I would report them to? I didn't have a clue, so I shook my head, sighed and dropped the idea.

By noon the next day my car had been put back together again. Now the thing I dreaded was upon me. How much would it cost me? Did I have enough money? When they told me the price, I knew I was in trouble. The price was far more than I could pay, so I asked to see the manager. They took me to the owner and he asked me to come with him to his office. He closed the door behind him, sat down on the other side of the desk and said, "What happened to you and your car?"

I sat there for at least fifteen minutes and told him the whole story. As he let me talk, I couldn't help noticing the large cross he had around his neck. In my upbringing as a child in the Catholic Church, I knew about the cross and what it represented. When I stopped talking, I also mentioned to him that the cross he was wearing around his neck reminded me of the guy who had gone to the cross and how he was falsely accused of something he had not done. I told him I now understood a little better how he must have felt because I had just been falsely accused of something I had not done.

When I finally shut up, the owner looked me over and said, "That's quite the story and I want you to go on your way in peace. I'll take care of the bill." Suddenly tears welled up in my eyes, a thing which had never happened to me before. Whatever was happening to me? First, hearing an inner voice and now tears.

I left the lot around 1:00 p.m. I had been wise enough to spread out my clothes in the sun and they were all dry. Maybe I wasn't losing my mind after all. I realized that this inner voice had not only saved me from jail with the lady's package, but also jail time for the drugs, had I left them in my car. Maybe I should pay more attention to it. It seemed to know what was going to happen in the future. Even though I found it confusing, it did keep me from a lot of trouble. I couldn't understand why the owner of the towing company would cover my costs either. Was it because of what I said or was it something else that caused him to do this unbelievable thing? I had many unanswered questions brewing.

SEVEN

Home Again at Last

It took me days to drive from Texas to the Canadian border. I can't explain why, but I was very happy to be going back to Montréal. A few years before, I sure would never have returned there. I drove many hours and long days, having lots of time to think about my life. A lot of it I wanted to forget. Where was my tumultuous past going to lead me in the future?

The closer I came to the Canadian border the better I felt about returning after such a long time away. The rest of my trip was uneventful—a welcome change. When I finally arrived at the border, I knew that I would have to repair the ragtop roof of the car, which had been cut in the Durango Mountains back when I had had my encounter with the Aztec Indians. It would have to be a quick and cheap fix, however, because money was quickly disappearing, so I opted for good old duct tape, which did the trick and waterproofed my vehicle.

As I finally entered Montréal, it was raining and snowing at the same time. *Good old Canadian weather,* I thought, chuckling to myself. I was so glad to be back that the weather was actually refreshing. All the hot weather in the past months was far behind me now. Happiness filled my soul. What was amazing was that the fear I had been running away from for the past two years was no longer there. I couldn't even pinpoint when it had left me. It could have disappeared gradually or instantly, I didn't remember.

I wasn't about to try and figure it out or look for it; I was just thrilled it was out of my life, once and for all…I hoped.

My first phone call was to my rich uncle to let him know I was back in town. I had kept in touch with him several times on my travels to let him know I was fine. He immediately invited me to stay at his home again if I so desired. Within thirty minutes I was at his doorstep. When he answered the door he took a second look to see if it was really me because my hair and beard were so long. He invited me in, but I could tell he didn't like the hair or the beard. I stepped in the house and realized I would be sleeping in a real bed, something I had not done for months. It took several days for me to recuperate from the long hours of driving and I slept twelve hours each night. What a thrill to experience real home-cooked food and a comfortable bed again. I'd had neither for the longest time.

Now that I was back in Canada, I didn't want to live alone the rest of my life, so the thought of marriage and settling down started coming to mind. I would definitely keep my eyes open for the right girl. Friendships with the opposite sex for the past years had been few and far between. It was definitely time for a change.

Within a few days I had sold my car and tent trailer and now had some disposable cash, which quickly went to buy new clothes, shoes, etc. I would have to look for employment in order to present myself properly, not with the rags I had worn in the past months. Cut-off jeans, sandals, and t-shirts would not do for an interview. I was starting a new life once again. Hopefully this one would be more positive and fulfilling.

My first interview was with a multi-national company, established in over eighty countries. It was a huge company and if I mentioned its name, most would recognize it. I trimmed my beard somewhat and styled my long hair; I thought it looked good on me. I was in for a surprise when I had my first interview. They said I had all the qualifications for the position and the right education to be able to do the job and offered me the position within ten minutes. But there was one condition. I would have to shave my beard and cut my hair. We compromised. I kept my long hair in a ponytail and changed my beard to a goatee. They were satisfied and told me I could start work in six days.

I worked seven years with this multi-national company and received nine promotions. I was being promoted into positions that other employees were sure they would receive because of their seniority, but I got them instead. This made me a few enemies. The company loved my work and whenever a new position came up, no matter what department it was, I was qualified for the job. Every time I applied, I was chosen. It came to the point where I could pick and choose whatever job I wanted. I thought I was the luckiest guy on earth. Positions were even available to me across Canada and around the world. It was a fantastic company to work for and I enjoyed every minute of it.

One day a girl caught my eye. I thought she was one of the most beautiful girls I had ever seen but she was different than the others. She caught my heart. I wanted to be with her the rest of my life. I rationalized that that would be impossible since I was convinced she would not have any interest in me. So instead of talking to her and trying to get a date with her, I would walk by her desk every morning as I went to my office just to have a look at her. Maybe one day she would show some interest in me as I passed her desk. She was working on the first floor of the building and I worked on the second floor on the opposite side of the building. Every morning I looked forward to making that detour just to see her. It made my day. Much to my disappointment, she never showed any visible interest in me.

When I got my eighth promotion, I was more nervous than ever, not because of the promotion, but because this girl I had been admiring all these years and secretly visiting every morning would now become my new secretary. Could this actually be happening to me? Now we had no choice but to talk to each other. My heart pounded just thinking about it. *I must be in love,* I thought. Nothing like this had ever happened to me before. I was to take over the position in one more week, the longest week of my life.

I couldn't wait to speak to her—about business, of course. I didn't think we had anything else to talk about, but my heart certainly felt drawn. I had so much to say to her, but knew she would not be interested so brushed all those thoughts aside, just being happy that I would be close to her every day. Maybe during our time together she would miraculously show some interest in me. Time would tell. I couldn't wait to find out.

The day I started my new position I was dressed to the hilt, shoes shined, wearing half a bottle of men's cologne. It was time to make a good impression on her. When I arrived at my new office, the first question I asked was, "Where is my new secretary?"

What I heard was absolutely devastating. I was told she was in the personnel office getting her last paycheque. Unbeknownst to me, she had resigned her position as secretary and was moving on to become an office manager of a new company that had offered her a job. It was a national company and a very lucrative promotion for her so she had accepted it. I was convinced she had quit her position as secretary as soon as she had found out I would become her boss. My suspicions had been right all along; she would never have any interest in me. I was broken-hearted and wanted to quit my job. I couldn't think straight and the same confusion started coming back on me that I had experienced on my travels. Life was not fair. Just when you thought everything would change for the better, there was nothing but disappointment.

Whenever an employee left, the company always held a farewell luncheon for him or her and everyone in that department would get together to say goodbye. The farewell luncheon was a smorgasbord at a very popular local restaurant and usually lasted an hour or so. I thought I would go since they had invited me as a new employee of that department. That would give me enough time to get drunk and forget what had just happened to the girl of my dreams. I left work early and arrived at the restaurant before everyone else. I had time for several drinks. As people arrived for the luncheon I joined them in line for the meal. Without any food in my stomach, the drinks were starting to take effect. To my surprise, the person who came in line right behind me was none other than the girl who was supposed to have become my secretary. With a few drinks under my belt, I was finally able to drum up enough courage to talk to her for the first time. Joy suddenly came back. Here we were side by side. It felt so right. To this day I don't remember what we talked about, but that was all it took to make my day. My heart pounded in my chest. Whether it was out of fear or love, I don't know, probably a little of both.

But one thing I do know, we have been talking now for some forty years, because that special girl, Joane, became my wife. One thing led to another and by the end of the luncheon, we had agreed to meet later that evening. Everything changed so fast. We met that evening after work, alone, and had so much to talk about. It seemed like I couldn't shut up. I found out things I didn't know about her feelings for me and told her how I felt about her. We had both kept silent up until now and discovered we had both been wrong about each other.

For the next two years Joane and I met almost every day. We made new friends, most of them married, but soon discovered they all flirted with others and even cheated on each other. Our relationship was much different. We didn't have eyes or a desire for anyone else. We were very faithful to each other and eventually decided to move in together.

We soon owned our own home, situated on a small island not far from Montréal, as well as two new vehicles. We were young, had everything money could buy but we also possessed what money could not buy—our love and faithfulness for each other. Not too long after we had moved in together, we both wanted to have children so decided to get married before the Justice of the Peace. Not wanting a big traditional wedding, we said our vows in front of only a few family members. Marriage would make our union legal in the eyes of the law and now we would have children together.

The truth was that we had more than a legal contract as husband and wife; we had actually made a covenant to stay together for the rest of our lives, a covenant before God that could not be broken. Our marriage was not just on paper; our marriage was written on our hearts, because of our true love for each other.

I kept working for the same company and my new bride worked as a manager at her job. Soon I was offered my ninth promotion. This one meant we would have to move to Western Canada if I accepted the promotion. Before I had been in sales and responsible for the customers in New Brunswick, Nova Scotia, Prince Edward Island, and Newfoundland—the Maritime provinces. I developed the territory, increased sales and found new customers. It was a large area and I drove to the Maritimes for a week once every six weeks.

I loved the job because I loved to travel and it took me out of Montréal and far from the possibility of meeting some of the people from my past in the underground world. I learned that in the years I had been gone, the friend I worked with at the oil company was now in jail and most of the top Mafia bosses were either killed or serving a life sentence in prison. I was extremely grateful I had escaped, even when getting out could have cost me my life.

The hardest part of my job was having to travel away from Joane and this influenced my decision to accept the offer when the position became available in Western Canada. I would be responsible to develop a brand new division of the company and become General Manager for all of Western Canada. I was considered for the promotion because of the way I had developed and increased sales in the Maritimes. They were very satisfied with my performance. The new territory would be a much bigger responsibility, which made me somewhat nervous, but just the fact they had considered me for the position was an honour. My new office and warehouse would be located in Calgary, Alberta. I had never lived there, only passed through years ago when I was fleeing by train to Vancouver.

Joane and I now had two children, a boy and a girl, the oldest being eighteen months old. We would be selling our home and cars, leaving our friends and family, to begin a new life on our own in a new place. It seemed overwhelming even to me. I was concerned whether Joane would accept or even entertain the possibility of moving. This would be the biggest decision we had made as a couple. The promotion would be my largest ever, monetarily. The company promised to sell our house in Quebec as well as finding a comparable house in Calgary and, of course, they would pay all moving expenses. The cost of our move would be very expensive for the company but they were more than willing to do it. They asked me to go to Calgary first and see if I liked the area and pick a house out of the six the real estate company had already selected for me. If I was satisfied with the houses, I would return to Montréal and they would fly our whole family to Calgary and have us live in a suite while Joane decided on the house and area she liked the best. We would continue to live in a suite until our furniture arrived, then move in to our new home.

I needed to know all these details before I even approached Joane with my new job offer. I knew it would probably be overwhelming for her, especially now that we had two young children and the fact that she had never lived outside the province of Quebec her entire life. But the fact that they would pay the difference between the market value for a comparable house in Calgary was reassuring. At that time, houses in Calgary cost 30% more than in Quebec. It meant we would not have to live in a smaller house in Calgary. They would take care of selling our house in Quebec regardless of how long it took to sell. The offer was a real advantage to us in every way. In the back of my mind, it also meant I would be moving far from the underground world, which was still a nagging concern for me, even though the dreadful fear was gone and I finally had some peace about it.

Again, just as in the years past, when some major decision needed to be made, I heard that inner voice giving me direction. I knew I was being told the right thing to do but whether my wife would agree was another story. But, just as in my past experiences, everything worked out to my advantage. I was very relieved. Things always turned out great whenever I obeyed that voice. It was still a mystery how I always seemed to hear it when I needed to know what to do.

Now it was time to let Joane in on this huge promotion that had been put in my lap. I had only a few days to give them an answer. I was anxious to see what her reaction would be. I told her all the details, including the extra money we would make, which would more than compensate for the job she'd have to leave. She would now be able to stay home and take care of the children. She had many questions we would need to sort out together, some I had never thought of. I saw that it would take more than a few days to give them an answer so I reluctantly asked them for an extension. They were gracious and gave us another week to decide. I thought to myself, *They must really want me to take this job.* After the extension was given, Joane's biggest concern was how long we would be gone before we could return. Not having even considered that before, I answered, without thinking, "Two years at the most." That answer seemed to help her finalize her decision and she agreed to two years.

It had been much easier than I thought! We came to an agreement. Now we had to prepare for the big move and both felt good about it. As a matter of fact, we were anxious to get started, even though we knew we would be leaving family and friends behind. The fact that we only had to be gone for two years made it much easier for all of us.

EIGHT

Calgary

Over thirty years later, we are still in Calgary. Those "two years" have come and gone many times over. In the years following our move to Calgary, many negative as well as positive things happened and our lives changed forever.

As the company had promised us, we stayed in a suite in downtown Calgary, all expenses paid, until we were finally ready to move into our new home. The market value for a comparable house in Calgary was $32,000.00 more than in Montréal so the company gave me the monetary difference to apply to the mortgage, saying I would not have to pay it back to them until I decided to sell that house. The loan was interest-free. We had been treated very well, far over and above anything I had expected.

It didn't take long to settle into our new home and I was immediately busy working to open up the market in Western Canada with a new concept for lighting. We manufactured energy-saving fluorescent lamps. I went to the major businesses in Western Canada and offered to take care of their lighting on a contractual basis for a period of two and a half years. We would go into their stores and offices and re-lamp their entire building with energy-saving lamps. We would wash all of their lighting fixtures, change all the defective ballasts and install new energy-efficient lamps. Just washing their existing fixtures increases the light output by 20 to 40 percent. It was a major expense, but we then put them under a two-and-a-half year contract with monthly payments that they could afford. The payback period was quick because of the savings on their electrical bill. We also included monthly service calls in our contract to maintain their new lighting system. All their lighting concerns were handled by us and, needless to say, not one customer refused.

Business boomed. My biggest concern was finding and training maintenance staff to keep up with the sales. New contracts were renewed every two and a half years. Renewals seem to be an automatic thing, with very few companies refusing to sign up again. It was the easiest sales job I'd ever had. I was beginning to have a lot of idle time on my hands because I had service managers running the ongoing monthly service work in all the major cities of Western Canada. It was all we could do to maintain the service to our many new customers. We really didn't need any more sales because of the tremendous growth we were experiencing. Some of our work was even generated by our head office in Toronto, which would sign up large companies that had stores right across Canada, including the area I was responsible for. Our sales were starting to surpass those in Eastern Canada. Because of this, I had one of the largest expense budgets in Canada. I was also able to drive the company car of my choice.

Unfortunately, all of this affected me in a negative way. Pride crept in and my lifestyle changed for the worse, although no one could have convinced me of that, not even Joane. My life started on a downhill spiral that soon became uncontrollable.

My boss was in Toronto and the only thing he knew was what I told him. Since sales were so good in Western Canada, I seldom heard from him. The only time I saw him was at our annual company seminar and budget meeting at head office, which occurred once a year. Otherwise I was completely on my own, accountable to no one, at least in my neck of the woods. I started entertaining customers on a daily basis at a certain bar, which I visited on a daily basis. Because of the many customers I had, I could entertain as many as four to five a day. By doing this, I knew I could get them to renew their existing contracts with the company, thereby guaranteeing a minimum amount of growth each year.

One thing led to another, until I was spending five days a week at the bar with all my customers. My entertaining budget had now reached $5000 a month—and that was for alcohol alone. I had personally become the biggest customer of that drinking establishment and was starting to receive royal treatment from the owner. He reserved, on a permanent basis, a six-person booth for me. No one else was allowed to sit in it but my customers and me. He also assigned the same waitress to my table on a daily basis, so that she would get to know what everyone drank, therefore giving everyone who sat with me priority service.

This did not help my pride at all and I even started to demand things from the owner. The first thing I asked for was a private phone line at my table. I could then conduct all my business there, without having to go into my office. A red phone was installed at my booth within two days. I seldom saw my secretary because I simply gave her instructions from the bar, my new office. I would only pay for drinks, not food. Customers had to pay for their own food if they wanted to eat. Whenever they decided to eat, they would graciously offer to pay for my food as well, although I seldom ate. My drinking became a major problem to the point where I would not go home until the wee hours of the morning, even if all my customers had left. I starting drinking on my own and even spent my Saturdays alone at the bar. I started drifting away from Joane and the children. Why she put up with it, I didn't know, but eventually found out.

Within two years I had become an alcoholic, although I would never have admitted it. I left home for the bar early every morning before anyone woke up. It was hard for me to face my family with the lifestyle I had. The bar didn't open until 10:00 a.m. but I arranged with the owner to have someone open early in the morning so that I could start making phone calls to my customers from my new office. I was the only one there until 10:00 a.m. and I was drinking the whole time I made calls. This drinking, I often had to admit to myself, was making me do things I really didn't want to do. The only time I saw my family was for a short period of time on Sunday afternoons when I got out of bed. I spent all Sunday morning in bed trying to catch up on the sleep I had missed during the rest of the week. It was quiet in the house on Sunday mornings, because Joane took the children to a church. I found it strange that they were not there on the only day I was home. I wondered why she even told me what she was doing, since I never gave her a clue what I was doing. I reasoned that it was actually better if she didn't know. Sunday was my day to try and recuperate and see my children. The first thing I did when I woke up every morning was to take another drink to try and help my hangover from the day before.

It was the best day of the week because after church was over I got to see and spend time with my kids. I didn't say much to Joane because I felt guilty about what I had done during the week and didn't want to talk about it, even though she had every right to know. After all, she was my wife. With the little communication we did have, I found out she had started a French Immersion School and spent all her time there with the kids. At least she had someone to talk to and our kids were making new friends. We, as a family, were drifting apart, though. Our relationship was getting worse and worse as time passed.

I then found out that Joane was contemplating leaving with the children and going back to Quebec. What a shock and wake-up call! I didn't let myself show any emotion but I couldn't fathom being separated from my family, even though we saw so little of each other. My destructive lifestyle still continued. It was like I couldn't stop even though I really wanted to change because I didn't want to lose my family.

This news only caused me to drink more and more, trying to forget what I had heard. Heavy drinking made me forget things, since many a night I would arrive home at two and three o'clock in the morning, not being able to remember what had happened the night before. I was so drunk, I had to close one eye to drive home, in order not to see everything double. If there were two lines on the road I saw four. I did this for months and couldn't understand why the police never stopped me. I even remember going through several police checkpoints. The police would stop one and let two or three go by and for some unknown reason, I always seemed to be one of the ones they let go. Had I been caught, my driver's license would certainly have been suspended. However, because they always did these checks at night, they couldn't see my face. If they had seen me they would have known right away that I was in no condition to drive. I always believed I was a lucky guy, just like in my travels in Mexico. Things always came out in my favour.

Suddenly, unexpectedly, Joane began acting very differently. When I arrived home in the early morning hours, she would often be at the door, asking me if I was OK and if she could cook something for me to eat. I was losing weight because of my lack of food during the day. Her actions towards me were very puzzling. Why would she treat me so kindly after the way I had been treating her and the children for years? I convinced myself she had found someone else in her life and was cheating on me, so she did this to get from me what she needed in order to be able to leave with this newfound man of hers. I could think of no other reason.

I told myself it was time to confront her, but I had to work up the courage and be sober enough to do it. I must put a stop to it before it went too far. We were still legally married and infidelity was not right in my eyes, even though my lifestyle was no better. *It's OK for me but not for her* was my thinking. I decided that Sunday afternoon would be a good time to confront her, while I was still sober.

The day finally arrived and after I had mustered up enough courage, I told Joane I had something serious to talk to her about. I asked her to tell the kids to do something on their own, because I didn't want them to hear what I was about to ask her. After the kids were alone in another room, I said to her, "I know what's going on here. I know you have another man in your life and I'm going to put a stop to this right away. This coming to meet me at the door in the early morning hours to see how I'm doing is only a cover-up. Because I'm drunk doesn't mean I can't see what's going on. Who is this guy anyway? Do I know him? Does he work for me?"

After my venting and complaining she finally had a chance to speak. What she told me was beyond my comprehension and now I was convinced she was lying to me.

She said, "As you know, I started a French Immersion School and have met many new housewives. Often they come over to visit at dinner time. I needed someone to talk to since you were never around, so I invited them to bring their kids so they could play with our kids. I have made many new friends and it has helped keep me going while you are out doing your thing, whatever that is. You're right. One of the ladies did introduce me to a man that has now become my best friend."

NINE

Joane's New Friend and My Strange Encounter

I stared at my wife in disbelief. Joane said, "I opened up to one of the ladies about my struggle with our marriage and your drinking. After I had spilled out my heart to her, hoping to get the help I needed, she told me about Jesus. She told me he was a real person and that he was the answer to all of our problems. She told me that if I personally invited him into my life I would have a genuine relationship with him. She told me what to do and after she had left and I had put the kids in bed, I came down to the living room, knelt down on the floor, and followed her instructions. I know what I'm about to say next will be hard for you to understand, but you can have the same experience I had if you want it and mean it from your heart."

She said that when she invited Jesus into her life, a mist completely enveloped her and seemed to spread throughout the whole living room. Then this peace that she had never experienced in her entire life filled her whole being. All she could do was weep. At that moment she knew something very real had happened to her. She felt completely different than ever before. She said, "Suddenly all my concerns about our marriage, our children and your drinking no longer seemed to weigh me down. It was as if everything was lifted off of my shoulders. I can't explain it. Ernie, believe me, that is what you need, and if you want, we can meet with my friends and they can tell you amazing things that Jesus did for their marriages and how he has totally changed their lives. You need to hear it with your own ears because you will have a hard time believing me."

I shrugged it off by saying that was OK for her but I didn't need this Jesus; she did. I was vividly remembering what happened to me at the seminary and how I was sure God had abandoned me and allowed despicable things to happen. I did not want anything to do with God, although I didn't know too much about Jesus, who was apparently his Son. But again, I reasoned that God allowed him to be crucified so why should I be interested in him?

Joane continued to attend church and fellowship with her new friends. She told me many of her questions had been answered by her newfound friend, Jesus, and because of the living room episode she had experienced. She was so excited about her life now that every time I saw her, she couldn't stop talking about something new that was happening. I was becoming frustrated because I had no idea what she was talking about. It couldn't be the same God I had experienced in my early years. Everything she told me was positive; everything I'd experienced had been negative. Every Sunday afternoon I would hear about all that had transpired in church that morning and the preceding week. It seemed to be the only topic that she was interested in. For me, it was the only topic I *didn't* want to talk about. But I could see an unmistakable change in her life.

It came to a point where deep down in my being I began to wonder if it was actually possible for me to feel that way. I quickly dismissed that thought, though, since I didn't want my lifestyle to change. My drinking continued but I started arriving home earlier at night, keeping an eye open for strange things that might be going on. One night as I was arriving home, I saw a group of people in my living room. They were singing and playing musical instruments and seemed so happy. They had to be drinking my booze, which was stored in my basement! I had two to three cases of liquor that customers had given me over the years. I didn't drink that liquor, because my company paid for all my drinks at the bar, where most of my time was spent. I was saving it for special occasions.

When I came into my house, for some reason everyone got up and started leaving. One gentleman who was playing the guitar said to me as he was going, "I'm praying for you." This shocked me because he didn't even know me, so why would he pray for me, and what would he pray? Anyway, I didn't need any prayers; I was fine the way I was. This would definitely be something to talk to Joane about next Sunday afternoon. What were all these people doing in my home? I would tell Joane to tell her friends to quit praying for me. I didn't need any prayer; I could take care of my own life, without anyone's help. That's what I had been doing since I left home at sixteen years old.

That Sunday the subject of conversation did not change. It was all about this Jesus again and I spent most of my time just listening to Joane because what could I say on the subject? She told me how her friends from church got together every week to sing songs and share what was happening in their lives. She said they always spent time praying for me. I was annoyed because prayer didn't work and was not part of my life. However, I finally admitted it couldn't hurt, even if I knew they were wasting their time.

Joane also shared how just before she had her encounter with Jesus, she had decided to pack up her bags and leave with the children. She wanted to go back to Montréal where her family lived. She couldn't continue living the way we were. I was no longer a husband to her or a father to my kids. As she was packing her suitcases one night, she suddenly had a vision of me on my knees with my hands lifted to the sky. Then and there she decided to stay and seriously pray for me. That only confirmed to me that prayer didn't work. My drinking became worse because I was so perplexed about everything she was telling me about this Jesus. I reasoned if I drank more I would forget all about it. But she was continuously meeting me at the door every night when I arrived home. It seemed the worse I treated her and the more drunk I was when I came home, the kinder she was to me, even if I came in as late as 2:00 a.m. This actually started to bug me. I would let her know about it the next time we talked. Enough was enough.

The following week I kept up my old habits, only now I made a point of coming home as late as possible. Because I drank more and more every day, I would hang around outside the bar, waiting to sober up enough to be able to drive. Many times I didn't even remember driving home. I was afraid that sooner or later my luck would run out and the police would stop me. One Friday I was drinking late at the bar, as usual, when something happened that scared the living daylights out of me. It was around 1:00 a.m. and most of the people had gone home and while I was sitting there alone at my table, I suddenly became aware of a presence standing next to me, like a silhouette. I knew someone was there but before I could actually turn to look, I heard an audible voice speak to me, loudly and clearly. It said, "Go home to your family where you belong."

The voice was so authoritative I froze and couldn't even look. Before I knew what I was doing, I found myself putting my drink back on the table, picking up my car keys, cigarettes and lighter and leaving. The fear of disobeying that voice was terrifying. I knew if I stayed, something awful would happen to me. I finally turned to see who was talking to me but no one was there. Was I hallucinating or losing my mind? That question had come to me before on my travels but this time it was much more serious. His words kept ringing in my ears. Even stranger, when I reached the outside, I realized I was completely sober. Whatever was going on? *I need to see a psychiatrist,* I thought, as I drove home. *I have a serious mental problem and it's just getting worse the more I drink.*

When I arrived home, again Joane was waiting for me at the door but this time she was shocked to see me sober. She asked if I was all right and if I would be coming to bed right away or if I wanted something to eat or drink. I answered, "I'm just going to stay up a while. I have something I need to think about and work out before I go to bed." She seemed quite happy to see me sober and went back upstairs to bed.

Alone in the living room, I sat down in a big arm chair in front of the TV, reached for the remote and turned it on. Programming was over for the night and all I could see on the screen was snow. I sat there and stared blankly at the screen. Then suddenly I was startled as I heard that same audible voice again. There was no mistaking it; it had followed me home. The voice said, "Monday morning you will go to the company office and write a letter of resignation to your head office. You will then start your own business."

I wanted to rush upstairs and ask Joane if she had heard anything, but quickly dismissed the idea. I was the only one hearing a voice. What would she say? She would ask questions I had no answers to. No, I would keep this all to myself until I got better. But I kept thinking, *How did I become sober outside the bar after drinking all night?* The thought troubled me enough to stay awake the rest of the night, staring at the ceiling. All night, questions bombarded my mind, but I had absolutely no reasonable answers.

The command to resign my position on Monday weighed heavily on me the next two days. It was the last straw. Going home to my family made some sense but resigning my position after fifteen years with the company, both in Montréal and Calgary, and starting my own business was the most ludicrous thing I had ever heard. Going to a psychiatrist on Monday morning made way more sense than going to the company office to give my resignation. I still had time to try and think things through. *Food and rest over the weekend will help me decide what to do,* I thought. I definitely needed time to think.

Even though I was at home all weekend, most of the valuable time that I needed to think was taken up, because it was such a treat for my children to have me at home. They wanted to be with me. Actually, I was happy about that. I hadn't spent quality time with them for months on end. I had forgotten how much fun it was playing and talking with them. They had so many things to share that I was only able to get a few words in edgewise but that was fine with me. I let them talk and enjoyed those precious moments that had somehow disappeared from my life. I even spent all day Sunday with them since there was no way I was going to church. I kept hoping that Monday would take care of itself, but wasn't too convinced. I kept wondering what a psychiatrist would have to say about my condition.

Monday morning came quicker than I had expected, and to my surprise I had a strong desire to go to the office instead of to the bar. I shrugged and figured the bar could wait a few hours. I had forgotten to tell the guy who opened the bar early for me that I would not be in. The truth was, I wasn't sure whether I would be at the office or visiting a psychiatrist. After getting ready, I found myself heading to the office, sitting at my desk, which hadn't been used for months and writing a letter of resignation. The words flowed freely until it was finished. It was a simple one-page fax, straightforward and to the point. I sent it to head office. For some inexplicable reason it seemed I was doing the right thing. I left the company office and headed straight to my usual "office" where my bottle was waiting for me. However, when I got there, everyone thought something serious had happened to me, since I hadn't come at my usual time. My arrival was always like clockwork, so everyone was concerned, especially the owner. I brushed the whole thing off by telling them an emergency had arisen that had to be taken care of right away. That satisfied their curiosity.

Two hours later I received a phone call from my secretary, telling me to call my boss in Toronto as soon as possible. I knew exactly why and after finishing my drink, I left the bar and headed straight back to the office so I could talk to my boss privately where no one could hear me. He answered his phone right away as if he had been anticipating my call. What came out of my mouth shocked me. I hadn't rehearsed what I would say, but suddenly blurted out, "I think I am losing my mind. I'm hearing voices and some of them are even audible, but no one's there. They're making me do things I don't want to do, but somehow I end up doing them anyway. I need to leave the company because I can't work in this frame of mind. I could end up doing things I regret. I need to get to the bottom of this so I have decided to resign and would appreciate it if you would accept my resignation and not ask me any questions."

My boss thought for a while then replied, "Let's give you one month's leave with pay until you get some needed rest. You must be extremely stressed out." Little did he know it had nothing to do with stress. With the lifestyle and the job I was doing, I had nothing that looked close to stress. I convinced him it wasn't stress without giving any details and he finally accepted my resignation, but made me promise I would stay on for three weeks to train someone else from head office. If at the end of three weeks I wanted my job back, he would gladly give it back to me.

I drove back to the bar with the sobering realization I would be out of a job and faced with my mountain of debts. I would have to sell my house in order to pay back the $32,000.00 advance given to me for my mortgage in Calgary. I would have to return or sell the new Impala station wagon I had bought for Joane. I would have to sell my motorhome because now there was no way to meet all those monthly payments. My credit cards were almost maxed out and I would also lose my company car. What compounded these worries even more was the fact that Joane knew nothing about what I had just done. How could I explain all of this to her, and what would she think? Now she would really have a reason to leave me and take the children back to Quebec.

Listening to that voice and obeying it had gotten me into this pickle. However, I clearly recalled some of the other things I was led to do because of that inner voice and had to admit it saved my life more than once! Could it happen again, since this command seemed bigger than all of the others combined? Over the next three weeks, while I was training my new replacement, my drinking diminished considerably since the gentleman didn't drink at all.

TEN

A Bizarre Meeting with Businessmen

I would have to stop putting off telling Joane and let her know what was going on. The fact that my drinking lessened was a pleasant surprise for her. She didn't question me so I didn't bring up the topic. Telling her about quitting my job was a much bigger problem than my drinking.

I spent more time at home and less time at the bar. I spent a lot of time thinking about my life and where it was all going. When I had left home as a teenager, there were only three people that had any directives for my life: me, myself and I. Things went pretty well, but now another person was trying to take control and I didn't enjoy it at all. He was making me to do things I didn't want to do and I was feeling bewildered by all of the unanswered questions bombarding my mind. I knew I should see a psychiatrist, but I really needed to tell Joane about this whole mess I had gotten myself into first.

I decided to speak to her the very next day and it was the best thing I ever did. Had I known the results, I could have saved myself a lot of misery and lost sleep. After the children were in bed, I began telling her what had happened to me. I spent hours trying to explain, hoping I wasn't sounding too crazy. I told her the decisions I had made since the encounter with this mysterious voice at the bar weeks ago and the command I'd received at home right afterwards.

When I had finished explaining my situation to the best of my ability, Joane did not react at all as I had expected. She told me she thought it was exciting and one day I would have all the answers to my questions. She said she could tell I'd had an encounter with Jesus and the sooner I accepted him into my life the better. *Well*, I thought, *it wouldn't take much to be better than what it is right now!*

However, the fact that she was at peace with the whole situation was a huge relief. The day my job finally ended I started to drink again. For some reason I thought drinking would make me forget my problems, but the relief was short-lived. It was like a vicious cycle. I was looking to Joane to give me answers to questions I had but she didn't. For the very first time I had to admit to myself that I did need someone to give me direction for my life, since I had no clue what to do next. I was facing a crossroads and desperately needed help.

A couple of days later at supper time, Joane turned to me and said, "How would you like to come to a banquet this coming weekend? It's put on by an organization called the Full Gospel Businessmen's Fellowship. Someone from the church gave me two free tickets. Most of the people there are businessmen and many of them own their own businesses here."

Since that voice had told me he wanted me to start my own business, all I heard was the word "businessmen" and immediately said, "Yes let's go."

Joane was shocked at my answer but assured me I would really enjoy the banquet, according to friends who had attended meetings before. I was more excited to go than she was and eagerly awaited the weekend. It was my chance to introduce my new business to all these potential customers that would soon be mine. I was already planning my approach and sales pitch to those businessmen. Then it dawned on me that I didn't have a business. I only had five days to get some kind of company started, register the name and have business cards printed and ready to be handed out at this banquet. I had a busy week ahead of me.

I sat and tried to come up with a name and business I could create. I spent the rest of the evening thinking but nothing seemed to come to mind, especially the type of company I could start. When I resigned from my position I had to sign a Non-Competition Agreement that stated I would not enter into the same type of business for the next five years. That was the only type of work I had done for fifteen years. I didn't know much about anything else. The more I thought about a new type of business, the less I knew what to do. It would have to be a service-type, where equipment would be minimal because my investment portfolio was non-existent.

Suddenly a crazy idea came to me. Why not ask the person who had gotten me into this whole mess in the first place and see what he says? What did I have to lose? It was a shot in the dark, but with no other options I was desperate to try any avenue that came to mind. But how could I get in touch with him? I knew he had gotten in touch with me by speaking to me out loud. Maybe I should do the same thing and see if he answers. It sounded like a far-fetched idea, but was the only logical thing that came to mind.

Looking around to make sure no one could hear me, I spoke these words, "Whoever you are, you're the one who got me into this mess, now get me out of it." I listened but didn't hear anything spoken back to me, so I repeated it again and again, getting louder and louder. After noticing I wasn't getting any answers, I stopped and sat there wondering what else I could do.

All of a sudden a thought came to me as clear as a bell. I recognized it gladly—it was that inner voice. I had experienced it many times before and things had always turned out amazingly well. These words started to replay over and over in my head: *I'm going to start an electrical contracting business.*

I knew absolutely nothing about the electrical business, except how to turn a light switch on and off, but I knew right away this was the answer to my dilemma. I would start an electrical contracting business as soon as possible. My reasoning was based on the fact that this voice always seemed to tell me to do things I didn't want to do. Now he wanted me to do something I knew absolutely nothing about. It was completely insane but the thought would not go away. The more I fought it, the more I thought about it. By the end of the day I was becoming half convinced it might work out. No other ideas had come to mind and the weekend for the banquet was fast approaching, so I kept entertaining this ludicrous idea that would not leave me alone.

Within three days, I came up with a company name, which was simply my three initials: EJF Electrical Contracting Company Ltd. It had a good ring to it somehow, so I went and had 500 business cards printed up.

By the time the Full Gospel Businessmen's banquet arrived, I'd accepted the fact that I was now an electrical contractor. That is what I would tell these businessmen. With 50 business cards stashed in my coat pocket, I arrived with Joane at the banquet hall. As we were approaching the entrance door, I noticed several men hanging around the entrance. When people came in, they started hugging them, whether they were male or female. I had a sudden flashback to a stopover I once had in San Francisco on my way to Mexico, where for the very first time I saw men hugging and kissing each other in public. I stopped, wondering if I should keep going towards the entrance or bolt for the exit. I reasoned that at least they were not kissing each other, so decided to brave it and continued to approach the entrance with my wife. Joane had no idea what was going through my mind. I let her enter first, staying closely behind, trying to hide behind her. Sure enough, one of the men gave her a big hug and as he did I quickly slid behind her and the door frame into the banquet hall without any human contact. Whew! What a relief. I had avoided that strange ritual.

I had never seen such a huge banqueting hall before. Tables and chairs were set up as far as the eye could see. I quickly scanned the room to see if I recognized anyone so we could sit with someone we knew. By this time I had been in Calgary for four years so there must be someone I knew, but to my disappointment I could spot no one. In order not to be too conspicuous, I decided to sit at a table near the back of the room and close to an exit, in case I suddenly needed to escape. From there, I could easily scan the room for potential customers without anyone noticing me.

At the front of the banqueting room a head table sat facing all the other tables. I concluded that this must be the table for the CEOs and owners of the multi-national companies, like the one I used to work for...only a few weeks ago. I thought, *These will be the guys I need to contact before I leave this place tonight.* Someone began introducing the head table and I quickly grabbed a pen out of my pocket and a napkin next to my plate, ready to jot down the names of my future customers. The first one they introduced was the main speaker of the night, obviously the one who would spend most of the evening explaining how his business had become so prosperous. I knew I was in the right place at the right time. The night was going to be exciting and I would get a good kick-start for my new electrical contracting business.

This is definitely the guy I need to talk to, I thought. *He already owns a prosperous company.* My hopes quickly faded when I found out he didn't live in Calgary but was actually an American who owned his own oil company in Tulsa, Oklahoma. *Well,* I thought, *There are quite a few more at the head table that I'm sure will be needing my services in Calgary, and what about all the ones at the other tables? They all need electrical work done. Who doesn't?* My mind was at rest with the whole thing when the MC asked everyone to stand. That was unusual but what he said next was even stranger.

He asked everyone to take a leaflet on the table and open it to the first song on the page. What was this all about anyway? People started singing songs and I moved my lips a little to make them think I was joining in their little sing-song. Fortunately, it only lasted a short time and then everyone sat down because dinner was about to be served. Another man at the head table was asked to say grace before the meal. Thankfully it was a short prayer and the dinner plates started to arrive. I tried to dismiss all these odd practices that were going on before the meal and focused on the real reason I was here. This was not the time to be distracted by what was happening around me. Everyone was eating and I was probably the first one at my table to finish my meal. I didn't want to talk to anyone. I was busy processing the weird things that were going on.

Dinner seemed to take forever, at least an hour or more. I was getting impatient to hear from the man at the head table. Finally everyone finished eating and the MC came to the mic. He asked for us all to applaud for the beautiful dinner we had just eaten and the wonderful service from all the staff. *What's with these people anyway?* I thought, *We all had to pay for our meals and I'm sure all the staff were well paid for their work.* Things were beginning to upset me but I reminded myself again to keep focused on the reason I had come here.

The MC spoke again, but instead of introducing the main speaker, he asked another person at the head table to, as he put it, give a five-minute testimony of how his life had been changed. I groaned inwardly at yet another delay but listened to see what some guy could say in five minutes. I was astounded, however, for he said a lot more that I related to in five minutes than I thought was possible. This guy had the same background as I did. He had been born in a Catholic family and because of what he experienced in the church, had left home at an early age to get away from it all. He spoke in detail of how he had cried out to God for help after he had hit rock bottom in his life with drugs, women and booze and how he had met Jesus, the Son of God, at one of these meetings. It was almost too much for me to process. How could his life have suddenly changed because of this Jesus? If Jesus met him at one of these meetings, I was wondering if he might have come to this one too, and if he did, where was he sitting? I had a good recollection from Sunday School what Jesus looked like. I scanned the whole room but couldn't see him there.

The gentleman said next that there was only one God, God the Father, and the only way to know him was through his Son Jesus. If we allowed him to come into our lives and take control, he would speak to us and give us direction. Suddenly a thought flashed through my head: *Is it possible that the voice I seem to keep hearing is this Jesus guy? Why would Jesus talk to someone with a lifestyle like mine?* It didn't make sense.

At last it was the main speaker's turn to come up and take over the meeting. I could finally glean information from him so that I could become as successful as he was in business. I was all ears and didn't want to miss a word. Even before hearing him, I was convinced that if I were to follow his example, I would be just as successful as he was. When he started to speak, nothing he said was what I was expecting to hear. In fact, everything he said was too good to be true—and I had been told all my life that if it sounds too good to be true, it usually is.

I tried to avoid accepting what he was saying but the more he talked the more convincing he became. He also said that the most important thing we could ever do in life was allow Jesus to take control. *I* had controlled my life ever since I left home and I wasn't about to let someone else take over, especially someone I didn't know. The man spoke for over an hour and all he talked about was this Jesus whom he had willingly made CEO of his business. He explained how Jesus gave him direction on a daily basis. He shared how finances would become available whenever a need came up. As he continued with his story, it became more and more the "too good to be true" story. He gave example after example how Jesus saved him from negative situations and how things always turned out for the best. Then he said, "I know this is hard for some of you here to believe and understand, but let me say that you will never really understand anything in life until you have experienced it for yourself personally." That statement stuck with me the rest of the meeting.

He finally completed his speech, then did something I had never seen before. He gave everyone an invitation. He seemed to be speaking directly to me. It was like he was zeroing in on me, even though I was at the very back of the banquet hall. He said, "If you want to make Jesus Lord of your life tonight, if you want him to prosper your business, if you want him to run your business, if you want to be successful in life and are willing to make him CEO of that business, come up here in front of this head table and I will be glad to pray for you. Jesus will change your life forever."

I'm sure he said other things but that is all I heard. Before I even knew what had happened, I found myself standing in front of the head table. I still have absolutely no idea how I got there. It was as though someone came up with me or someone carried me up there. All I knew was I was standing in front of all those people in that massive banqueting hall. I had a sudden urge to run but realized it probably wasn't a good idea, since the speaker was looking right at me.

I thought, *What am I doing here and what is going to happen next?* Before that thought was over I felt a hand on my shoulder. A man asked me if he could pray for me. What was I to say? No?

So I let him pray for me. He came around to the front, facing me, and asked me to repeat a prayer after him. I repeated everything he said as though I was hypnotized. Then he asked me, "Do you want to receive the baptism of the Holy Spirit?"

Without thinking I said, "Yes," because in the Catholic Church I had heard of water baptism so I thought this must be something like it. Soon he had me speaking this strange language, nothing like the two other languages I already knew and spoke fluently. The words I spoke made absolutely no sense to me, so I just chalked up everything that had happened to me in the last ten minutes as the most bizarre experience I'd ever had.

When I looked around, I saw many others had come up to the front as well. Some were weeping, some were shouting and some were even dancing. I was glad that I was calm and collected and quietly made my way back to my table before some other weird thing happened to me. As I slowly walked back, I was suddenly aware that all the worries and concerns for my life, my business and what would happen to me and my family had completely left me. It felt like a ton of weight had been lifted off of my shoulders. Peace and joy filled my being and for the first time in my life, I knew everything was going to be all right. I knew that deep down inside I was not the same person I had been twenty minutes before. Something had really changed but I couldn't put my finger on it.

I had so many questions brewing in my head, but even they didn't seem to bother me. What had happened to me I could not comprehend but tomorrow was another day and maybe I would get some clarity about the whole evening. All I knew was what I had experienced was not bad; it actually felt really good for once.

ELEVEN

A Whole New Kind of Life

It was truly an evening I would never forget, Good Friday, April 8th, 1983. I had so many questions for Joane, if I could just locate her in that massive crowd. I finally found her. She was grinning from ear to ear, crying and laughing all at the same time. I guess I would have to wait until we got home.

I asked Joane to drive home because I felt light-headed, even though I had not had a drink all day. She kept trying to describe what had happened to me. She told me how she and many others had been praying for this to happen to me for months and months. She explained what I had done and how my life would never be the same. Now it would be important for me to read the Bible because it would have the answer for every question I had. She kept talking so long I didn't have an opportunity to ask her anything. I was OK with that since many of my questions were being answered as she spoke.

By the time we got home, I had received enough information to last me a week. Now I would have to process everything. We paid the baby sitter, went to bed, and went straight to sleep. I woke up rested and still full of peace and joy. Everything I had experienced the night before was still fresh to me. Something mysterious had taken place inside of me and the whole day Joane kept explaining in detail what had happened.

The same thing had happened to her in the living room the evening she had experienced Jesus in the form of a mist. She had said the same prayer as I had the night before. A friend from the school had told her, "When you are ready to make Jesus your best friend and want him to turn your life around, just pray this prayer. You don't need anyone else to be there, just you and him. What we all need is a personal relationship with him on a daily basis and he's waiting for us to make the first step."

That morning Joane gave me a Bible she had bought for me and told me that everything I needed to know (and more) was in that book. It was the only truth and that truth had the ability to change any circumstance in our lives, if we obeyed it. I took the book and it opened in the middle. The first line my eyes fell upon said, "Trust in the Lord with all of your heart; don't lean on your own understanding. In everything you do, acknowledge him and he will direct all of your steps" (Proverbs 3:5-6). That was a sweet sight to my eyes and confirmed what the main speaker had said the night before. He had said that Jesus wanted to give us direction for our businesses and our daily lives.

However, that very first scripture I'd ever read completely contradicted what I had been taught in the Catholic Church. We were told, first of all, that we shouldn't read the Bible, because we wouldn't understand it and that is why God had put priests in the church. The other thing I couldn't understand was why Mass was in Latin. Nobody understood anything except the announcements and a five-minute lecture in English on sin. Everything else was in Latin. We were so sin-conscious after these services that we flocked to confess our sins to a priest every month just to stay in God's good books. We were then assured that if we died that month we would not spend too much time in Purgatory before going to meet Peter at the pearly gates. I had tried to find these things in the Bible before but with no success.

What else had I been told that was not true? I remembered having to eat fish on Fridays because we were not allowed to eat meat. I couldn't find that in the Bible either. I was curious as to how else we had been brainwashed with so for the next month I spent eight hours a day devouring the Word of God. I was finally getting to know the truth and this truth was setting me free from religion—all the beliefs that were man-made, by priests or anyone else. I was finally finding the truth about God and life and the purpose we were put on this planet as well as what was right and what was wrong.

I started to realize that the Bible was the road map for our lives and unless we believed it and received it personally as the truth, we could be deceived by the teachings of man. Human beings need to follow the wisdom of God or they will remain in bondage and confusion their entire time here on earth. I certainly had tried everything else, but nothing had worked for me.

I thought of people all over the world following different man-made religions. They all contradicted each other and wars were fought over these beliefs. Some went as far as to kill each other in the name of their gods. They argued with each other, trying to prove they were right and others were wrong, families were divided, and the world was in chaos. All because of religion. I had finally found out that my personal relationship with Jesus and the road map for my life, the Bible, were the only things I needed to fulfill the plan and destiny God had for me.

I had walked this planet for thirty-eight years, convinced beyond a shadow of a doubt that I was right and everyone else was wrong concerning God and religion. Why? I had allowed my personal negative experiences, along with man's teachings, paint a picture of who God was and what life was all about here on earth. I had been deceived.

While reading the Bible, I found that my personal experience could not be taken away from me. No one could convince me it wasn't real. I would now embark on a journey to find out the truth, once and for all. I read in the Bible that knowledge on its own puffs us up or causes us to be proud, but if we actually do what God says in the Bible, it will transform us.

The Full Gospel Businessmen's meeting I attended on Good Friday was the day my life was turned upside down forever. It was the beginning of a new life with Jesus. I was "saved," or "born again," as the Bible puts it. I had to discard everything I had learned and been told before. Now I would have to find out the truth for myself in the Bible.

The Lord Jesus lovingly took me back to my early life and showed me every negative experience I had faced and how he had been there by my side to protect me from harm. He confirmed that the promptings and the inner voice I had experienced over the years were indeed him speaking to me. He was causing me to be led by him, even though I didn't understand at all what was going on. I realized this after reading the Bible verse that says, "My sheep hear my voice; I know them, and they follow me."

It never dawned on me that God had been guiding me in my travels. I had been taught that God only spoke to holy people that followed him and obeyed him. I sure didn't fit into that group. I was a sinner and a drunk, and I was convinced God was not at all interested in that kind of person.

I believe he also wants me to let you know, through this book I'm writing, that he loves everyone the same, no matter what lifestyle you have chosen for yourself. He doesn't like you entertaining sin in your life because he knows, sooner or later, that sin will destroy your life. You don't have to live with it, however. You can make a choice in your life that will set you free.

God has given us a free will to choose and will not force us to do anything. All he will do is love us unconditionally and try and get us somehow to see him in our difficult moments in life. I was so glad to find out that God was not my enemy, although that is how I had seen him all those years. I had put God and religion in the same boat. Now I have found out he is my best friend. The person who is my enemy is the devil, and he is also very real. The Bible says that he is constantly prowling around trying to destroy us before we find the truth. He only comes to steal, kill, and destroy us, but Jesus came to give us life and this life more abundantly.

The first thirty-eight years of my life were a result of the choices I had made, based on my ignorance of the truth. The last years of my life would be different, but again they would be shaped by my choices.

Before I was born again, Jesus had spared my life six times—three times when I was with the underground world, twice in accidents and once he spared me from going to prison for life. Had he not been with me in those times, protecting me, this book would have never been written.

I was in a different "fold" the first thirty-eight years of my life but I was still in God's heart. Let me explain. The scripture I quoted earlier in John 10:27 said, "My sheep hear my voice; I know them and they follow me." Most people agree that happens once someone is born again and decides to follow God. But I was not following him and did not know him personally at all, yet I still heard his voice. Why?

John 10:16 goes on to say, "I have other sheep that are not of this 'fold.' I must bring them also, and they will hear my voice, and they will become one flock with one shepherd." This verse refers to all who are not yet born again and have not yet chosen to follow God. God wants them to know that they are continually on his heart and he wants to bring them to himself even though they have no interest in him right now.

I had always seen myself as a loner, thinking no one ever cared for me, but when I read John 10:16 I realized that all this time, unknowingly, Jesus was by my side taking care of me. I was overwhelmed by his love for me and couldn't help but weep. I had angrily pushed God out of my life and all that time he continued to be my protection from my enemy, the devil, who had been trying to kill me the whole time, to keep me from entering into God's plan for my life.

The more I read the Bible, the more I desired to know the whole truth and nothing but the truth. One day I decided I would only follow the Word of God from that day forward and receive all the direction I needed for my life from him alone. I had no more time to waste. The devil had already stolen thirty-eight years of my life. As I was thinking about those wasted years, an old song came to my memory, which I used to sing as a boy. It was "Old McDonald had a farm, E I E I O." When I thought of those five letters, I said to myself, *Why did they use those five letters and not other letters of the alphabet?*

Immediately the Lord spoke to my spirit. He said, "Those letters are telling you how your life is going to change now. E I E I O means 'Enough Is Enough It's Over.'" God can speak to us in unusual ways, even through an old children's song. From that day forward I endeavoured to keep my ears and eyes open to the Lord. He wanted to communicate with me on a regular basis, his way, not mine.

Even today, whenever I read the Bible, there are passages I do not fully understand, but that's OK. He will give me understanding at the right time, when I need it for my life. If I reflect back on the thirty years since I first accepted Jesus as my Saviour, there were many scriptures I didn't understand. When I did finally receive the understanding, it was at the exact time I needed it. God wants to be my counsellor, my teacher, my lawyer, my healer—everything. He began to make himself known to me in all those areas. I remind myself every day that he wants to guide every step I take that day.

Today as God directs me to travel to many countries all over the world, I see so many who seem like robots, practising their religious beliefs, doing horrific things in the name of their gods.

That is when I realize that our greatest enemy is religion. My Bible tells me that pure religion is taking care of widows, the poor, and the children. People will read many different books, including their own man-made bibles, and practice their beliefs, convinced they are doing the right thing. Some of it may be true, but most of it is far from the truth. What they don't understand is that there is only one true God, God the Father, and the one and only way to get to know him is through his Son Jesus. When we come to that realization, our whole life will be turned around.

I had to learn this the hard way. Don't make the same mistakes I did by following the teachings of men. Find the truth for your life, which is only in one place, the Holy Bible. It's better late than never.

TWELVE

Putting the Bible to the Test

Whatever we hear is only good if it works in our lives. I found that when I did what the Bible says to do, I got results.

There are hundreds and hundreds of promises in the Bible, but I noticed that most were conditional. I had my part to do. If I did my part, believing it was the truth for my life, then Jesus would do his part. Guaranteed.

I couldn't wait to put the Bible to the test. My first test hit me where it hurts the most—my pocketbook. I had read in the Bible that (not money, but) the "love of money was the root of every kind of evil." I realized that was exactly what had enticed me to work with the underground world—the love of money.

My financial situation, because of my past lifestyle, and now spending all this time reading the Bible every day, was not bringing in any money. But my newfound faith in God was showing me what he wanted to do for me. I took a good long look at my financial situation and realized I definitely needed help to get out of the hole I had gotten myself and my family into. I needed to bring the situation before the Lord to see what he thought about it and what he could do about it. I had read in the Bible that God would take care of all our needs. I was experiencing this promise on a daily basis through people I knew. God didn't rain paper money down from heaven, but he used people in my life to meet our needs.

Joane and I have experienced that for years now. That doesn't mean God doesn't want us to work, but whenever we have been short of work or finances, God has always stepped in to help. We had made him Lord of our lives and it is a two-way relationship. I remember reading in the Bible that God wanted to be my provider and these provisions would come according to his riches, not mine. That was easy to accept. I didn't have any riches of my own, so I guessed we would work with his riches. I didn't have a clue how it could happen but I was open to his instructions and wanted to obey them, since I didn't have any ideas of my own.

Our financial burden had become a big mountain in my life and I didn't know what to do. That can be a good thing, since it means we have no choice but to rely on someone else, but that person has to be the right one. I decided to rely on the Lord and see if he would do what he said he would do. That became my first major test.

I got alone with the Lord in a quiet place out in a field, Bible in hand, not far from the city—God and I alone trying to figure out my next step. I felt he led me to the Book of Malachi. I started to read the whole book since I didn't know any specific place to start. The thing that stood out the most to me was the third chapter, a passage that spoke about finances. That was my worst problem, so I knew I better stop and see what God had to say about it. It stated that if I was faithful to give ten percent (he called it the "tithe") of everything that came into my life, God would stop the devil, the devourer, from stealing any more of my finances. The picture that came to my mind was God plugging up a hole in the dam so a leak would stop.

I was excited about that because it was a solution for my future. The devil could no longer steal my finances if I kept my side of the deal and faithfully gave ten percent of everything I got. That was a good start, but what about my bills that were past due? I kept reading. It said that if I was faithful in my tithing and giving, he would open the gates of heaven and pour out a blessing to me that was so big I would not be able to contain it. This was getting better and better. I didn't have to worry too much at this time about giving more than ten percent (called offerings) because I didn't have anything to give…I thought.

I immediately put this tithing principle to work and when people gave us money or food I made sure ten percent was put aside to give away. I saw that we could tithe food if we didn't have money. I could also tithe my time (which was money) to people in need of services or help. I wanted to make sure this principle was followed because I was certain God would keep his promise. I definitely needed "windows opened" and the sooner the better. Things were very tight. I had already experienced times when God met my needs through others. It was exactly like it said in the Bible: all God's promises are "Yes!" and "Amen!" That sounded pretty positive to me.

Now that I had opened my life to all the promises I could find, I wanted so much to fulfil my end of the deal. I was excited to wake up each day to see what the Lord had in store for me. I didn't want to miss a thing. Day after day he miraculously worked wonders before my eyes. What an exciting life I had entered into. It was like day and night compared to my previous life (and it still goes on to this very day some thirty years later, getting more exciting year by year).

My financial situation was about to change. Husbands and wives are under tremendous pressure to provide for their families but my Bible says that if we surrender our lives to him, God will become our provider.

Most people struggle because they still want to keep some control. If we get to know God, we will find he's more concerned about our well-being than we are. He's more concerned about our health, finances, and all our problems than we are. Why? Because he wants us to fulfill his plan on this earth before he returns to take us home to heaven. He also wants us free from the pressures of this world; he wants us to be available to do whatever he asks us to do. We can't do this if we are burdened down or broke.

The Bible says in 2 Chronicles 16:9 that the eyes of the Lord are looking throughout the whole earth, so that he can strongly support those whose hearts are fully committed to him. If God is continually looking, there must be a shortage of available and willing people. I want to be part of that group he is looking for. If we are not aware of this truth, we will struggle and strive all our lives, trying to be our own provider.

The gospel is called the good news. That means we don't have to do everything ourselves without God's help. The Lord was preparing me for the next phase of my life and believe me, he had a real challenge with the likes of me. I didn't know what to expect. All I knew was that the more truth I received, the more I was put to the test. Would I do what I read and heard from him? I found that it was by "doing" what God asked that freedom came into my life, not just by hearing or reading.

After having reviewed and calculated all my debts, the amount I owed totalled $110,000.00. I had maxed out two major credit cards to the tune of $25,000.00 each. I was shocked to see how alcohol and drugs had taken their toll on my finances. I was in a serious dilemma.

Our family was now going to church every Sunday. I went as well, even though I was still battling my drinking habit and smoking like a chimney, but much less than before. At this church, I was told about a well-known preacher in the States that went from complete poverty to being a millionaire in a matter of a few years. I was interested to find out what he had done to change his situation so I bought a book he had written. I read that when he was in debt, because he had no money, he would give anything he had. He even put a pencil in the offering once. He explained that if we were always faithful to tithe and give, no matter what our financial situation was like, then when we were in need of a financial miracle, we had ammunition to work with against the devourer of our money, the devil.

It was as though he knew exactly what my situation was and had written this book just for me. He continued by saying, "If you are in a financial crisis, make a list of all the people you owe money to and total it up." I had already done that and the total was $110,000.00. He went on, "After you have done this, get out a copy of your latest tithe receipt you have received from your church for income tax purposes, place it on top of the list of the people you owe money to and speak to your debt out loud, so you can hear yourself speak. Say this and direct it toward your enemy the devil: 'Devil, here is my receipt for my tithing and giving for the past months. I place it on top of all my debts and, according to the Bible, God will rebuke the devourer for my sake and open up the windows of heaven and pour out a blessing in my life that I will not be able to contain, that will take care of all my bills.' Thank you Lord, I receive your abundance right now, in Jesus' name, amen." As I did that, a peace came over me. I knew God was about to do something for me. I didn't have a clue what he would do. I would have to wait and see.

The very next day, the Lord spoke with that inner voice again. I was getting pretty good at knowing when it was him speaking to me, and whenever he did, I paid attention to what he said and made every effort to obey. What he said to me this time was a shocker. What would Joane say?

The Lord told me to look at all the assets I still owned, list them all out on a piece of paper and find out how much equity I had in each one. The items with equity I was to put up for sale immediately. The list was not very long but the items on the list were items I really wanted to hold onto. Joane had a new Impala that I had bought for her only a year ago. That went on the list. I wanted to hold onto it, but I knew it had some equity in it so it would have to go. We owned a ten-year-old motorhome that had been completely paid for the year before. This item was nice and handy for our family to get out of town on weekends and the children were always excited when we used it, but it had to go too if I was going to be obedient to God's instructions. I had a little equity left over in our house that the company had help me buy and after having paid back their $32,000.00 and re-mortgaging our home at a higher interest rate, our monthly payments were more than we could really afford. So the house would have to be sold as well. My company car was given to the employee I had trained to take my place after I had resigned. This would leave us with absolutely nothing to our name.

It was one of the toughest things the Lord had asked me to do, and it took me a while to digest what was actually going on. Joane would have to agree with what I was about to do and she did. Within a couple of weeks, everything had been sold and after calculating how much revenue had come in from the sales, the total amount was slightly over $30,000.00. *Had it been worth all the effort?* I wondered, but that wasn't the right question to ask. The right question was, *Had I obeyed the Lord?* I could truthfully answer that question with a resounding, "YES!" I had done what he had asked me to do and Joane had agreed to everything. But what was the next step?

The Lord didn't waste any time in giving me my next assignment. It was just as difficult as the last one, if not harder. I was to call everyone I owed money to, explain my financial situation to them and promise to pay them back as soon as possible. That was the most humbling experience of my entire life, but somehow I made it through and felt so relieved after it was all done. Again, a weight was lifted off of my shoulders. It felt so good. What amazed me was after having been bluntly honest with all of them, many people forgave me my debt and told me I didn't have to pay it back. That was nothing short of a miracle.

The Lord then told me to apply the $30,000.00 to the creditors who wouldn't wait, such as the banks. This made sense, since they were charging me a lot of interest every month. I was able to come up with a monthly payment plan that, to my amazement, they approved. I asked them to charge me no interest on the balance owing each month. That was unheard of, but miraculously they agreed and even put it into writing. I guessed that after they reviewed my financial situation, they must have been concerned that there was a very good possibility of me declaring bankruptcy. They didn't know I was merely following the Lord's instructions and that the thought of bankruptcy had never even crossed my mind.

A careful review of my new financial situation didn't paint a very good picture. After being freed from owing money to some of the creditors that had forgiven me my debt, after having sold all of the things that had equity in them and receiving approximately $30,000.00 and after having struck a deal with the banks with a monthly payment plan, I still owed $70,000.00. It was such a huge amount to me, even though it was $40,000.00 less than before.

I felt it was now time to review my personal situation. I still smoked two packs of cigarettes a day, I still had a drinking problem, even though I was reluctant to admit it, but I reasoned it was probably because I was attending these Alcoholics Anonymous meetings and they had me state at every meeting that "Once an alcoholic, always an alcoholic." I didn't feel right about saying that because, in contrast, the Bible said, "Whom the Lord sets free is free indeed" and "Nothing is impossible with God." Besides, I had already experienced that truth when he completely freed me and delivered me from drugs at that Good Friday meeting when I was born again. The craving for drugs had never come back. So I decided to quit going to the AA meetings and trust God instead.

I justified my smoking by believing it was calming my nerves while I was going through the mess I was in and of course the alcohol helped to some extent as well, as long as I didn't drink too much. It looked like everything was in control. Shortly after quitting the AA meetings, I concluded that what I could do was bring my drinking habit to the Lord and see what he had to say about it. Did I really need help and could he really help me? It was worth a try.

One day, in the middle of the afternoon, I felt I was to go home and talk to the Lord about my drinking. There would be less distractions there and the children were still in school. For some reason I felt he had an answer for me and that, once again, he would give me direction on the issue. I wasn't disappointed and before I could finish my inquiry to the Lord, he gave me a very clear instruction. Some are clearer than others, and this one was crystal clear. I had no doubt whatsoever that it was the Lord talking to me, because he asked me to do something I would never have done in a million years. This would prove to be one of the hardest things for me to do so far, but it would also bring me the greatest freedom I'd ever experienced in my life.

As I entered the house, I clearly heard the Lord tell me to go to the basement and bring upstairs all the bottles of cognac that had been there for months. My former customers all knew I loved cognac and every so often would buy it for me as a gift. I had not drunk the majority of it, because they would also buy me these drinks at the bar and what they didn't buy I would drink and charge to the company. There were bottles in two different cardboard boxes and I carried them upstairs to the kitchen. I discovered I had accumulated twenty-one bottles of cognac. Most of them were very expensive. If I were to go out and buy these bottles, it would cost me around $2000.00.

The Lord told me to get rid of those bottles that had been sitting there for all those months. The first thing that came to mind was to go to the bar where I had spent years drinking and sell the bottles to the bar owner at a discounted price and make some money. I sure could use that money. Then this thought instantly came to me, *What if this same booze is bought by someone and causes them to have an accident?*

I didn't know why that had come to my mind, because if they did, that would be their problem, not mine, so I quickly dismissed that thought and was about to load the liquor into my vehicle when I received another message from the Lord that was loud and clear: "I want you to pour this liquor down the sink one bottle at a time."

I was absolutely sure this was the Lord speaking and I didn't dare disobey Him. I knew it wasn't a suggestion but a command. I reluctantly put several bottles on the kitchen counter and started uncorking the first one. When I had the cork off, I could smell its beautiful aroma. The first few bottles I had put on the counter were the cheaper brands of cognac. I picked up the first bottle to pour it down the sink, in obedience to the Lord, but just couldn't do it. Something was stopping me. This struggle went on for approximately ten minutes until I started to pray in my heavenly language I had received on Good Friday and suddenly I started to pour it down the sink. It started with a small quantity at a time, but soon the bottle was upside down and in a couple of minutes it was empty. To my surprise, I felt good about it and proceeded with the second bottle. It was easier to pour out the second than the first one and again it was soon gone. What I noticed next, but didn't understand, was that I actually started to enjoy what I was doing. It felt like I was getting a desire never to drink this stuff again. Now I know that with every bottle I was pouring down the sink, the Lord was delivering me from my addiction to alcohol, like he had done with my habit of taking drugs. This time instead of it being instant, it was gradual, until every last bottle had been poured down the sink.

When I was doing this, I had turned on the water to try and get the smell of the cognac out of the kitchen, but I accidentally turned on the hot water and steam began drifting upstairs. Soon Joane came down to see what was going on and I joyfully explained to her what the Lord had directed me to do. When she saw all the empty bottles, she didn't need any convincing. It was truly the Lord and definitely not my idea. I had been completely delivered from being an alcoholic in a matter of thirty minutes or so. We both rejoiced and as I picked up the empty bottles. I realized that obedience to the Lord always brings blessing. Some might believe that "Once an alcoholic, always an alcoholic" but God's power and grace had proven it wrong. How many more things I'd once believed would be proven wrong?

THIRTEEN

Goodbye, Addictions—Hello, Freedom!

The two major things that the devil had used to bring me to financial ruin were drugs and alcohol. Now, I had been set free by the Lord in both of these areas. The third area that bothered me was the fact I still smoked two packages of cigarettes every day. For some reason, this was the one thing I couldn't get rid of. I tried to quit so many times but would soon fall back into my bad habit. Every time I would smell someone else's cigarette smoke, I would find the smell irresistible and before long I was smoking again. Then I decided to change the brand of my cigarette and go to one with a filter, to cut down on the amount of nicotine I was inhaling. That didn't help me quit either, so I kept changing brands until there was hardly any nicotine in the cigarette. I had gone to the lowest amount of nicotine available, but to no avail. All it did was to cause me to increase the quantity of cigarettes smoked. I was still getting the same amount of nicotine as in the stronger non-filtered brand.

This struggle went on for months after I was born again. I didn't bring this issue to the Lord because I realized I wasn't really serious about quitting, even though I tried to quit many times. I realized I was simply justifying my habit by being convinced that the lesser amount of nicotine wasn't really that bad for me and my health. Justification of sin doesn't work. What we are really telling the Lord is that we don't need his help in that area; we have everything under control.

That was about to change as well. The Lord was cleansing me of everything that was hindering my walk with him. He saw that in my heart I had the desire to obey him. He was simply removing things from my life that would hinder my walk with him.

I had a very good friend in Calgary. He was the one who had brought me to my first AA meeting, wanting me to quit drinking, because he saw what it was doing to my life and my family. He was about to go on a two-week vacation with his family in Europe, but he owned a small deli business in Calgary and needed someone to take care of it while he was gone. He asked me if I would do it for him since he saw I was not really doing much with my own business. I agreed to do it and in those two weeks I had a lot of time between customers to sit at a small table in the deli and study the Word of God. It was like I was becoming addicted to the Word of God and couldn't get enough of it. The two weeks went by so fast that before I knew it my friend would be back in a couple of days. The day before he was to arrive, I was sitting in the deli on a relatively quiet afternoon. I reached over to get a cigarette from my package, only to find it was empty. I didn't have far to go, so I went behind the counter and got another package and at the same time bought a new cigarette lighter. I was tired of carrying matches around in my pocket, since they were forever getting wet. I put my money in the till and went back to the table to continue my study of the Bible and have another cigarette. I reached over to open my new pack of cigarettes and try out my new lighter. I took out a cigarette and put it in my mouth.

The minute I took the lighter the Lord spoke to me in a gentle but authoritative way, "You don't need to have that cigarette. Today I'm giving you the choice to decide, one way or the other. If you have it, you're on your own, but if you choose to not have it, I will help you quit."

I instantly picked up the package of cigarettes and crushed it with my hands, including the one I had in my mouth. I got up from the table and threw them all into the garbage can, along with the new lighter I had just bought. I was acting mechanically, like a robot, not totally conscious of what I was doing. It reminded me of Good Friday, when I found myself at the head table without knowing how I had gotten there.

There was my bad habit in the garbage can, along with my new lighter, in a matter of a few seconds. I knew it was the Lord's doing and I was very thankful for what had just transpired. I thought to myself, *He must have just set me free from nicotine.* Five minutes later, a customer came in the door of the deli, cigarette in hand, and walked up to the counter. I got up from the table and proceeded to serve him. As he was ordering a sandwich, he blew some cigarette smoke in my face. To my utter amazement, his smoke reeked so much of nicotine and smelled so bad I almost gagged. That instant I knew I had been delivered from nicotine by the Lord and again I was so thankful. I was being cleansed by him, one step at a time. Obedience to God's voice was turning everything around. I was realizing that the Lord wanted to set me free from all the things that had been ruining my life for so many years. He wanted me to be free from each thing that hindered my life and health before my new business would be fully operational. This had been his plan all along.

Shortly after my deliverance from alcohol in my kitchen, the Lord seemed to prompt me to go back to the bar once again. That didn't seem right to me but again I remembered that often the Lord told me things that I would never do otherwise. It was hard to believe that he would send me back to the place that had almost ruined my life and marriage. A scripture came to mind that I had read a few weeks prior, which said that God's ways are greater than our ways and his thoughts are higher than ours. I also remembered reading that the Lord works in mysterious ways. This was certainly mysterious to me.

I was getting better at recognizing his voice. I was also realizing it was imperative that I follow the directives of the Lord. Every time I did I experienced positive results. This one was very different, though. Yet I knew I had to obey, no matter what I thought about it. I had learned that the greatest enemy to following the Lord's voice was my mind. We will never be able to understand spiritual things with our minds. Our minds operate in the natural realm, but the Lord works through our spirits and wants to bypass our minds. He wants us to cooperate with him, spirit to spirit.

One significant thing I had learned was that we, as born again believers, are spiritual beings. God communicates with our spirits (hearts) and not our minds. That revelation made it much easier for me to follow the promptings of the Lord. Even though I didn't understand why the Lord wanted me to do the things he asked me to do, I did want to obey, so I decided to go back to the bar. I was very curious to find out why he wanted me to go back.

I still remember the look on the faces of the regular customers as I walked through the door of the establishment. Of course I recognized most of them and they recognized me as well. They had all come to the conclusion that I was either very sick and in the hospital or had died, probably in a car accident, because I was never in any condition to drive when I left the bar.

I sat down and began talking to some of the men sitting at the bar. They seemed to have a greater concern about what had happened to me. The first thing they wanted to do was to buy me a drink, so I obliged and ordered a cola with ice. The same look that had been on their faces when I entered the bar was back on their faces again—a look of disbelief.

I spent about two hours at the bar, telling all who were willing to listen what had transpired in my life since the last time

I had seen them. There was a mixed reaction. Some were genuinely happy for me, some were skeptical about the whole thing and some didn't believe a thing I said. I was OK with that because I know if I had been in their shoes and they were telling me the same thing had happened to them, I probably would not have believed a word either. Both the group that was happy for me and the group that was skeptical had dozens of questions to ask but I didn't have time to hang around. I promised them I would be back some day and continue our conversation. They seemed to be glad that I would return, especially the skeptics.

On the way out, a hand touched my shoulder. I looked and saw it was the waitress that had been serving me all those months at my booth. She was the owner's daughter and she wanted to know what had happened to me. I told her I would be back soon and would explain everything that had happened to me since the last time I had been here. She made me promise and I did.

I looked for her dad but he wasn't around that day, which was a little strange since he had never missed a day of showing up to oversee his business the whole time I had been there. I would see him the next time I came. I knew in my heart the Lord wanted me to come here again.

I ended up coming back a little over a month later and that time my waitress, the owner's daughter, gave her life to the Lord and was born again. So did her dad. At least a dozen of the customers did the same thing. This was all happening in a bar! They would never have gone to a church. That is when I realized that we must go to the sinners instead of waiting for them to come to us, and tell them that they do not have to stay bound with addictions, but can be free. They need to know that although God hates the sins that are ruining their lives, he truly loves them, the sinners, unconditionally. Their deliverer is the one they are rejecting.

I used to be convinced that God didn't care about me, especially in the condition I was in and doing the things I was doing. Only the truth in the Bible will set people free—and since they will probably never pick one up, we can be the bearers of the good news and bring it to them, the captives.

FOURTEEN

God's Electrical Business

I was finally as ready as I could be to consider going ahead with the new electrical business the Lord wanted me to start. He had to help me do it, because I knew absolutely nothing about the electrical field. What I did know frightened me whenever I thought about it. I knew you needed to be a master electrician in order to take out permits to do work. I knew it took four years of on-the-job training for apprenticeship before you could become a journeyman and then at least another four years to become a master electrician, after passing the exam, which not everybody does. So I had to force myself not to dwell on these facts but on the fact that this was the Lord's idea in the first place, so it was up to him to make it happen, not me. To me this was an impossible task but I was quickly reminded of the Word of God that said, "With God all things are possible." That brought me a little peace. Anything positive would be a miracle.

I knew I would have to hear his voice more clearly than ever or this business would never get off the ground. I read in the Bible that we are to imitate Jesus. I started to study Jesus, especially his last three years of ministry where many impossible things happened wherever he went. Jesus said he only did the things he saw his Father do and only spoke the things he heard his Father say. That is what I needed to do, but how could I? I would have to be so in tune with Jesus that I wouldn't do or say anything unless he prompted me.

That seemed impossible for me to attain, but the Bible said we were to do the same things Jesus did, so I needed to know what was expected of me, because the Lord doesn't work on his own here on earth. He needs people to be his hands and his feet, to do and to go wherever he directs. When did the Lord see and hear his Father? I found it was when he spent hours, early in the morning, alone with him in prayer. I knew I would have to do the same thing in order to achieve the same results as Jesus. I decided I would get up every morning, five days a week, at 3:00 and pray for a minimum of three hours. I knew I would need his supernatural help to do this. But when the Lord puts on your heart to do something he always gives you the grace (the supernatural ability) to do it. So I faithfully got up every morning at 3:00 and prayed fervently for my business. It made my days long, but the effort and the results were nothing short of miraculous.

The first morning I got up to pray, after ten or fifteen minutes praying in English and French, I had no more words to express what I had to say. I then decided I would try out the new language I had received on Good Friday, the day I was born again. It seemed fruitless to my mind because I didn't understand anything I was saying. I was praying in tongues and I wasn't very fluent; it seemed that I was saying the same words over and over. I decided, though, that I would stick it out, keeping my side of the deal to pray for three hours. The hours surprisingly went by quicker than I anticipated and soon it was time to eat and go to work. Where or how, I didn't know.

I decided not to go anywhere until the Lord showed me where. That seemed to be the way it worked in the Bible. My whole reason for getting up early in the morning had been to receive direction from the Lord about my new business. As I was eating breakfast, suddenly I had a picture of myself driving up and down Deerfoot Trail, Calgary's main freeway. I was so excited that the

Lord was starting to show me things. All I had to do was follow and the result should follow, just like they did for Jesus.

In my excitement I left the house without finishing my breakfast and headed straight for Deerfoot Trail. Since I didn't really know where to begin, I started from one edge of the city and drove all the way down to the other side of town. That way I would cover all of Deerfoot Trail. As I started to drive, suddenly I began to hear an unfamiliar voice, saying things like, "You don't really think this praying in tongues works, do you? I mean you're the one who made up those few words of gibberish and you will soon find out that it doesn't work at all. You can spend all day driving up and down this highway and it will accomplish nothing. The only thing that will happen is wasting your money on gasoline, nothing else."

Entertaining that thought for a second made me begin to doubt I had received a prayer language. Then it dawned on me that I was hearing that old enemy from my past, the devil, who was trying to abort what the Lord wanted to do with my business. I pulled over to the side of the highway and spoke out loud to the devil and told him where to go, in Jesus' name. I knew I had been given authority over his works so I simply exercised that authority and as quickly as those thoughts had come to me, they left. I had read in the Bible that he was nothing but a liar so why would I ever entertain anything he had to say?

I then asked the Lord to give me the assurance that my new tongues were enough to get whatever direction I needed for the business. I asked him to increase my vocabulary, so that it didn't sound like I was praying the same words over and over again. I started back onto the highway and continued my trip, still not sure of where I was going.

As I reached the end of Deerfoot Trail, I turned around and started back again. I quietly spoke in tongues as I drove, resting in the Lord's peace, now that the devil's voice was gone. Suddenly my tongues seemed to shift gears and I heard myself speaking new words with a different kind of force behind them. It was as though I had switched into overdrive and I was going somewhere fast with the Lord. I felt a much greater authority in these new words. I could clearly sense that something was happening in the spirit realm. I also noticed something happening in the natural realm when my car started to sway back and forth as if I were drunk so I quickly pulled off, where I could focus on what the Lord was saying, without being distracted by the traffic.

I don't know how long I parked on the side of the freeway, but I do know that when I stopped I felt like a superman. It was as though nothing could possibly keep me from doing what I was called to do. Praying in tongues was a marvellous new experience and I could hardly wait to see what would happen next. I thought to myself as I pulled back onto the highway, *There never seems to be a dull moment with the Lord.* I always had anticipation in my heart. My eyes were constantly looking for what he might show me and my ears tuned to what he would tell me.

Heading towards the north of the city, I clearly heard the Lord say, "I want you to take the next exit and make a right hand turn at the intersection."

It startled me, because it was the first time the Lord had acted like a GPS while I was driving. The next exit was Peigan Trail. I had never exited there before in all the years I had driven in Calgary.

As I exited, I felt impressed to make a right turn and the minute I did, the instructions continued. "Drive until you come to railway tracks and make a left turn." These instructions continued for several streets until I turned into the parking lot of a huge manufacturing company that I recognized right away. Everyone in Calgary knew this company, because everyone consumed their product.

I thought, *What am I doing here? This is a huge company.* So I said, "Lord, why did you have me come here?"

All I heard in my spirit was, "You need work, don't you?" I waited for more information but it didn't come so I decided to go inside to see what the Lord had in mind. Did he want to give me some business with this company? Why would he pick such a huge corporation? I had no employees, no vehicles, no electricians, no tools, no electrical knowledge, no money, so nothing made sense to me. I would just have to by-pass my mind in order to stay tuned to my spirit; otherwise I would just turn around and go back home.

It took me a while to decide I would finally obey and go inside. The main entrance and the reception desk were right in the front. I was sweating bullets, not knowing what to say. I didn't want to lie to them, but on the other hand, I didn't have to tell them everything about my business either. When I approached the front desk, the receptionist asked me my name and the name of my business and whom I was here to see. I told her I wanted to see the person in charge of hiring different trades to do their service work. She immediately knew I had no appointment since I didn't even know the name of the person I was looking for. But without further questions she gave me the man's name and phone number along with his extension number.

I asked her if she could inquire whether I could see him for a minute so I could introduce myself. She giggled and said, "It usually takes a week before you can get to see him; he's a very busy man, so I suggest you call and make an appointment."

I thanked her for her information and as I was about to leave, I felt the Lord prompting me to wait. I turned back and asked her if she would mind if I just stayed in the sitting area for a while. I told her I had a few things to go over before I left. She was very gracious and let me stay. As I was reflecting on what had just transpired, I wondered why the Lord had brought me all the way here for nothing, since the person in charge was not available. Regardless, I decided to obey the Lord. I sat in the reception sitting area for almost half an hour with my nose buried in a magazine. It seemed like an hour but my watch told me it had only been twenty-five minutes.

Suddenly, the receptionist called my name. She said, "Sir, this is your lucky day. It's a good thing you stayed! The customer who was scheduled to meet him in thirty minutes just called to let us know there was an emergency and he would not be able to come. I called the person you need to see and he will be able to see you in ten minutes. If you want to go up to the second floor and just wait outside his office, he will come and get you when he is ready to see you."

Feeling like cheering, I thanked her and proceeded toward the elevator. My whole being was overflowing with thanks to the Lord as I made my way to the second floor. Then I thought, *When the gentleman comes out to meet me, what will I tell him about my company?* This troubled me since I didn't want to lie. I would soon find out. Those were the fastest ten minutes I had ever known. Then I found myself face to face with the superintendent of this huge multi-million dollar corporation. I could feel the sweat pouring down. What would I say?

However, I was about to discover the miraculous ways of God. It was one of the greatest challenges of my life. I was being trained to walk in blind faith when I couldn't see what was ahead at all. I would find out firsthand what the Lord would do. He only needed my obedience. I could either let him come through for me and win…or fail by doing it myself.

The first time you go through an experience like this, it's a scary place to find yourself, but oh, what a joy it is to get to the other side of the situation and realize you could never have made it without the Lord. I was finding out that the more I trusted him, the more mightily he worked on my behalf—in spite of me. I was about to learn a very important lesson: the more yielded I was to Him, the less struggle I had in my mind. I could clearly see it was not my business that was about to begin, it was God's business and all I had to do was follow his instructions and make him CEO from that day forward. That decision was easy, since I knew nothing about the electrical industry. I realized that when the Lord sent me somewhere he always had a reason for doing it and the results would always turn out to be very beneficial.

The superintendent introduced himself to me with a handshake and said, "Come on in."

I explained to him that I had been working for a multi-national company for over fifteen years and now I was ready to branch out on my own. I told him I was starting my own business and I needed some work to get it off the ground. I had come there to see if there was any possibility of getting some electrical work.

He looked at me and said, "Well you may have come to the right place. Right now, I'm in the process of buying two new pieces of equipment from Minnesota. It will be the first time this equipment has been used in Canada and by acquiring it, I will be able to sell my products to Japan and be a step ahead of the competition. I will require two electricians for at least thirty days. This is new equipment, so there are still a lot of unknowns. I have full-time electricians working for me, but they are busy with the every-day maintenance of this company. I need to look outside for help since this is not permanent work. By the way, if these two pieces of equipment work out for us, we will be buying four more this year. I'm willing to give you this work if you promise me I can have the same two electricians, should we decide to buy the other four pieces. By then your boys should know exactly how they are to be wired up and I don't have to be concerned about looking for another electrical company. They will already possess the knowledge to handle this equipment and should also be able to wire them up much faster than the initial ones. If you agree to this, then it's your job, based on the hourly rate you just quoted me. The equipment won't be in for another four to six weeks. Does that work for you?"

I agreed, we shook hands and it was a done deal. What an awesome day it had turned out to be, simply by obeying the Lord's directives. It had been too easy to be true, but I couldn't deny it. Had this gentleman wanted me to start immediately, I would have been in a pickle, since I still didn't have any employees. The Lord knew this and that is why the meeting went the way it did. He was giving me time to find reliable electricians. They would have to be reliable, dealing with such a large manufacturing company that was in the process of supplying the market in Japan. It meant at least three months' work, should the other four machines be purchased as well.

Thanksgiving to the Lord filled my heart and I had a new assurance that everything was going to be OK. I needed to stay focused on his plan for my business and continue praying every morning. *This stuff works*, I thought, as I made my way to the parking lot. I had a new bounce in my steps and couldn't wait to get home to tell Joane the good news. I was amazed at the confidence this gentleman had in me, a complete stranger. I was sure that the Lord had something to do with it.

FIFTEEN

God, My CEO

My time with the Lord every morning became very precious to me and I let nothing come in the way of it. Three days later the Lord spoke to me again. In my spirit I heard him say, "I want you to go downtown today, park the car, and look around at all the different businesses."

Downtown Calgary is quite large. I tried to hear more details from the Lord because his instructions were pretty vague but nothing else came so I decided simply to obey and go. I spent the first four hours of the morning looking at different businesses, trying to memorize the names of the companies in my head, since I had forgotten paper and pen in my car. I began to get hungry and decided to find a place to grab some soup and a sandwich. My hours of walking had not borne much fruit. All I knew is that the Lord had a purpose for me being there and it looked like he wasn't in any hurry to let me in on his plan.

I walked by a huge department store that took up the whole block and heard in my spirit, "Go in there."

That was the last place I wanted to go. I didn't need a department store. I needed a restaurant or deli to appease my hunger pains from walking all morning. I reluctantly obeyed and as I entered one of the doors, I found myself in the women's clothing department. I knew this definitely wasn't the right place for me and continued to make my way across the first floor. As I approached the escalator, I saw a sign that said, "Washroom and

Deli in Basement." Maybe I was in the right place after all, since I desperately needed both these services.

I went down the escalator and into the washroom. As I came out, I noticed there was only one place to sit at the bar-like table. I took the seat and immediately overheard an interesting conversation. This department store was the largest in Calgary, seven stories high and covering an entire block.

I heard, "I'm not looking forward to the renovation that is starting in six weeks. They're going to gut this whole basement floor and make it into a food market for the public. There's going to be such a mess in here for at least three months with all the renovations going on, and I'm really not looking forward to it at all."

All of a sudden this crazy thought came to mind, *I should quote on this job.* I answered myself, *How crazy is that?* I dismissed that thought as fast as it had come but as I was having my soup and sandwich, it kept coming back to me again and again. Then a light bulb went on in my head and I wondered if the Lord had planned this. Reflecting over the guidance I had received to come to this store and go to the basement floor, I thought I'd better pursue the thought, just in case the Lord was in it. *I'm already here now and I have nothing else to do downtown after all my walking this morning, so why not check it out—but where am I to start?*

I decided that when I had finished eating, I would find the reception area, wondering if they even had such a thing in a large department store. I spent some time searching with no luck and decided to ask an employee where the offices were located and was told to go to the second floor. As the doors of the elevator opened, there was clothing as far as the eye could see. Finally I located the offices situated in a far corner. They took up almost a quarter of the floor. *This must be the Canadian head office for this store.* These stores were all across Canada, the majority of them being in Western Canada.

I came to the offices and there in front of me was the reception desk. I introduced myself to the receptionist and boldly told her I was here to pick up a set of the blueprints for the basement renovations. She said, "Aren't you a little late? They came out a week ago and all the quotes are due in four days."

Not knowing quite what to say, I blurted out that I had just heard about it today and could she find out if I was too late to submit my quote. Within a few minutes she came back and said, "The gentleman in charge of the quotes, the one in charge of the renovations, would like to speak to you. He's busy right now, answering questions with another electrical contractor, but if you want to take a seat in front of his office, he will be with you soon."

She brought me to his office. His door was closed so I took a seat and a picked up a magazine. Right in the middle of an interesting article, his door swung open and he invited me in. He was bidding farewell to another gentleman. He went back into his office, seemingly in a rush, with me following close behind. As I entered his office, an unbelievable conversation started up between two different voices. The whole thing transpired in about thirty seconds and took me completely by surprise. The first voice said, "I want you to talk to him about Jesus."

The second voice immediately said, "If you do, you'll lose all their business."

The first voice came back in a split second and said, "What business? You don't have any from them so what do you have to lose?"

My mind was reeling and here I was meeting with the person in charge of all Western Canada's renovations in the largest department store chain in Canada. He extended his hand to me and told me his name and title. I shook his hand, told him my name and my company name.

Then I looked at him, and said. "Do you know Jesus?"

I expected him to show me the door but to my amazement he smiled and said, "I've been in the business and with this company for thirty years but I've never met anyone like you before. It looks like your religious beliefs are more important to you than the business you came here for. As a matter of fact, to answer your question, I'm Catholic."

Coming from the Catholic background, I knew this didn't necessarily mean he was born again. I briefly gave my testimony and he wanted to know more about being born again. Before I knew it, he was praying the sinner's prayer with me and was gloriously born again! I was as shocked at what had transpired as he was. With what had happened in just five minutes, the voices arguing in my head and this person receiving Jesus as his Saviour, I had almost forgotten what I was there for.

For the next twenty minutes the gentleman talked and talked about what had just happened to him and I could tell that business was the farthest thing from his mind. I listened to him until he was finished and then brought up the subject of the renovations. Coming back to the subject at hand, he explained to me that for the last ten days all the other contractors already had the blueprints for the job in their possession and they were, unfortunately for me, due back in four days.

He said, "You can have a copy of the prints if you want and if you have time to quote the job, just have them back in my office before 10:00 AM, four days from now."

I told him I would give it a try and let him know. He said, "If you have any questions whatsoever about the job, call me any time and here's my home number. You'll definitely be working over the week-end." He couldn't thank me enough for what I had shared with him in his office and for leading him in the prayer of salvation. He made me promise I would come back to see him whether I had time to finish the quote or not. He wanted to spend time with me after working hours. I could see he had many unanswered questions, just as I did when I was born again. ✔

He called someone to bring me a set of blueprints and to my amazement it was the man I had overheard while having my soup and sandwich. The Lord had orchestrated the whole thing as plain as day. Did that mean he would allow me to get this contract? That was impossible since I didn't even know how to read blueprints.

A couple of days before, I had taken a business card from a man from Nova Scotia, where I was born. He was an electrician with another company. I thought I might just call him up and ask him if he could help me read these blueprints. I didn't have any time to lose and had no other option. I hoped he wouldn't ask me to pay him for his service, should he accept. Money was scarce but work was on the horizon.

I didn't lose any time in calling him. He said, "I'm busy right now, but I can take a look at them on the week-end and let you know what I think about the job. Tell me what hourly rate you're planning to use. I pretty well know the cost of the materials and will try and come up with a price for you by Monday. It will only be my estimate and I don't want you to hold me responsible for the outcome of the quote. I'm just helping you out here. You can compare my figure with the one you get."

Little did he know I had given only him a set of blueprints and he was the only one helping me with my quote. I happily agreed and gave him the blueprints, again thanking the Lord for allowing this person to come into my life at such an opportune moment, when I desperately needed his expertise. I spent the weekend praying for this newfound friend, asking the Lord to give him wisdom while going over the prints.

This contract would mean the world to me since it would really get my business started. The week-end took forever to pass. We had agreed to meet Monday morning at the department store. If he had any questions, he could look at the job site and see what was involved. We would meet at 7:00 a.m. sharp at the shipping and receiving area, the only way into the store before the store opened to the public. I had already made arrangements with security and since I was quoting on the renovations, I would be permitted to come inside early.

Monday morning arrived and I anxiously waited to hear what the quote would be. We were shown inside by security, quickly grabbed a coffee from a vending machine, took it to a table in the deli and sat down. What he told me was frustrating and disappointing. He said, "You'll have to go with your quote because this is much more complicated than I thought."

What he didn't know is that I wasn't even able to quote, but I wasn't about to tell him that. He continued by saying, "There are so many unknowns here that your price could be out in left field and you wouldn't find out until you were well into the job. If the demolition was already done it would be a different story, but the demolition is part of your quotation. If you're not certain about your price then I would forget about this job."

By now I was trying to understand why the Lord had me go through all of this. It appeared to be for nothing. I thought it might be just for the man's salvation and that brought me some relief. Then out of the blue, the man said, "The strangest thing happened to me last night. Around 3:00 in the morning I suddenly found myself sitting straight up in bed and this large sum of money kept flashing through my mind. Nothing like that has ever happened to me before. You know what, I think I'm going to win the lottery."

In curiosity, I asked him, "What was the large sum of money that kept flashing in your head?" He said, "$355,000.00."

The instant he said the amount the Lord said to me, "That's the amount of the quote you are to submit for this job."

I looked up at the man and said, "You're not going to win any lottery; that's the price I need to quote on this job."

He started to laugh and said. "You're crazy, that's impossible."

I said, "No, it's not impossible, that's the number I'm submitting for my quote."

He said, "That's the craziest thing I have ever heard, but it's your company and you can do what you want, but if you go with that number, you could lose your shirt, and don't come back and blame me for it."

I said, "Thank you very much for all your work last weekend on this quote."

He replied, "I didn't spend that much time on it anyway. I saw right away that it was going to be too complicated for me to work out in just a few days. Best of luck with your quote, but I would be interested to find out how far off you were on it. It seems way too high to me."

I said, "I'll keep in touch with you and let you know what happens."

"That's great," he answered and chuckled, "and if you get the job, I might just come and work for you."

I prepared the letter with my quote and submitted it the next morning at 9:30 a.m. I felt good about the price and I had total peace about it. *My Nova Scotian friend thinks I am quoting way too high and if I am I won't get the job anyway.* Four days later I got a call from the gentleman with regards to the tender. Lo and behold, I had won the bid by coming below everyone else's price by $5000.00. The Lord had come through for me in an amazingly miraculous way.

The renovations would be starting in two weeks with the demolition of the whole basement floor and a week later the electrical work would begin. The only people I needed to do the demolition were some strong, able-bodied men and I knew enough of those guys. Within two days I told the electrician about my quote. He was in awe and wanted to know if he could come and work for me, starting with this job. He knew from the blueprints he had seen it would give him steady work for at least three months.

SIXTEEN

Divine Instructions and Astonishing Meetings

I was rejoicing at what the Lord was doing with my business but now things would have to come in line with all the work that was coming in. I needed a master electrician to take out permits and I would need at least half a dozen electricians to do the work after the demolition was completed.

I had to open accounts with suppliers in order to get all the materials for this huge project. I would need to set up an office with someone to do the billing and everything else this contract required, such as paying the employees, accounts payable, etc. My very first requirement was a master electrician. I soon found out that all the master electricians had businesses of their own. What should I do?

I decided to talk to the Lord about it in prayer and not do anything until he spoke to me—clearly. I realized this was the most important part of my business. No master electrician, no permits; no permits, no work. I need to hear from the Lord for sure. While in prayer I sensed he was telling me to go to this electrician from Nova Scotia and talk to him about my predicament. The Lord was working in a different way with me by not directly giving me the answer I needed but leading me to the person who had the answer. Unfortunately, he would find out that I was not a master electrician and would wonder why in the world I had quoted this huge job in the first place, if I couldn't take out the needed permits.

This would be a humbling experience for me, but if he was to work for me, it was important that he knew the truth. After spending time in prayer, I called the electrician and met with him over lunch. I explained my situation and how the Lord had directed me in all my recent business affairs. He told me he was also a born again Christian, but none of the things that were happening to me had ever occurred in his life. He also told me that the master electrician he had worked for was also born again and that he only did a minimum amount of work because he was now semi-retired.

He said, "You should talk to him about the possibility of him taking out the permits for you, at a cost of course. I'll introduce you to him tomorrow and maybe you guys can work something out together."

That gave me great hope and I realized now why the Lord had asked me to talk to this man. Things were falling into place and I could tell in my spirit that I was about to have a wonderful meeting with the master electrician the next day. I couldn't wait to see what the Lord had in store. The electrician arranged for me to meet the master electrician at the deli in the store where the job would take place. We would have lunch and discuss the possibility of him taking out the permits.

We had a wonderful two-hour meeting, the subject turning towards the Lord and the wonderful things he was doing. After several hours of getting to know each other, he agreed to take out all necessary permits for a fixed rate and after the work was done by my electrician, he would come again and look at the finished work to make sure it had been done according to specifications. When he was satisfied that all had been done properly he would call the city to come and do the official inspection.

He was paid strictly on an hourly basis which worked well for both of us. He even suggested I call certain electricians he knew that did excellent work but were no longer happy at the places they were working. They used to work for him, but because of his semi-retirement, he was not able to keep them busy enough and had to lay them off. Thanks to the Lord, I would be able to start the job on time, with enough electricians to do the work. My biggest concern, about the necessity of acquiring a master electrician, had suddenly been solved. I kept thinking, *The Lord's ways are so good and so much higher than ours. I need to have a greater trust in him. After all, the responsibility for the success of this business is on his shoulders, not on mine because I've made him my CEO.* I would have to remind myself of that fact continually. I was simply his employee.

My morning prayer times continued and were the best part of my day. The business continued to grow and so did God's instructions. One morning the Lord dropped a company's name into my mind and told me to call them around 9:00 a.m. His instruction was more specific for some reason. I wondered, *Why at 9:00?*

It didn't make any sense to call this company, because I had tried to get business from them countless times, but to no avail. I must have called them fifty times, but the person in charge of operations never seemed to be there and I never did get a response from the messages I left for him. I came to the conclusion he didn't want to do business with us, for whatever reason. He could have at least had the decency to call me up and let me know why. His company had left a bad taste in my mouth and would have been the last place I would have called for my services with my new business. Who needed someone like that?

But the Lord seemed to think they should be one of my customers, so that was a good enough reason for me. I thought, *I'll call but I wonder how long it will take for me to talk to the operations manager—if I talk to him at all?* His was the largest grocery chain in Canada and their headquarters were based in California. That much I knew. At 9:00 a.m. sharp, I picked up the phone and called the company, merely out of obedience to the Lord's voice, but my whole being resisted the idea. The phone must have rung eight or nine times. When someone finally did pick up the phone, it was a man's voice on the other end and it took me off guard because all the other times I called during those three years I only talked to the receptionist. Who was this man and why was he answering the receptionist's phone? Both questions were immediately answered as he gave the company's name and his name. Miraculously it was the Operations Manager I had been trying to reach for three years.

He apologized for the phone not being answered sooner and explained that the receptionist must have gone to the washroom. He just happened to be passing by her desk on his way to a meeting. "I usually don't answer any phones personally; my secretary takes all my phone calls, but for some reason, I just felt I was supposed to answer this one."

I gave him a brief explanation why I was calling, saying that I had been trying to talk to him for a long time, but now I had started my own business and was looking for potential customers.

What he said next floored me. He asked, "What are you doing for lunch today? I have lunch at this small cafe next to my office every day at 11:00 a.m. in order to avoid the crowds and if you can meet me there, that would be great. I would like to talk to you about something. Are you able to make it?"

I didn't take long to answer and in less than two hours, I was finally talking to the man that had been absolutely impossible to reach. How quickly things can change when the Lord gives instructions.

I arrived at the cafe fifteen minutes early to find a seat facing the entrance. That way I could see everyone coming in and hopefully we would recognize each other, even though we had never met. I left my name with the waiter in case he asked for me. I had done my homework and was ready to meet him. At 11:00 a.m. sharp, a well-dressed gentleman with a three-piece suit walked in. I knew it was him, and was further assured when I heard the waiter call him by name.

I was dressed in jeans and felt quite out of place, but I waved to him and he came over to my table and introduced himself with a handshake and a smile. My first impression of him was good, but I wondered what he thought of me and the way I was dressed. He said, "I see you took some time off of work to see me. I appreciate that. I only have thirty minutes for lunch, so I'll get right to the point. By the way, I've seen your name on some of the phone memos on my desk several times over the years, but we were not ready to look at anyone new to do our work until a major change in our company was finalized. I have now been made President of all the Canadian stores and I'm sure you can imagine how busy I've been with this whole affair. Much of my time has been spent in California over the past year, dealing with head office and their re-organization. It's a good thing I know the Lord or this transition would have been much worse."

I could hardly believe my ears at what just came out of his mouth, but at the same time I was rejoicing. I thought, *A potential Christian company as a customer—wow!*

He didn't skip a beat and continued, "I have forty-three stores in Alberta and Saskatchewan. We want to renovate and change the lighting in all of them and provide extra power for our new fridges and freezers. The job will take about three to four months and my question to you is, can you put a group of men on the road, travelling to all our stores and get this job done? If you can't, I will understand. I know you still have to service your existing customers in this city."

Little did he know, I had almost no customers, but the few I did have were very big jobs. Before I realized what I was saying, I told him I could. He pulled out his purchase order book and started giving me orders for all the stores. The purchase orders already had the name, address, phone number and the manager of each store. They were in duplicate form and he simply asked me to return him a copy of the P.O. every time I finished a store and I would be paid within five working days. He said with a smile, "Don't forget to put the name of your company on them if you want to be paid."

I then briefly told him about my experience with the Lord and how this had all come about, as we both finished our soup. He smiled and said, "I feel good about this meeting and I'm looking forward to talking with you in the months to come. Let me know how things are going and you can start the work as soon as you are set up and ready to go. Just keep in touch with me on a weekly basis and if you have any problems send me a fax. Here's my card with my private phone number written on the back."

He got up, picked up his briefcase, and said, "It was nice meeting you. Have fun." It had been too simple a meeting, but this was further proof to me that I had the best CEO for my business. Business had never come that easily before. I picked up my forty-three purchase orders and by the time I was ready to leave, he had already disappeared out of the restaurant.

When I went to pay for the lunch on my way out the waitress said, "It's taken care of. He has a running tab with us; he's here every day."

Another excellent day with the Lord, I thought. *It doesn't get much better than this.* I smiled all the way home. These were the kind of meetings I really enjoyed, the ones orchestrated by the Lord.

What was in store next?

SEVENTEEN

A Hopeless Case

The job I had just received would be the first one I would have to start. I needed scaffolding, ladders, special tools, and above all a new reliable vehicle that would be able to transport at least four guys and all the necessary equipment to do all these stores. Supplies coming to me every week would need to be paid for. Salaries would have to be paid every week, along with my travelling and living expenses. I had an open P.O. with this company and was able to tack on all these extra expenses, since I'd been told I would be paid within five working days.

I needed cash flow and it was relatively easy for me to get a line of credit with the bank, especially when I showed them the three P.O.s I had with these three major organizations. They asked me how much I needed and of course I gave them a figure that would give me a good cushion, should anything unexpected occur.

My next task was somehow to buy an expensive, oversized van with no credit record and with no receivables in the company as yet. The bank had used my P.O.s as collateral but car dealers were not interested in future business coming in. They were interested in whether I could afford to buy the vehicle now, today, period. The next morning, I was switching through several radio stations trying to find some suitable music. Suddenly I heard an ad for a car dealer. It said that no one was ever refused.

That was the only thing I heard in the ad. I immediately turned the car around and drove straight to that dealership in the north end of Calgary. They sold Dodge cars and trucks. As I entered the show room I was greeted as someone important. Two salesmen were jockeying for my business but I quickly told them I wanted to talk to the owner if he was in. They assured me he was but didn't like the idea I didn't want to deal with them. With no money and no receivables coming in, they were not the ones who could give me the answer I needed. It would be up to the owner to decide if he wanted to sell me a vehicle or not.

I waited about fifteen minutes until he was available. He was alone in his office so I didn't know why he hadn't seen me right away. When he finally signalled for me to come in, I could see he was going through something serious. Something definitely was wrong. Before I sat down, I told him, "If you want me to come back tomorrow, that's OK. I can see you're struggling with something."

He assured me he would be OK and asked me to take a seat. Before I could say anything he jumped right in. "I'm just going through something difficult with my family, but I'll be all right. It's not the first time I've gone through this. What can I do for you today?"

Before I explained to him why I was there, I told him I had also just recently gone through some rough things with my family and if God had not intervened, we wouldn't be together today. I would have probably even lost my children. That seemed to strike a chord with him and he wanted to know more about what God had done to save my marriage and kids.

For the next hour and a half I told him in detail where I had been with my drinking problem, drugs, and smoking and how God had delivered me from all of them. I shared how God told me to start my own business and what had transpired in the past couple of weeks. He was totally amazed. When I stopped long enough for him to get a few words in, he said, with tears in his eyes, "I'm in the same boat right now you were in. How can this

God of yours help me? I'm so glad you came here today. This is exactly what I needed to hear, because all hope has been slowly fading away from me over the last few months. I was certain everything was over, but today you've given me hope."

Within fifteen minutes he had prayed the sinner's prayer and was gloriously born again. His whole countenance changed and he wore a huge smile on his face. He said to me, "I know something happened to me just now, but I don't know what. I know it's OK and I believe everything is going to be all right with my family. I feel peace in my life again." He couldn't stop telling me how glad he was that I had showed up that afternoon.

When he finally realized I had come for some other reason, he asked me what kind of vehicle I was looking for to do all those jobs God had gotten for me. I told him I didn't really know, so he looked at me and said, "You go out there and pick out any vehicle you need and let me know which one it is. I need to call my wife right now and try and tell her what just happened to me and how I now know there is hope for our marriage. Once you know what vehicle you want, come back in and see me."

I looked around the dealership at all the different options and decided on an extended van called a Dodge Prospector, fully loaded with room for seven passengers. I found out later the seats could be folded down to make a queen-sized bed. What a beauty! The price did make me a little nervous. The owner didn't know my financial situation or he wouldn't have told me to go out and pick out what I needed. *He is about to find out,* I thought as I came back into his office.

He was still on the phone, so I waited until he hung up and gently knocked on his glass door. He looked up and signalled for me to enter. He had a huge smile on his face and looked far better than the first time I saw him. He told me that his wife was excited about what had happened to him and wanted to know all about it herself but that he couldn't answer any of her questions. He asked me if I would come back tomorrow, after he talked to his wife, so he could ask me her questions and some of his own. I agreed and he was very thankful.

He then said, "By tomorrow morning I'll have your vehicle ready for you to pick up."

I said, "We haven't even talked about finances yet and you're asking me to come tomorrow to pick up my vehicle?"

"That's right," he said. "I know your financial situation by all the things you told me. Don't worry about the financing, leave that with me, and when you get some receivables coming in with all these contracts, come back and we'll sit down and work things out. I'll see you tomorrow."

Another amazing miracle. As usual with God, everything fell into place.

A few days later, I bumped into the service manager from the last company I worked for. He had become so good at it, I could leave him in charge of all the service work and not worry about the quality or quantity of work. Before I had been glad for that because the less time I needed to spend checking out his work, the more time I could spend at the bar. I was pleased to see him but he was even happier to see me.

He said, "I've been looking for you for the past couple of weeks but you're no longer at the bar and no one seems to know where you've gone. I'm glad I bumped into you. I don't work for the company any more because I could never do enough for them. They were never satisfied, so I quit. By the way, what are you up to these days?"

For the next twenty minutes I talked to him about all that had happened to me and how God had miraculously provided all these jobs to do. I told him I was looking for employees. He immediately offered me his services and said, "I'll do a good job for you if you'll hire me."

He was the exact person I needed for a foreman to oversee the work at these forty-three stores. I hired him on the spot. Another divine appointment, orchestrated by the Lord. I told him I needed a total of four guys for the work and one of them had to be an electrician. Within two days, he called me to let me know he had found the people I needed and asked if I wanted to interview them. I agreed to interview the electrician but I knew that he was very capable of interviewing the others himself. After all, they would be working for him and he knew exactly what type of employees he wanted.

In a few days my crew was on the road. I arranged for my suppliers to drop-ship all the materials where they were needed at each location, prior to my crew's arrival. Everything was working like clockwork; the jobs were all running smoothly with very few hitches—nothing my new foreman couldn't solve. I sure had chosen the right guy for the job, or should I say God had arranged for us to meet again for that very purpose.

I went back to talk with the owner of the truck dealership several times over the next few weeks and he was amazed how his marriage was being restored to even better than it had been years before. He couldn't thank me enough. I just pointed my finger to heaven and smiled and he knew exactly what I meant.

The next thing on the horizon was the $355,000.00 renovation job that would be starting. At the beginning, all I needed was one electrician to supervise and labourers to demolish the place. That electrician was the man who had the dream of winning the lottery but it was God's way of letting me know the exact amount to be quoted. *God has a good sense of humour*, I smiled.

While the demolition was taking place, I put an ad in the newspaper for electricians. When the contract was awarded to me, all the ones who had lost the bid wanted to know who this new kid on the block was and where he had come from. It didn't take long before phone calls started coming in from curious contractors. Resumes for electricians poured in but since I didn't know anything about the electrical business, and not being an electrician myself, or having gone to trade school a day of my life, I didn't hire them based on their skills. I chose them based on their character instead. I knew if they had a good character, I could work with them. It was obvious they had skills or they wouldn't have applied for the job.

During the interviews I listened carefully for the Lord's promptings and only hired the ones I felt peace about in my heart. I didn't allow my head to come into the equation at all. It was uncanny how simple it was. This business was coming together and prospering seemingly without any input from me. I had no electrical knowledge to offer, so it made God's job easier. We made a good team and he kept leading me to new jobs the minute another one was needed.

For some reason the Lord seemed to be leading me to one of the biggest companies in the city. I could only guess he was doing that because he didn't want me to have the headache of trying to collect payment from these jobs. Because of the magnitude of business he was getting me into, I needed a good cash flow but that was always available when required. Some days I would have to pinch myself to see if I was really awake and all of this was truly happening to me. *Why me, Lord?*

I was directed to one new customer, though, that became a real thorn in my side. I began to wonder if the Lord had made a mistake on this one. It was a huge, Canada-wide company that was having major problems with its lighting. Their warehouse was the size of a football field and their shipping across Canada was all computerized. Trollies went around each aisle, guided by wiring in the concrete flooring. The trollies would automatically go right to the exact product that needed to be shipped.

The major problem was the gentleman in charge of the whole operation. His language was so profane that I dreaded seeing him.

I thought I had heard all the swearing possible in my earlier years before being born again. But this man took the cake, icing and all. I spent the absolute least amount of time possible around him. He used the name of Jesus Christ in almost every sentence and every third or fourth word was the "F" word. He was the most bitter man I had ever met. He definitely had a huge chip on his shoulder about something.

One day I decided to talk to him about Jesus to see what would happen. *It couldn't get any worse, could it?* Oh, how wrong I was. It got way worse. He now started swearing whenever he caught sight of me far away and would shout louder to make sure I and everyone else heard him. This was getting nowhere, so I did what I should have done weeks before and brought the matter to the Lord.

I got up early the next morning to pray in tongues as usual and brought this problem to the Lord. I didn't hear any response from him. I just couldn't see his purpose in this case. Why would he allow or want me to be in this terrible situation?

I got my answer that very day. That morning I was asked to check out this company's problem with their lighting and come up with a solution. As I drove to the warehouse, the Lord began allowing me to feel the hurt that foul-mouthed man had within him, a brand new experience for me. I had never felt someone else's hurts before. I ached so much inside it became almost more than I could bear. It took me right back to my experience as a boy at the seminary where the brothers and priests were abusing all those students. This guy seemed to have the same type of hurt within him, only magnified several times over.

Then I heard the Lord speak to my spirit as plain as day: "You have this job, because I'm going to use you to lead this guy to the Lord."

I felt completely helpless because I had already experienced his strong reaction when I had mentioned God to him. I just couldn't imagine him ever becoming interested in God. He looked like a totally hopeless case. The Lord reminded me where I had been in the past and how people must have thought what a hopeless case I was. I realized then that the Lord specializes in hopeless cases. *Look at what he did with me,* I thought.

Meanwhile, I was doing electrical work with other major companies, replacing mercury vapour ballasts with the latest craze, high-pressure sodium (HPS) ballasts. Much of Calgary still had the old mercury vapour fixtures, but the new high pressure sodium fixtures gave much more light so large warehouses were wanting to switch their fixtures over to the brighter ones. A prominent carpet company had decided to change the lighting in all their warehouses to HPS. They had hired a big electrical company to do all their work but after the job was done, they started noticing a large return of their products. People were complaining they were not receiving what they had ordered.

They had found out about me through an electrical distributor who was one of my suppliers. They phoned me asking if I had a solution to their problem. I decided to go visit them, because I knew right away what the problem was, as well as the solution. It would be easy and simple work for me; a first-year apprentice could have done the work. They had done the right thing in wanting to get rid of their old mercury vapour fixtures, but they had replaced them with the wrong fixture type. What they didn't know is that the HPS lamp gives off an orange light and that orange light changes the colour of their carpets, the reason for the high return from their customers.

The solution to their problem would be expensive. I suggested they change all their lamps to metal-halide lamps, the bright white light lamps car dealers use. This light does not change the colour of the product. They were happy about the solution but concerned about the cost. Instead of asking them to buy all new fixtures, I would simply take out the HPS ballasts and replace them with metal-halide ballasts. They would have to replace the ballast and the lamp.

The new HPS system had been in operation for less than six months but because of the high return of their products, it needed to be changed right away. They understood that when the customers chose the colour of carpet they needed under those orange lights, it did not look the same as in the natural light of their homes. They had learned an expensive lesson. I could see they were struggling to give me a "go ahead" because of the exorbitant cost, but they knew the obvious answer. It looked like they wanted me to give them a break, financially.

Because I knew it was the current craze for people to switch over to HPS and I knew the supplier of the fixtures and lamps would not take them back, I decided to buy their HPS ballasts and HPS lamps from them for 20 cents on the dollar if they would promise to give me the job right away. It was a good deal for both them and me, and what I would give them for the HPS products was more than they could ever get on their own. We agreed to the deal.

I now had a warehouse full of HPS ballasts and lamps in my inventory, which I could eventually sell and install for an incredible profit, but right now I had more work than I could handle. The Lord's blessings were overtaking me; he was opening the gates of heaven and pouring me out such a blessing I could hardly contain it, just as he said he would in the book of Malachi.

One day I again had to go see my "hopeless case," as I called him. He was standing on the loading dock, swearing at the truckers who were delivering merchandise. Nothing had changed and I wondered why the company kept him as an employee. I would have gotten rid of him long ago. I thought he was a disgrace to the company, but again, maybe they didn't know what was going on, or maybe they didn't care. He was a good worker.

All these thoughts were going through my mind and the more I thought about it the more bitter I became towards him. I knew that wasn't right. After all, the Lord had told me he would use me to help him. I admitted, *The sooner the better. This is seriously starting to affect my attitude towards him.* What troubled me the most was his use of Jesus' name. He was swearing about the one who had set me completely free from a living hell and was now my dearest friend.

I stayed in my car until he was finished dealing with the truckers at the loading dock. I then reluctantly walked towards his office, hoping I wouldn't have to spend too much time and quickly let him know what had to be done to rectify his lighting problem in this massive warehouse. They still had the old mercury vapour lamps and ballasts and I knew that because of the two new products on the market, metal-halide and high-pressure sodium, these old ballasts and lamps had already been phased out and would be hard to obtain in Canada. After I told him, his response, using his favourite adjectives, wasn't too gentle. He answered, "Do you think I'm some kind of idiot? Do you think I didn't check all this out? Do you think I don't know what you just told me? I don't need your information crap about it. I need your solution. What are you going to do about my problem?"

He then let me know that he had already spoken to the manufacturer of the mercury ballasts and they were no longer producing that product, but because of the quantity they needed for their warehouse, they would be willing to re-tool their equipment to produce the product for them at cost, which would probably be double the original price they had paid. When he'd heard about the cost, he already decided he would have to get all new high-bay fixtures. I had to admit he had done his homework but had come to a brick wall as far as being able to stay within his budget.

He told me he would have to do it in stages because the company didn't want to give him any more money to rectify the problem. His budget was quite high since he had been changing the existing lamps and ballasts on a daily basis for the past year. I suggested he go with HPS ballasts and lamps, which would dramatically increase his light output, but keep and use the existing fixtures. That would save him a fair amount of money.

For the first time ever, he seemed to be happy about my idea. He asked me, "Get back to me with your costs as soon as possible, before my warehouse is in complete darkness."

I told him I would get back to him in twenty-four hours and his answer was, "You better or I'll find someone else to do it." That was the kind of treatment I received every time I went there. No wonder I dreaded being around him. He truly was a thorn in my side, but obviously the Lord didn't see him that way.

At that moment, an HPS light bulb went off in my head. *Jesus does hate the sin, but he sure loves the sinner,* I thought, *and I have to learn to do the same thing, no matter how hard it is.* This was another important lesson; now it was time to put it to work.

As I drove away, shaking my head, the Lord spoke to me and reminded me that I had accumulated enough HPS ballasts and HPS lamps from the carpet company to do the complete job. They were sitting in my warehouse waiting for jobs to come up, and lo and behold, they could be used on this one job. I saw dollar signs swirling in front of my eyes. This would mean thousands upon thousands of dollars of profit. My cash flow would double in size with just this one job. I was so excited; I struggled to concentrate on my driving. This would become my most profitable job ever. What an awesome blessing from the Lord. I was so glad he had reminded me about it, since I had promised this guy an answer within twenty-four hours. I would be able to tell him I could start the job right away and that I already had all the product in stock. Hopefully this would make his day and cause a change of attitude in him.

I would call him and give him the good news tomorrow morning. What I had to do now was come up with a fair price for the products, obviously not based on my costs (twenty cents on the dollar), but on the present market value of the product. I also took into consideration that they were not brand new because they had been used for six months. That was no big deal since these ballasts last a minimum of ten years. I would figure out the cost of the equipment to do the job and all the labour separately. I decided I would give him a very fair price on the products and in return he could use my men to do the work. Everything was falling smoothly into place.

I awoke the next morning for my time with the Lord. The only thing different was that the Lord spoke to me very clearly that morning. I couldn't understand how he could ask me to do something I so completely did not want to do. If I weren't so familiar with his voice, I would have been sure it was the devil speaking to me. It would be my biggest test so far. I heard the Lord plainly command me, not ask me, but command me to give this hopeless, profane man the products for free and incorporate my twenty cent cost of the products into the cost of my labour and equipment rental. This was the same authoritative voice that had commanded me to go home the first time the Lord had visited me at the bar at 1:00 AM, only this time his voice wasn't audible. Just like that time, I knew he meant what he said and I was to obey him without question. I groaned inwardly and struggled with the Lord's request because these products could be sold for a hefty profit, which would be a tremendous help to me financially.

Reluctantly, I finally decided to obey. After breakfast, I sat down and figured out the cost for my labour and rental of the equipment to do the job. It was still a good-sized job, but it could have been so much bigger. Around 10:00 a.m. I called the customer and told him the good news about what his cost for my work would be. I even told him my reason for giving him such a deal. I was very aware of his reaction the last time I mentioned God and this time was no different. The minute I said that God had directed me to give him the product free of charge, he absolutely flipped out and swore like never before.

Suddenly the phone went dead. He had hung up on me. I called him right back and politely asked him please not to hang up on me again but to listen to what I had to say, which he did for a few more minutes then hung up on me again, ending his conversation with the same filthy language. I called back again but this time he didn't answer. I decided to load up all the product, go to the warehouse and give it to him, regardless of his attitude. I had to obey the Lord.

I arrived there shortly before noon. He wasn't in his office. When I inquired as to his whereabouts, I was told he was in the cafeteria having lunch. I walked into the cafeteria and saw him sitting alone at a table, even though many other people were around. I thought, *I don't blame everyone for not wanting to sit with him.* He saw me coming, and his look was not inviting at all. He immediately started telling me never to do that again.

I didn't know what he meant by that statement, so I said, "I don't understand what you mean. Could you clarify for me?"

He was convinced I was blatantly lying to him and that I was just pulling his leg as a joke, which he said was not funny at all and never to try that again. I assured him it wasn't a joke. I assured him I had the product with me, ready to unload from my van if I was given the OK to do the job. I was holding my quote in my hand. I had typed out a letter on my letterhead, stating in detail what the cost would be, excluding the product—because it would be free of charge—and I would be available to start the job immediately. The product was free on the condition I would get to do the work.

He grabbed the letter out of my hands, quickly read it and said, "Follow me."

Where was he taking me? We went directly to his office, he closed the door behind us and we both sat down. He read my quote again and looked up at me to speak, but before he could say a word, I said, "I know it's hard for you to believe this, but let me tell you, it was just as hard for me, when I was told to do it. The Lord must really love you to make me do such a thing. You know, you're not the easiest guy to get along with and if it had been my decision, I would never have done this for you. I believe the Lord wants to touch your hardened heart in spite of whatever you have done against him. He wants you to have no doubt how much he loves you."

As I spoke, tears welled up in his eyes and he started to weep uncontrollably. The more he tried to stop, the worse it got, to the point where I decided to leave his office and let him have time alone with the Lord. I could tell God was really working in his heart to heal the wounds that had accumulated during his lifetime. I knew he would be a new person after the Lord was done with him.

I went to my van and started unloading the products onto different pallets on the loading dock. I was amazed at how many ballasts and lamps there were and unfortunately didn't have any help, because God was still dealing with him. He wasn't there to ask his employees to help me. Half way through my backbreaking work I looked up to see him walking towards me. When he opened his mouth, no swear words came out, but what he said was music to my ears. For five solid minutes, he apologized profusely for his rude behaviour toward me. Like I had done, he had turned away from God for he was convinced beyond a shadow of a doubt that God hated him and had allowed a whole bunch of negative things to happen in his life. He didn't want to go into detail at that time, but said he did want to have the same experience I had with regards to this "God thing."

We left everything on the dock and went back to his office where I was able to lead him in the sinner's prayer. He was wonderfully born again. His countenance completely changed. The Lord had done a miracle with that totally "hopeless" guy. He was a changed man. We kept in touch with each other for weeks while my boys were doing the job. All he could talk about was the Lord. I didn't think anyone could have so many questions and fortunately I was able to answer most of them. Swearing had completely disappeared from his vocabulary and, believe me, it was a welcome relief. He was a new man, thanks to the Lord and my reluctant obedience.

The Lord asked me a question that day as I drove away from the loading dock, thinking of all the money I could have made with those products. He said, "What price can you put on a person's salvation?"

I knew a person's salvation was beyond any price. The Lord had paid the ultimate price for sin. Not long after the job was completed, the man left town and moved back to his former home. I never saw or heard of him again but I knew that with his newfound Friend everything was going to be all right. The Lord had decided to work through me and with me to touch the lives of people in the business world. They were ones who had written God out of their lives and the very last place they would have gone would have been to a church, just as I wouldn't have darkened a church door for anything a few years before.

EIGHTEEN

From Booming Business to Struggling Students

We had a contract with another large company who supplied three quarters of the city's restaurants with produce and supplies. It had grown so much over the years it had become one of a kind, with little to no competition. Everyone was using their services, even the Calgary Stampede, where in ten days every year literally tons of food and supplies were delivered. I was impressed with their operation and warehousing. Tons of fruit and vegetables were brought in each week and placed in gas chambers for ripening. Tons of soup were made right on the premises in large vats, then bagged and frozen and sent to various restaurants and fast food establishments. Potatoes were prepared, washed, and peeled and put in individual see-through bags for delivery. Motorized lifts buzzed through the huge warehouse, preparing pallets for their customers. They would then be loaded into many refrigerated trucks for same-day delivery.

Because the warehouse traffic went on all day, our lighting and electrical maintenance had to be done at night or on the weekends when it was closed for business. The gentleman in charge of the warehouse operation and maintenance was from the Maritimes, just like I was, and we hit it off well and soon became good friends. He opened up to me and started talking to me about his drug problem. He had been hooked on cocaine for

132

years, from a time when he'd hung around with a biker gang. I slowly started to talk to him about how the Lord had set me free from drugs and alcohol. He didn't reject what I shared with him but didn't embrace it either or seem to be interested. It was like he was saying, "I'm glad for you, but that's not for me."

I visited him over the months and continued sharing the things of the Lord with him and he never reacted negatively to anything I said. It was confusing to me because most people immediately let me know where they stood when I shared the Lord with them, but not this guy. One Saturday morning I went to visit him because he wanted me to quote on a new system they were about to install for their loading docks. I arrived a bit early for my appointment, which I always preferred to do. It gave me time to think about why I was there so that when I walked in I knew exactly what direction to go. As I walked toward his office in the warehouse, I could see him holding his head in his hands, staring at the desk. He was either catching a nap or something was bothering him. I waited about five minutes before I placed myself in front of his window where he could see me. It took a while but he then noticed me and signalled for me to come in. He had a worried look on his face and I knew something was wrong, so immediately asked him, "Are you OK? Is something wrong?"

Instead of giving me an answer, he started asking me questions about this God I had been talking to him about for months. He remembered everything I had told him about how the Lord had gotten me out of trouble again and again even before I knew him or wanted anything to do with him. After talking for ten minutes or so, I found out that the biggest concern he had was if the Lord would do the same thing for him. I assured him he would because God was no respecter of persons. The Lord loved him unconditionally no matter what kind of life he lived.

He confessed to me what had happened to him the day before and even though he had been with the company fifteen years, they would decide next week whether they would keep him as an employee or let him go. They had finally found out he had a drug problem, leaked to them by another employee. He had been told who the employee was. He had been good friends with this employee and thought it would be safe to talk to him about his drug problem. He needed to talk to someone. Unfortunately, it had backfired because this supposed friend of his had wanted his job for years and seemed to want to hang out with him so that he could learn all the ins and out of his job.

He felt like someone he had trusted had stabbed him in the back. After he finished telling me the whole story, I saw that he had been betrayed. He was definitely at a crossroads in his life and his next decision would change the course of his life forever. I explained to him that the first step he needed to take was to put the whole situation in the Lord's hands, repent of his sins and accept Jesus as his Lord and Saviour. He decided to accept the invitation and the Lord not only saved him but delivered him from his cocaine habit over the next few weeks as he began to learn truth from the Word of God. That truth set him free as he cried out to God for his deliverance. He was able to keep his job but the hardest thing he had to do was to forgive that employee for turning against him.

He told me later that he was able to talk to that guy again without any bad feelings. He also told me he believed the Lord had not only used me to help him get saved but he believed this guy would as well.

Through this experience I learned that the Lord can use things in our life which look so negative and turn them around for our benefit. We spent months together after his salvation. I found out that he had been born into a Christian family and his mother had been praying for his salvation for years. Another fascinating thing he told me was that his dream had been to practice dentistry and he had actually purchased all the necessary dentistry tools, which were at his home in a wooden case. He never followed this dream because of his drug problem, one of the biggest disappointments in his life.

About a year later, we took a team to Manila, Philippines to work in the slums. We had become friends with a Canadian couple who had been missionaries there for years. They had spoken several times at the church we attended and needed help with the children in these slums. We decided we would go and take our own family with us, along with eight other people from the church. What an eye-opener it turned out to be for everyone. Before we left, we were asked to bring medicine, toothbrushes, and toothpaste because these poor people had a very serious problem with their teeth. Most of them had decayed teeth and on one of the days we were to be there, we were going to go help relieve them from their pain by pulling teeth. The missionary wife had learned how to administer pain killers and pull teeth but she needed help, since so many people were showing up with teeth problems. When she told me that, I remembered the guy with the former cocaine problem who always wanted to be a dentist. I still saw and met with him at least once a month. He continued to grow and flourish in his Christian life. I went to see him and told him about our upcoming trip to Manila and what we would be doing for a couple of weeks. He immediately asked me if it would be possible for him to come with us. He would be able to fulfil his lifelong dream of doing dentistry work. Of course I told him he could come and help.

In just one day in Manila, we treated about three hundred people and my newly-saved friend was absolutely in his element, doing what he had always dreamt of doing, dental work. I was thrilled at how the Lord had made his dream come true. While there, he noticed how the women in Manila were gentle and loving towards him and upon his arrival back in Calgary he asked me if I knew of a Filipino Church. I did, so he attended that church for several months, fell in love with a girl from Manila and they eventually married. Today they are happily married with children; he has started his own business and is prospering.

By now, the two new machines that were coming in from Minnesota arrived and were installed. Three more were installed that same year. The contract for $355,000.00 was completed and we ended up doing not only the basement of the large department store but another four floors. The company was so impressed by our work and service we were then asked to do all their stores in Alberta.

The forty-three grocery stores across Saskatchewan and Alberta were also completed, with a very good profit margin, and our new van was now completely paid for. Because the business was doing so well, I had time to become quite involved with our church and soon had been appointed to many of their boards. Most of the church's work was inside the four walls of the church but my passion was to help the people outside who wouldn't ever go to church.

Every day, in the business world I would ask the Lord to bring people across my path that needed to know about God. I wanted to meet those who had lost all hope in their personal lives, like I had years ago. I wasn't disappointed. The Lord brought many people my way every week and I was much more interested in them than in my business. It got to the point where most of my time was being spent ministering to people and taking hardly any initiative in my business.

One morning during my time of prayer I brought this concern to the Lord. In my spirit I heard his words to me, "The more time you spend doing my business, the more I will be involved in doing your business."

I placed some of my Christian employees in positions of authority, which gave me more time to fulfil my passion outside the church and out in the business world. Jesus said, "Go into all the world and preach the good news," so I had a great desire to go and not just stay still and do nothing. It wasn't long before I did go but not in the way I had imagined. I first had to be prepared to go and that meant obtaining a solid foundation of Bible knowledge and experience.

One evening a well-known preacher came from the United States to speak at our church. Joane and I went to hear him speak. He preached on how important it was for Christians to be grounded in the Word of God so that they would become strong by studying it for themselves. He continued stressing the point that without faith it was impossible to please God, but that faith comes from a knowledge of God's Word.

He spoke of a man in Tulsa, Oklahoma whom the Lord had called to preach specifically on faith. His name was Kenneth Hagin and he was known as the "father of faith" in many circles. He had started a school in Tulsa called Rhema Bible Training Centre. Students came from all over the world to attend this college for a minimum of two years. The minute I heard this, I heard the Lord say, "I'm going to send you there for training."

This seemed impossible because of my business and my involvement with the church, but I remembered that if he wanted me there he could make it happen. First he would have to convince Joane. With everything she was involved in and our children in school, it looked impossible for all of us. We also had a dog we all loved.

The thought was so overwhelming I didn't hear another word the preacher said that night. I was too occupied trying to figure out how it could work out. I came to the conclusion that it was too much for me to think about so I would just have to leave it in the Lord's hands. If he wanted us there, he would have to do everything on his own, without any help from me.

To my surprise, as Joane and I were driving home, she said out of the blue, "Wouldn't it be nice if we could go for this training in Tulsa? We need to pray about it because with God nothing is impossible."

I was stunned that the Lord had spoken about it to her so fast. Was it possible that he was really going to make it happen? Several months later, the whole family, including our dog, were on our way to Oklahoma in a new van that had entirely been paid for through our business.

Before leaving Canada, we needed a minimum of $15,000.00 USD in a U.S. bank account, since our commitment was for two years and we were not allowed to work during that time. We had either sold or given away all of our furniture because we would be living in a rented home. Storing all our furniture would have been too costly. The hardest test for me was to entrust my business to my employees while I was gone for two years. I was so glad I had already given many of them authority to run many aspects of the business. God knew months before and had already been preparing things for me.

A big consolation for me was that my Christian accountant would oversee the business and send me financial reports on a monthly basis.

The hardest thing for the family, especially the children, was leaving their friends behind and having to make new friends. I could see their sad faces in my rear view mirror and tried to think of something to cheer them up when suddenly a thought came to me out of nowhere. I heard myself saying, "Before we come back home to Canada we are all going to spend a week at Disney World and have fun together." This seemed to work as I noticed big smiles forming on their faces. For the next few hours all they could talk about was what they wanted to do while in Disney World. The dog seemed to be the only one with no concerns and he peacefully slept at the back of the van.

All our possessions, also in the back of the van, were contained in three suitcases. It was an adventure that we still talk of to this day. Our whole family experienced so many miracles in those two years from the love of our Father towards us as a family.

After travelling for several days, we arrived at Tulsa. We needed a place to live and a school for the children and were really trying not to be overwhelmed with it all. The day we arrived we found out that there was a huge, three-day revival meeting starting that evening, which thousands of people would be attending. There was no admission fee so the price was right. We went that night and met people from all over the world. What made us most happy, though, were the local people we met who could answer our dozens of questions. That night we found the church we would attend, and a place to live, which was only a few blocks from the college. The children even made new friends. Things were falling into place faster than we had ever imagined, which was amazing since we were in a brand new country when just hours before we were among complete strangers.

That evening at the revival meeting they must have taken up three different offerings, specifically targeted to urgent needs around the world. Both Joane and I had in our hearts to give towards these needs, so we did, giving more in each offering, not realizing at the time that we were spending the money that had been allotted to our living expenses. By the end of the three days we had given almost 30% of the money in our U.S. bank account. But it was too late to change anything; it was done. So we just thanked the Lord for meeting all of our needs according to his riches in glory. We would have to look to his bank account in heaven, not ours here on earth. After all, we were at Rhema to become grounded in faith and those offerings were given in faith. We would soon find out if this "faith stuff" really worked. We decided not just to talk about it but actually do it.

It is easier to do something in faith when both husband and wife are in agreement. We had arrived in Oklahoma a week before the classes were to begin, and found we had other needs with different people we were starting to meet. By the time we were settled in and ready to start our classes, much more money had been spent than expected, including sending our children to one of the most recognized Christian private schools in all of the U.S. They would be getting the best education possible, but we knew we were serving a big God who wanted to give us the best he had while we were here in Tulsa doing His will for our lives. So far, He was meeting every need over and above anything we could have thought of or imagined.

We were a big, happy family and even the dog got used to the heat of Oklahoma. After classes were in full swing, we had a desire to become involved in ministry on the weekends. During the week we were busy with our children's homework and our own studies as well. We started attending one of the largest churches in Tulsa with over ten thousand members. We could learn things about faith there as well and before long we found ourselves pastoring over 600 children from ages eight to twelve years old, including our own children. We did this at the second Sunday service, as well as attending the first service so it made for long Sunday mornings for both our kids and us. The kids didn't mind, because they had the opportunity to meet many new friends, and it took their minds off the friends they had left behind in Canada.

The two years we spent at Rhema Bible Training Centre in Tulsa, Oklahoma, changed our lives forever. We received some of the best teaching on faith and healing in the world. We experienced financial miracles and witnessed many healing miracles. We attended numerous special meetings held by various ministries in Tulsa. Some of the best known and biggest ministries had their bases there, such as Oral Roberts, T.L Osborne, Bob Yandian and Billy Joe Doherty, to name a few. We were growing by leaps and bounds spiritually. The two best recognized Christian schools in North America were located in

Tulsa and our children were able to attend both of them, a year at each school.

The Lord was also blessing us financially. The more money we gave to meet the needs of people all over the world, through different ministries and meetings we attended, the more the Lord prospered my business back in Canada. We never had any lack and all our daily needs were being met. We saw people come out of wheel chairs and walk. At some of these meetings we saw demon-possessed people completely set free by the power of God and of course we saw many salvations, where people with addictions were also instantly set free. Every summer, Kenneth Hagin Ministries would have a camp meeting and ten thousand people from all over the world would gather for a week. All employees and students of Rhema Bible Training Centre would attend those meetings.

At one of these meetings, I noticed a man sitting in the front row among some of our Bible School teachers. He looked very familiar and I suddenly realized he had been the speaker that Good Friday in Calgary where I had accepted Jesus into my life. I later found out that he was one of the ministers who was on the Board of Directors for Kenneth Hagin Ministries. I was amazed. Imagine that the Lord would use someone to lead me to the Lord from the same ministry I would years later attend.

One evening at a camp meeting that I will never forget was when Kenneth Hagin was preaching. Suddenly, in the middle of his message he stopped talking and walked over to the edge of the platform. You could have heard a pin drop. Everyone's eyes were glued to him, not knowing what to expect. When he reached the edge of the platform he pointed to the eleven wheelchairs that were lined up there. In one of these wheelchairs was a classmate that had to be wheeled into our classes every day. He had been born completely crippled and had never walked in his life. Kenneth Hagin spoke, gently and quietly, and said, "The Lord just showed me that you were to get out of your wheelchair and walk."

My eyes were glued to that student to see what would happen. Suddenly his legs began to straighten out and within minutes he was up and walking. I had to hold my jaw up before it hit the floor. I had just witnessed a most incredible miracle. Then I noticed seven more people had gotten out of their wheelchairs and were all standing up and rejoicing. Kenneth Hagin simply walked back to his spot in the middle of the platform and continued his message, as if nothing unusual had happened. From that day forward the scripture that became the most real to me was, "With God nothing is impossible."

As I left the meeting that night, I wondered why not all eleven had been healed. Immediately this scripture came to mind, "According to your faith be it done unto you." I still had a lot to learn about faith but at least I was in the right place, being taught by a father of the faith, Kenneth Hagin. In fact, as international students we were privileged to meet him privately. On many occasions, he would have an international evening just for us, so we got to know him well, asking him questions that we would otherwise never have been able to ask in class.

NINETEEN

God's Big Treat for Our Family

Those two years of Bible School will be engrafted on our hearts forever. In December we spent our last Christmas in Tulsa. In three months we would be packing up to go back to Canada. A few weeks before Christmas, I received a phone call from my accountant telling me that things in the business were not doing very well. An unexpected expense had come up and had to be paid and we were making less and less profit on our different jobs. He assured me it wasn't the end of the world but that cash flow was very tight and we all had to tighten our belts and spend money only when absolutely necessary. "Something is going on with the business, but I haven't put my finger on it as yet," he said, "but I will keep you informed, if something turns up."

The timing could not have been worse. To top it off, my children were now reminding me that I had promised to take them to Disney World before we returned to Calgary. I remembered seeing the joy on their faces in my rear view mirror when I had promised them we could go. I had to keep my promise. The only time we could go was during our Christmas break. The next three months after that would be so busy with final exams and assignments that we only had this little window of time.

Fortunately, we had made good friends with a couple who were from Orlando, Florida who could give us all the information we needed about Disney World with regards to food costs, hotels, admission, etc. We set up a time to meet with them. What we heard was anything but encouraging. They told us to expect our cost for a week to be around $3000.00. We were going at the busiest and most expensive time of year. Apparently, more people attend Disney World at Christmas than any other time of the year. Not only was their news anything but exciting but our chances of going looked impossible, thanks to the recent news from my accountant.

We thanked them for their time and information and went home, hardly saying a word in the car. I couldn't break my promise to our children. Somehow God would have to come through for us. I checked my bank balance and it read $1,100.00. If we were to go to Disney World, by some unforeseen miracle, we would have to leave within a few days.

It was out of the question for the business to help pay for this trip. God would have to do something for us. Forty eight hours came and went and the Lord's miracle was nowhere to be seen. I was puzzled and wondered why the Lord had not come through for us. It was most important to me, because of the promise I had made to the children. As I was thinking about our trip, the Lord spoke to my spirit loudly and clearly: "Just go!"

It took me completely off guard, because it contradicted all logic, but then I thought, *God doesn't operate with logic. He does the impossible when things are not possible to the natural mind.*

Peace enveloped me and I heard myself telling the family, "We leave for Florida tomorrow morning." Excited, the children began packing their clothes within minutes. We found someone to take care of our dog and bright and early the next morning we were on the road. As I drove, my bank account balance kept flashing before my mind. I knew where that was coming from, so I quickly took authority over the enemy and was at peace again. Florida was a lot farther from Tulsa than I had expected.

After filling up the van with gas and making our way to the next state, the Lord suddenly spoke to me and said, "I want you to take the next exit and stop at the first gas station you see."

I had experienced the Lord's GPS before with my business so I knew something was waiting for me at the next destination. I had coined the phrase that GPS stood for "God's Purposefully Speaking."

I glanced at my gas gauge and knew the purpose he had was not for gas, since my tank was between half and three quarters full. He had something else in mind and I couldn't wait to see what it was. Our trip was getting off to a good start and faith was rising up in me. The question of the lack of money was far from my mind. I saw the next exit sign, took the exit and within a few minutes drove into a service station. As I pulled up (and since I didn't need any gas) I parked in front of the door. We could at least get a cup of coffee and something for the children, since they were always hungry, and see what happens.

As I turned the van off and was getting ready to step outside, a gentleman with a business suit came towards my door, clipboard in hand. He said, "You're from Canada aren't you?"

I was surprised and asked him how he had known, to which he replied, "I saw your licence plate. Where are you off to?"

I was skeptical about his question so asked, "Who wants to know?"

He told me he was a sales manager for the Days Inn chain of hotels and that they were in the process of buying out other hotels across the United States and Canada. I told him where we were going and he smiled back at me and said, "Let me tell you, sir, this is your lucky day. You will probably never get another offer like this again. What hotel are you booked into in Orlando?"

I said, "None as yet." He looked surprised.

"Did you know you are going to Disney World at the worst possible time and your chances of getting a hotel close to Disney

World are nil? You might have to stay as far as five miles away because everything is already reserved for the Christmas holidays." He was only confirming what my Florida friends at Rhema had told me. He continued, "I can see now that this is really your lucky day, because with this promotion of ours, I can book you into one of our newly-acquired hotels only minutes away from Disney World. When are you getting there and how long are you staying?"

I told him we were on our way right then and would be staying for at least four days. He asked me to wait just a minute while he made a phone call to see what he could find for us. No details about the promotion had yet been discussed and no costs mentioned. Being only a few minutes from Disney World, I could just imagine the cost. Within minutes he was back at my door. The family had gone into the service station to buy a few goodies for our trip. He said he could put us up at a hotel for three days, but unfortunately, we would have to move across the street to another of their newly-acquired hotels for the last night of our stay in Orlando.

Now I would find out the famous deal they were promoting. He started to explain to me what they were doing. These newly acquired hotels in Orlando all needed to be renovated to their standards and while awaiting these renovations, they were offering rooms free of charge to anyone who would agree to go to Daytona Beach to visit their hotel on the beach which had already been refurbished, where we would have to spend several hours of our time at a presentation. Breakfast was included and there was no obligation to purchase their timeshare.

It sounded far too good to be true but since the Lord had led me to that gas station, I knew I should agree to the deal. I was assured by this gentleman that Daytona Beach was not far from Orlando and we could stop there on our way back to Tulsa. I agreed to do it and signed the paper on his clipboard. I had read all of the conditions and they were as he had said but I noticed at the bottom I would have to make a deposit of $25.00 for each hotel in Orlando where we would be staying free of charge. I asked him why the $25.00 charge; he explained to me it was a guarantee to them that we would actually go and stay at those hotels. But upon our arrival we would be reimbursed the total amount. I could tell the Lord was involved in all this so gave him $50.00.

After we left the gas station and had gotten back onto the freeway, we noticed fire trucks and police cars everywhere and a huge pileup of cars. Traffic was backed up a fair distance. I realized that had we not obeyed the Lord and stopped at the gas station, we could have been involved in that pileup, but the Lord had protected us.

I was now bombarded with new thoughts that maybe *that* was the reason for our stop, and we had fallen for a scam with this gentleman who had taken us for $50.00 cash. I struggled with these thoughts for a while and before long I was thinking the worst. What had I gotten myself, and my family, into? Was there such a hotel and if there was, would the rooms be like a dive with rats running across the floors? If so, I would just have to kiss my money goodbye. I reasoned we could always sleep in the van.

I eventually snapped out of it, recognizing the enemy's thoughts, and realized I was falling for his lies. We arrived at the address just before dinner and sure enough there was a hotel, just as the man said. We walked into the lobby, which looked like anything but a dive. I wondered why renovations even needed to be done. As we walked through the door I heard a voice say, "Welcome to Orlando."

We turned around and there was a woman sitting behind a small desk. She asked the kids if they were going to Disney World and received their enthusiastic answer. Part of the promotion was to give free tickets for every day that people stayed at their hotel. They usually gave four per family. We were handed

12 tickets for all the rides at Disney World, which included the entry fee for each day we attended. When I looked at the tickets I saw they were worth $105.00 each. We had just been handed over $1200.00 worth of tickets! With the Lord running things, they really can be too good to be true.

She continued by saying, "While you are here, you need to go visit Sea World."

I explained to her we were on a tight budget and couldn't really take on any added attractions.

She replied, "Aren't you staying here with our promotion?"

I said, "Yes."

She then asked me how much I had paid before getting here and I told her $50.00. She said, "This is what I will do for you. I will give you four tickets to Sea World for your $50.00, if that's OK with you and I'll even throw in special tickets where they will take you into the back area to see all the sick animals they are taking care of. I know the children would love that."

I could see the excitement on the children's faces, so how could I say no? We accepted her generous offer and she also threw in a coupon book for meals all across Orlando. Most of the coupons were two-for-one deals with some places throwing in a free dessert. How much better could it have gotten?

After spending twenty minutes with this lady I made my way up to the reception desk to book into our room. They asked me my name and asked when I had reserved. I told them I had met a representative of theirs at a gas station and he had reserved for us, including one more night at one of their hotels across the street. They checked their computer reservations and my name was nowhere to be found. They asked me for the gentleman's name, which I didn't know, since he had never given it to me, but I told them the details about Daytona Beach and their timeshare deal. She said, "I can't find you in the computer. Wait just a minute." She disappeared into the back office. While she was gone, I pictured myself having to give back all our Disney World tickets. But that thought quickly vanished when she came through the door saying she had found it. It had not been posted in the computer as yet and was sitting in someone's basket. What a relief. She handed me my $50.00 deposit along with two sets of keys to our room. On the way out to get our suitcases, I handed the women at the desk my $50.00 and she gave me all my tickets to Sea World, including the special ones for the kids. Everyone was happy and we could hardly wait to see our room and relax from our long trip.

As we opened the door to the room we were all shocked. It was nothing like what I had imagined. The entrance brought us into a large sitting room with a sofa and chairs. To the right was a beautiful kitchen completely furnished with dishes, pots and pans. Farther down a corridor were two large bedrooms. This place was more than we could ask for and the price was perfect.

Behind the door, we read that the price of this unit was $187.00 per night. How wonderfully the Lord was taking care of us, in spite of all the doubts and unbelief that had bombarded my mind.

We had the most wonderful four days in Orlando, especially the kids, an experience they never forgot. It turned out that Sea World was the highlight of their trip. They got to hold baby animals in their hands and bottle feed them, only a few days after they were born. They got to pet dolphins and manatees and do many other wonderful things not allowed to the general public.

We then went to Daytona Beach to fulfill our part of the deal. Upon arrival we were given the keys to our room. This hotel would also be free, including a free breakfast for everyone. As we opened the door to our room we noticed that it had to be at least 40 feet wide with drapes spanning the entire wall. For some reason they had not been opened and as we opened them we gasped in awe. The whole wall was glass and there in front of us was a panoramic ocean view. It was an absolutely spectacular sight. We noticed that there were vehicles on the beach. It seemed everyone was allowed on the beach with their cars. We just stood there for a long time, looking and taking it all in. The goodness of God overwhelmed us.

I decided to check behind the door to see if there was a price per night for this suite and as in the other place I saw the price was $243.00 per night. We spent the rest of the day on the beach and the next morning we went to the two-hour timeshare meeting during breakfast. We made it through the presentation but there was no way we could afford the timeshare. A little pressure was applied on us to buy one but after explaining our financial situation, they reluctantly let us alone and we were back on our way to Tulsa.

God had given a glorious experience to our whole family. As soon as we were back in Tulsa, I checked our bank balance and, to my surprise, we still had close to $700.00. Our trip of miracles had not cost us $3000.00 but a mere $400.00. Only God could have done that, and he did it because of my obedience to go, even when it seemed impossible with the amount of money we had in the bank. What a valuable lesson I had learned, one that would always stay with me.

Where God guides, he provides.

TWENTY

Ministry in the Church and in the Marketplace

In the spring, Joane and I both graduated from Bible College and were on our way back to Calgary, after having spent two unforgettable years in Oklahoma. Incidentally, before we had ever gone to Tulsa, for two years Joane and I both spent several hours every morning taking live teaching via satellite. Some of the best Bible teachers from around the world taught us the Word of God. We grew by leaps and bounds. Every few weeks we would write exams via satellite and at the end of the two years we went to Dallas, Texas to attend a Graduation Ceremony and meet some of the teachers face to face. So in reality, along with our two years in Tulsa, we had actually completed four years of Bible School.

The church we attended began putting pressure on both of us to enter into full-time ministry. Fortunately, I had learned not to succumb to pressure but to continue being led by the Holy Spirit. I felt the Lord wanted me to commit half of my time to the ministry of the church and the other half to my business.

Soon we were asked to oversee weekly small home groups. We were also hired as assistant pastors of the church. Joane worked full-time supervising the children's ministry and I was involved on all the boards of the church, including planning and finances. I was also appointed Dean of the church's Bible School, which took a few hours of my time every morning. I enjoyed this

151

position the most because I was able to share everything I had learned over the past four years. The students were eager and hungry to learn the Word of God.

There was a major move of God in the city at that time. The Lord was working mightily both in the church and in the business world. My business was improving, now that I was working there again. But I started to spend more and more time with church affairs. I was at peace with it because of the way the Lord had taken care of my business while I was away in Tulsa. I knew it would continue to run smoothly now that I was back.

I found it harder and harder to spend long hours in prayer early each morning. If I did, I would have little time to sleep because of my now hectic schedule each weekday as well as weekends. I was spending less time one-on-one with the Lord. In spite of this, the Lord continued to be faithful in leading and giving me direction for my life. I had learned in my relatively short time of walking with him that my sole responsibility was to follow his directives. When I did this, he took responsibility to make things come to pass in his timing.

Mind you, his timing is not our timing and everything we want is not necessarily what we really need. The Lord showed me this one day when I was driving by many houses having garage sales. He said to me, "A garage sale is merely people selling off, at a much lower price, all the things they thought they wanted or needed, but didn't really."

I was so excited with what the Lord was doing in my life and my family. I wanted to tell the whole world about his goodness and the miracles that happen when we hear his voice. People in the business world seemed interested, but unfortunately, I didn't get the same reception in the church. I was continually told that I was so spiritually-minded I was of no earthly good. So I started to spend more time with business people than with church people and became cautious about whom I shared my experiences with at the church.

Even with God's own children I needed his direction. Because I grew up with a lot of rejection, these Christians were creating a big problem for me. I took their unbelief personally regarding the things I shared with them. I felt that they were rejecting me and was tremendously hurt by their attitude. However, I continued to believe the Lord to help me conquer this problem.

The business kept growing and prospering in spite of the few hours I was spending running its daily operations. Most of my employees were now saved so I was able to trust the Holy Spirit in them to help them do their job with integrity. In our business, we exchanged employees when needed. If one electrical business had a slow period, we would hire some of their electricians that were about to be laid off and vice versa. Whenever I traded one of my electricians to my competition, I would make sure to give them the best one I had. I had learned the principle that we reap what we sow. I made sure my employee was born again so he could influence the other workers for God. Whenever I received an employee from another company, he became a potential candidate for the kingdom of God. Happily, many came to know the Lord over the years. We had "church" going on right in the marketplace.

It came to the point where I often had as many as twenty-five electricians on payroll. This really tested my faith. Every fifteen days, money had to be in my bank account to meet a large payroll, as well as the monthly tax remittance to the government. Many, many times the funds would arrive on the very day payroll was due. I learned that the Lord never seems to be early in what he does, but, let me assure you, he is never late. He is always faithful.

One of my major responsibilities in the business was to look at every job before it started and at every quote before it was mailed. I had made a habit of inquiring of the Lord every time.

Some jobs looked real promising at first sight. I remember one particular job that was handed right into my lap without me having to quote it. It would have given us a huge profit margin. In fact, it would be twice as high as usual because most of the product needed for the job was dead stock in our inventory. I was ready to accept it without praying about it. I thought it was obvious that the Lord wanted us to do this job so we could get rid of this stock that was no longer moving. Nevertheless, I briefly brought it before the Lord, and amazingly, I immediately sensed in my spirit that we were not to accept the job. I also knew that it was the Lord telling me, because if it had been left up to me, accepting this job would have been a no brainer.

When I told my manager we were not going to quote on it, he almost had a meltdown. To him this was a once-in-a-lifetime opportunity to make a huge profit and move a lot of dead stock. He just couldn't understand my decision not to accept it. But since I was the boss, he had no choice but to go along with my decision. We found out many months later who had taken the job and unfortunately, well into the work being done, the customer declared bankruptcy and the contractor lost his shirt, to the point where he didn't know if he could continue in business. He had extended their credit to ninety days and had not been paid one cent for all his work. Needless to say, my manager respected my decisions from that day forward. God had indeed directed and come to my rescue.

I wish I could say I diligently followed my decision always to inquire of the Lord before doing any job, but sadly, on one particular job I didn't and it actually destroyed my company. I share this particular situation to show how our enemy, the devil, is very ruthless and out to get us at every opportunity. His only goal is to steal from, kill, and destroy us, especially if we are fully committed to the Lord. Sometimes when he tries to destroy us, he will use the people closest to us, people we think we know well. He knows we won't suspect them and let our guard down, opening the door for him to attack us through them. That is what happened to me.

My company name was becoming well known and accepted in the business world and in Christian circles. The history of my work for these large companies that the Lord had given me over all these years was well known and respected in the electrical industry. We were known for our integrity and good morals. One day I received a phone call from a well-known church in the city. They were about to build a brand new, large church. They asked if I would be interested in doing all their electrical work. It would include supplying and installing all products as well as designing their lighting, both indoors as well as outside in their parking lot and any lighting required on the actual building at entrances. It would be a large project but I was up for the challenge. I had designed and done all the electrical work for a Christian School years before so already had experience with this type of work. I had been highly recommended by this Christian School to this church. The job also meant supplying and installing their sound system, data cables, telephone system, back-up generator and a theatrical lighting system and would take eight to nine months to complete. It would mean setting up an outdoor construction office on the premises, plus the rental of several semi-trailers to store all the products and equipment needed for the work. There would have to be a foreman on site at all times, in order to answer questions the other trades might have. It was a huge undertaking, but I was eager to get started. The project would not be going out to tender as far as the electrical was concerned. The job was mine if I agreed to take it on. It took me a week to quote on it according to the specification on the blueprints. All extras encountered would be paid on a monthly basis. I accepted the challenge and, after receiving my quotation, was given the go-ahead to do the project.

I had crossed every "t" and dotted every "i" many times over with my master electrician and the foreman that would be responsible to get the job done. The only thing and the most important thing that I had neglected to do was to inquire of the Lord. I thought it was a job that would be done for the Kingdom of God and the Lord would undoubtedly be happy about me doing it. This new church would be used to introduce the gospel to many people in our city. The first scripture I had read in the Bible after I was born again plainly said, "Trust in the Lord with all your heart." I was getting good at doing that by now, but I missed the next two phrases which say, "Don't lean on your own understanding but acknowledge me in EVERYTHING you do, and I will direct your steps."

I was leaning on my own understanding and had not acknowledged him in this project at all. The consequences of not fulfilling all the conditions of that scripture became devastating, not only to my business, but to me personally as well. I would soon learn that "in everything you do" meant everything, without exception.

Halfway through the project, the church ran out of finances and the bank would no longer extend their line of credit. It was going to cost them much more than they had anticipated. An urgent meeting was called by the senior pastor to let us know about their unfortunate situation. They had decided as a church to stop the project and would immediately start a fund-raising campaign to get the finances needed to complete the job. The only trades that would continue the work in the months ahead would be the trades needed to complete the outside of the building and install power for heat before it started to snow. All the underground work for the parking lot would also have to be completed before the frost would set in. This created an immense problem for us. We had to be on site at all times, because as the brick for the building was being installed, we needed to set in place all the electrical boxes for lighting and power on the outside of the building. For some unknown reason, all the outside electrical boxes needed to be surface-mounted. It had to be done according to the prints and I was sure they had made a mistake in showing them as surface mounted instead of being recessed. There was no question of going back to the city to have changes done at this time although it would have meant a large savings in cost.

The only reason I could understand was that if they needed more outdoor plugs for car heaters in the future it would be easier to install more of them. We could not return all the units that had been rented for a minimum of nine months for our office and all our supplies. They were still needed on site even though our work had come to a standstill. We still needed our office there and we required a secure place to store all the materials that had already been ordered and delivered for the entire project. Whether my foreman worked only one or four hours each day, I still had to pay him for eight. All of these factors came into play and it was getting very complicated.

I called for a meeting with the senior pastor and before the meeting was over, he had assured me that any extra expenses would all be paid for at the end of the contract. I just had to submit the invoices with the extra expenses to him personally and he would take care of them. The project extended three months beyond the original due date. By now a nine-month project had taken a full year. I was struggling financially to complete the work and needed extra financing from my bank to meet all the expenses that kept coming in. I knew I wouldn't get paid for all the extras incurred during those three months until the contract was completed. I agreed to be paid at the end of the contract because I knew the church was financially strapped but now I was in the same situation.

In addition, many things were not going well with this project. In order to get extra financing to run my business and finish this job, I now had to give personal guarantees in order for the bank to extend my line of credit, which I foolishly did, still thinking the Lord would see me through this mess I had gotten myself into by not acknowledging him in the first place.

When the project was complete I would submit my invoices and be paid for all the extras incurred, then I would be able to go to the bank and have all my personal guarantees removed. Surely it would only be a short time before my business would be up and running the way it operated before I took on this disastrous contract. Oh, how I looked forward to that day.

Three days after I had submitted all my invoices, I received a phone call from the senior pastor. He wanted to see me at his office. I set up a time to meet him and went to his office, expecting to get a cheque and be paid in full, not only for the holdbacks, but for all the extras that had been incurred. I was in for the shock of my life.

I entered his office and was barely seated when he handed me a cheque for all the holdbacks, which I was pretty glad to see. I then asked him, "When can I be expect a cheque for all the extras, since my bank is starting to put pressure on me for paying down my line of credit?"

What he said next was unbelievable and I asked him to repeat it, since I was sure I had heard wrong. He said, "There is no place in the contract where it stipulates we are to pay any extras, should there be a delay on the work to be done. That's just the cost of doing business."

I reminded him of the meeting we had had together, specifically to address that very issue and reminded him that he had personally assured me that all extras would be paid in full when I submitted invoices to him after completing the project.

He answered once again, "There was no clause in the contract that obligated us to any extra expenses. The church board has voted on the issue and this was their conclusion. If you want to pursue it further in court, you are welcome to do so, but as far as we are concerned the matter is closed."

I decided to go to my accountant to get some advice. He was in his office so I went right away. Surely he would know what I should do. After telling him my situation, he simply said, "Take them to court; they don't have a leg to stand on."

My accountant suggested I call a lawyer that he knew personally and gave me his number. I made the call right from his office and this lawyer said, "Based upon the information you've given me, you have a very good case and I would be glad to represent you and help you get back the money owed to your company. Let me know when you are ready to pursue this issue."

Everyone was giving me the same information about what I should do, but I knew very well I couldn't do it because the Word of God simply and plainly states we are not to sue a (Christian) brother in court but rather let ourselves be wronged.

I broke out into a cold sweat and my mind went blank. I had no clue what to do. The same fear I had experienced during the years I was running away from the underground world suddenly hit me again. How could this happen, now that I was a Christian? I felt so confused and it took everything within me not to head back to my old drinking hole to try and forget what had just happened. It must be a bad dream, but I knew it was not.

I was in a place I had never been before. I felt completely alone, with no one to help me. Sometimes that is a good place to be, because then we are forced to go to the one person we know is always there for us, no matter what. And that is what I did. I prayed to the Lord for hours and was finally able to go home and tell Joane what had transpired and what would happen when the bank eventually demanded their money. We could lose everything, even our dream home, which we had recently built together. It was hard to be positive about anything right then but fortunately Joane encouraged me that we still had the Lord on our side and he would definitely see us through this mess. We simply had to leave everything in his hands. It was time to put our faith to its biggest test. We had been grounded in faith for years and now we were being given the opportunity to see it work in a humanly impossible situation. Would we be able to pass this test? Time would tell.

TWENTY-ONE

The Test

I knew that if I allowed my company to go bankrupt, it would affect all my employees and all my customers. I still had ongoing business with them all and didn't want this financial situation to ruin my reputation in the business world. I decided to go see a bankruptcy lawyer and get some advice on what to do. He told me to try and work out a repayment plan with the bank to avoid bankruptcy and if that didn't work I should declare personal bankruptcy.

I went to see the bank and they would not cooperate whatsoever so I made the decision to declare personal bankruptcy. The consequences were miserable. I would have a bad credit rating for seven years during which time it would BE impossible to acquire any credit. Joane and I sold everything we owned that had any equity in it, even our house and vehicle. That helped to pay off some personal debt with the bank, but I still owed them thousands of dollars, which ended up not being paid. It would have been far better for them to strike a deal with me for a repayment plan but they had refused my offer.

Although it was a very tough time for all of us, the Lord was there to see us through. I strongly felt I should get out of business completely and work full-time at our own church as an associate pastor. I inquired of the Lord to see what I should do with my business and whether I should try and sell it or not. He instructed me to give the business to my master electrician, who had loyally and faithfully run it while I had been at Bible School. During my years in business, I'd had many opportunities to purchase electrical inventory from job sites and auctions with my personal money, and it was all stored in the business warehouse. The new owners of my business wanted to pay me for this, as it was used up on future jobs. We came to a mutual agreement and both of us were satisfied.

I wanted to get this whole situation behind me and try and forget what had happened. One of my employees decided to go into partnership with my master electrician. They changed the name of my company and all of this was smoothly done, without affecting the operation and service to the customers. I called all the customers to explain that I was no longer in charge of the company and was moving on to bigger and better things. I also assured them that the work and service they would receive would not change in the least; the only thing that would change would be the company name and its ownership. It was an easy transition since all the customers had already worked with these two men over the years and knew them well.

Within just a few weeks, I received all my money for the inventory. The new owners both felt that they were to pay me immediately and that helped me get back on my feet. Joane and I were hired by the church on a full-time basis. I was being paid far below the income I had been getting through my business, but nevertheless I was very thankful to the Lord for seeing us through the whole mess. We were able to acquire a small condo with the help of some church friends and life went on. We had the Lord and a close-knit family. We had each other and nothing else mattered.

To this day, the company is still servicing all the customers the Lord had brought to the business. Only the name and ownership changed and I am very happy for that. The Lord gave me the desire of my heart.

Because of the sudden change in our income, our lifestyle changed considerably. I missed being in business and had to try somehow to supplement my income. I didn't like being cooped up in an office every day and I also missed the friendship I used to have with my employees. Something kept pulling my heart towards the marketplace.

I brought all of these feelings to the Lord to see what he would say. He said something that I had never considered. I knew it would be a very humbling experience, but I knew I had heard his voice, so I pursued the idea. I was to approach the new owner to whom I had given my business to see if I could get some part time work from him. He agreed to give me as much work as I wanted, since they were extremely busy doing many different maintenance jobs throughout the city. The business was continuing to prosper and I was glad to hear that. He mentioned that he would have to pay me the hourly wage of an apprentice. I had no training whatsoever as an electrician and to pay me any more would not be fair to the other apprentices.

It was a humbling situation, but I knew he was doing the right thing. I decided to work for him starting the very next day. I could work as many or as few hours as I wanted to; the choice would be completely mine. It was a good arrangement for me since I still had a full-time position at the church. I would either work nights or on weekends. Since most of the employees didn't work these hours, he gave me the keys and combinations to all the padlocks of his tools and warehouse doors. I would have access to everything. No matter what time of day I decided to work, I would have everything I needed at my disposal. It was an ideal arrangement for all of us.

During the first month I worked quite a few hours. Since my work at the church didn't start until 9:00 AM, I would sometimes work two or three hours before coming to the church. I always had two sets of clothes with me, many times not knowing whether I could work that day or not; but there was almost never any lack of work.

One morning I had an encounter with the Lord in a way I had never experienced before and, to be honest, it actually freaked me out. My part-time employer called me because he knew I was up very early every morning. It was not even 6:00 AM when the phone rang. I was surprised to hear him at the other end of the line because he had never done that before. He explained that he was working on a new job out of town and that he and all the employees were there. They had all driven the night before and were staying at a motel—to avoid the heavy morning traffic and get an early jump-start at this new job. Unfortunately, they had forgotten to bring some important materials that were needed on the job that day and I could tell by his voice that he was stressed out about it. If the material didn't get there on time that morning, he would have a lot of idle men on his hands. I was the only one left in town who had the keys to his warehouse and he asked me to do him a big favour. He said he would make it worth my while if I could get the product there before 9:00 AM.

I was happy to be of assistance, since I understood the predicament he was in. I assured him I would do everything in my power to accommodate him and would leave the house right away. He gave me the address where they were working. I hung up and was out the door headed for his warehouse. By the time I arrived, traffic was just starting to get heavy. It was pitch dark outside as I pulled up to the warehouse entrance and for some reason the lights in the parking lot were not on. I had been there a few times before so I had no problem finding the stairs to the door. I backed up my vehicle to the door to make it easier for loading. I knew this material was not bulky and would all fit into my trunk. As I got out of the car and walked up to the door, suddenly I was horrified to find out I had forgotten the keys to the warehouse at home.

Now suddenly it was my turn to be stressed out. I didn't know what to do except go back to the vehicle and see if they were there by some miracle. They could have dropped out of my pockets and might be lying on the seat. I searched everywhere I could think of, but to no avail. What should I do? If I drove back home to get the keys, I would now be in the heaviest traffic of morning rush hour and that could cost me hours. I dismissed that idea and was about to call my employer when suddenly I noticed a bright light in both my side mirror and my rear view mirror. It was impossible to miss since it was so dark outside. I saw a man standing at the doorway, holding the door wide open. I leapt out of my vehicle and ran towards him before he had time to close it again.

As I approached him, I noticed he was well dressed in a sports coat and grey trousers. I wondered what in the world he was doing there, dressed the way he was and at that time of day. But these concerns were really not important, so I greeted him, quickly explained my predicament to him and how glad I was that he was there. Now I could get the stock from the storage area, since the padlock on that door had a combination lock. (That eliminated the possibility of other employees forgetting their key, like I had done that morning.)

What I found very strange with this man was that he never made eye contact with me as I spoke to him. He never uttered a single word. He had a different look about him, like someone from the Middle East, so I assumed he didn't understand or speak English. This was not important at this particular time since I needed to stay focused on my assignment. As I entered the building and proceeded down the long corridor leading to the storage area, I heard the door close behind me. I looked back and saw this gentleman following me down the corridor. I could hear his footsteps behind me and halfway down the corridor. I stopped at the storage door and punched in the four-digit combination number. It opened so I turned to see where the man was going.

He was nowhere to be seen. He had vanished from sight. I knew it would have taken him at least two minutes to get to the other end of the corridor where the washrooms were located. I had taken a few seconds to unlock the door. Between that door and the washrooms there were no other doors to enter and the walls, floor and ceiling were solid concrete. There was absolutely nowhere else to go.

At that point I realized what had happened and literally freaked out. That man had vanished in thin air. I had heard of Houdini, but this was even more impossible than anything I had ever seen him do. Before I entered the doorway to pick up my stock, I decided to go to the washrooms down the corridor and see if, by some unexplainable way, he had been able to get there within a few seconds. My mind was in full gear, trying to make some kind of sense of all this. I started with the women's washroom and checked every cubicle to see if he was hiding there, then went to the men's next door but this man was nowhere to be found.

I looked back up the corridor and noticed I had left the door ajar. I wondered if I missed seeing him behind me and now he was in my storage area. My mind was playing havoc with me and I quickly ran to the open door, gathered all the material I needed to pick up and rushed out of the building to my vehicle. It was still dark outside. I kept glancing over my shoulder to see if the man would reappear. My mind was not thinking logically and I had to get out of there.

I spun out of the parking lot, gravel flying everywhere and was back on the main road in no time. I headed towards my destination out of town but was still nervous because I had no logical explanation about what I had just experienced. It puzzled me so much that it started to affect my concentration. I pulled over to the side of the road and when I came to a complete stop the Lord spoke to my spirit. He said, "I am the Master Key. I can open any door."

I realized I had encountered an angel of the Lord who had come to my rescue when I had no solution to my problem. Immediately a peace that passes all understanding rested upon me and all fear disappeared. I wondered why fear had been present during the entire experience, since it was the Lord's doing but I remembered reading many times in the Bible that whenever an angel appeared to someone the first thing he said was, "Do not fear." In my experience, this angel didn't say a word.

Since that time, Joane has also seen an angel and on another occasion an angel appeared when our whole family was in danger, which I will elaborate on later. Angels are very real.

Miracles are for real. Impossible things in life suddenly become possible with the Lord's intervention. However, people will not experience miracles unless they believe in them. Very early in my walk with the Lord I understood that without faith it was impossible to please Him. My greatest desire in life is to please him because of everything he has done for me and my family.

TWENTY-TWO

An Impossible Prophecy Comes to Pass

A miracle I once experienced was the time the Lord gave me a new vehicle. You read it right—he gave me a brand new vehicle. One day Joane and I were sitting at our kitchen table with very good friends of ours. They were pastors of a church in Edmonton. As we were enjoying our coffee and visit together, one of them spoke up and said, "I sense that the Lord wants you to have a new vehicle. I just heard him say that."

That was new to me because my experience had always been that when the Lord wanted to do something in my life he spoke to me directly, so why the sudden change in procedure? This was my first introduction to the prophetic ministry. Our friends belonged to an organization from Florida where the founder was a prophet who ministered all over the world. I had been studying under the "father of faith" in Tulsa and now I was being introduced by my friends to the "father of the prophetic." Prophecy is when the Lord speaks a word to you through someone else. This was new to me and I had a lot to learn.

After their visit, I pondered what they had told me about the new car, knowing that it was completely impossible for me to get a new car because of my bankruptcy and the bad credit rating hanging around my neck for seven years. But this word would not leave me alone so I discussed it with Joane and we decided we should go check out some new cars. What did we have to lose? We would just do some window-shopping together.

Since we had been very pleased with our past vehicles, we decided to visit the same dealer. We arrived just before they were closing on a Thursday evening. Looking around the lot, we were drawn to their new SUVs. We checked out several and as we were peering inside one to see the interior console, a gentleman behind us offered us a key to the vehicle. He had been watching us from inside.

He said, "Would you like to take it for a test drive?"

I said, "No, we are just looking right now."

To my surprise, Joane said, "I would like to take it out for a spin." He reached out and handed her the keys.

He looked at me and said, "Why don't you to go with her?" I wasn't going to say no again.

Here we were in this new vehicle driving down the road, my wife at the wheel. That wasn't in my plan at all. When we arrived back at the dealership, the gentleman was waiting in the parking lot for our return. He invited us to come in for a cup of coffee, to which my wife gladly agreed. I, on the other hand, just wanted to leave and was not feeling very happy about having come there in the first place. I knew far too well what my financial situation was and going inside would just be a waste of our time. I knew exactly what their answer would be if I said I wanted to buy a vehicle.

I couldn't understand why Joane was doing everything opposite to what I wanted. *Maybe*, I thought, *we shouldn't have come together.*

I reluctantly followed them inside. We sat at his desk, coffees in hand, when the salesman asked what colour of vehicle we liked the best. Of course Joane was quick to answer once again and chose her favourite colour, gold. The next thing I knew, I was facing the paperwork they wanted filled out. All this was happening so fast I didn't have time to speak to my wife privately, to let her know we had to get out of there before we became the laughing stock of the entire place. We were wasting our time but, more seriously, we were wasting everyone else's time and would just be humiliated when we finally left.

I was into this too far now, though, so I went through the motions of filling in the information they needed, wanting desperately to get out of the mess. Our past pleasant involvement with this dealer would disappear forever after this fiasco. After I filled out the forms and we had both signed them, they were taken to the sales manager for approval. I knew what the answer would be, but it was too late to do anything about it. We would just have to face the music and suffer the consequences of our immature behaviour.

While we were alone, I tried to let my wife know it was mostly her fault that all of this had happened, but she refused to accept what I was saying. Things were starting to heat up between us, but didn't go too far because the salesman came back with the paperwork. Oh, how I didn't want to hear what he was about to say but what choice did I have?

The next words that came out of his mouth didn't make any sense whatsoever. He asked us if we would be able to pick up the car in a few days. They still had a few things to do with the vehicle, like spray a rustproof coating on the under-carriage, Scotch Guard the seats and do a few other minor things. He then asked us if we wanted a roof rack and automatic car starter installed to which I was quick to answer, "Yes, sure go ahead and do that." All of a sudden Mr. Faith Man came alive. Since I didn't know why we had ever been approved, I figured I had better take advantage of it while the going was good and before they changed their minds.

We agreed to pick up the vehicle the following Saturday afternoon. As we walked out of the dealership that night, I felt a new bounce in my steps but I had a very serious conversation with the Lord the minute I got into the parking lot. I was far enough away from the building that no one could hear me except

Joane. I said, "Lord, I don't know what you did or how you did it but I do know one thing. In thirty days a car payment has to be made and I want to make this very clear before a witness, my wife, that it will be your responsibility to meet this payment as well as all the others, because I had nothing to do with what just transpired in there. It was all your idea...and to some extent Joane's as well."

We drove home without saying another word to each other, both stunned at the goodness of the Lord. It was a mystery to us and reminded us that the Lord works in mysterious ways. To this day I don't know what the Lord did to get that loan approved. Did he blind their eyes with regards to my salary or did he let them see another zero on my salary? I may never know, but what I did know was the fact that we were soon to be the proud owners of a brand new vehicle, just as the prophet had told me.

In thirty days when the first car payment was due, miraculously unexpected money came into our hands. In fact, the amount was sufficient to pay off the whole car. We never did make a single monthly payment. God paid for the whole thing.

One day, several months after getting our new vehicle, I was invited to attend an all-men's prayer meeting by a good friend of mine, who had been attending these weekly meetings for months. After the prayer meeting was over, we were all sitting around the kitchen table having coffee. It was a regular get together for men to share what the Lord was doing in their lives. Several shared about their experiences and then my friend asked me if I would share about the recent experience with the car dealership. You could have heard a pin drop as I shared what the Lord had miraculously done.

After I had finished my story, one man stood up and said, "Why don't we take up an offering for this guy? We could be a part of this miracle and what the Lord has done by helping pay for gas to put into his vehicle." Nothing like this had ever happened to me before. The men started putting money on the table and when it was counted they handed it to me. They had collected just under $300.00. That would buy a lot of gas.

On my way home with my friend, he said to me, "This is what I want to do for you. I want to pay for the insurance on that vehicle." To this day, many, many years later, he still has continued to pay my insurance every year for every car I've purchased.

I'd had no problem giving to various needs, but now the Lord wanted to teach me how to receive from others. I always felt I owed people something after they had blessed me financially but I had to learn that receiving was also from God, and he was merely putting on different people's hearts the desire to give. The more I understood this, the easier it was to receive. I was discovering the truth of the verse, "Whatever a man sows, that he will also reap" (Galatians 6:7). It would make no sense for a farmer to continue sowing seed and not reap a harvest. It was slowly sinking in and soon I began looking expectantly for harvests in my life. They started to happen all around me.

TWENTY-THREE

The Lighthouse

Our very good prophetic friends from Edmonton invited Joane and me to a conference about hearing the voice of God—not for yourself, but for prophesying to others. This was new to us and we were excited to hear more. Hearing the voice of the Lord for myself had been going on in my life since I was a child. But hearing prophetically for others was a different story.

After the conference we spent a few days with our friends and one morning during breakfast the Lord started speaking to us through them. The Lord showed them that one day Joane and I were to start our own church in Calgary. The name of the church was to be "The Lighthouse." It would become a place of insight. That seemed like an awful lot of revelation in a span of a few minutes. We couldn't fathom how it could ever happen because we had both been associate pastors in our church in Calgary for over a decade. However, by now I was beginning to realize that when the Lord wants to bring change into your life, many times it doesn't make sense. If it was logical, I could have thought it up myself.

A few months later, things were not going smoothly in our church in Calgary. I will simply say that before we knew it, we were no longer needed or a part of that church, after fourteen years of ministry there.

The prophetic word we had received from our friends made more sense now and within six months we were ordained under our friends' prophetic ministry in Florida, ready to start a new prophetic church in Calgary. This would be a major change in our lives. The Lord would begin to use us to introduce the prophetic ministry in Calgary. I was sure that everyone would be excited about this new revelation from the Lord. I couldn't have been more wrong. The first thing we wanted to do as new pastors was network together with other churches. When we had been associate pastors for many years, we were known to some extent, but now we were no longer with that church and our teachings would be different. We believed the Lord wanted to introduce a new thing to the church in Calgary called the Prophetic Movement. Many believed that prophets were no longer for the church, only a thing of the past. We were realizing the Lord wanted it to become a major part of the present-day church. We soon discovered that change and new ideas for the church are not always received with open arms. My first challenge was about to unfold.

We had heard about and had even attended some of a certain minister's meetings in Edmonton. The Lord was using him to bring deliverance and healing through laughter. It was very hard for the religious people to accept it, again, because it was new. Nevertheless, the Lord wanted me to invite him to come and minister to the churches in Calgary. I didn't really know if he was available to come or not, since he was in great demand all over Canada and even in the States. I had his phone number so gave him a call, wanting to know if he was available to come to our city to minister. He told me what dates were available and that the Lord had put a strong desire for him to come to our city. He asked me the name of the church and other questions about accommodations and transportation. It had been much easier than I had anticipated. I hung up the phone and realized this would be our first invited guest to our new church, The Lighthouse.

After our conversation I suddenly remembered we had no church building as yet, and there were only a few people attending our church at this time. I was surprised he had not asked me what size our church was, since the first question we are asked when we tell people we have our own church now, is "How many people do you have?" If he had asked that question, I was quite sure he wouldn't have accepted my invitation; but he didn't ask, so he would arrive in our city in about thirty days. Since the Lord had put in my heart to do this, I expected him to take care of the logistics for me. This is how it always happened in the past, so why should it be any different now? A couple of weeks later as I was doing part time work in the same warehouse where I had encountered the angel of the Lord, it suddenly occurred to me that we only had two more weeks left before this minister would be at our church. We had no church building, so where would we hold our meetings? With such a few people, how could we meet all the expenses of a special speaker? All of a sudden a whole bunch of questions came to mind and I had no answers. I had been at the warehouse all day assembling lighting fixtures and I was just about to finish, when a man's name, "Craig" popped up in my head. I just knew in my spirit that the Lord was trying to help, since all these questions were brewing in my head about our upcoming meeting. The only problem was the fact I knew absolutely no one by that name, so I was no further ahead. I left it at that, packed up my belongings and headed for home.

As I entered the house, Joane said to me, "There's this pastor in town who called. His name is Craig and he wants to know who we are and why he hasn't heard of our church before." That very same day he had called this same minister, wanting to invite him to our city and that's when he found out that he was already booked to come to The Lighthouse and would be here in two weeks. Joane took Craig's phone number and told him I would call him back. I took the number and immediately called him.

As I was speaking to him, I found out he had also graduated, years ago, from the same Bible College in Tulsa, Oklahoma that we had. He asked me where the meetings were, the exact days they were going to be held and if we could work together on the meeting. After letting him know I had not as yet secured a meeting place he offered to let me use his church building and added that he would not charge me anything for it. Things were falling into place and the Lord was once again taking care of the details.

We had wonderful meetings and the Lord worked mightily during this time together. Other churches attended as well. We soon began to become acquainted with other churches in the city and they were getting to know us. This would prove to be beneficial for us, as the Lord continued to have us bring the churches together through other city-wide meetings. The next such meeting was at the same church building a month later. The Lord had directed us to invite a prophetic minister to teach on the new prophetic movement and on hearing the voice of God and about thirteen different churches from different denominations attended. It was a first for the city. The Lord was bringing the churches together as he had promised to do, through us. It was exciting to see the Lord using a little-known church called The Lighthouse to accomplish his will in our city. A scripture came to mind: "He uses the foolish things of this world to confound the wise."

We had become good friends with this pastor, Craig Buroker, and at one point he even offered his building for us to use for our regular services. Since we were not adamant that our service be held on Sunday, we started meeting on Saturday evenings. We were anything but a traditional church because our focus was on meeting the needs of the poor, the orphans, the widows, and the elderly. We were not trying to get people to a building; we as a church wanted to go out to meet people's needs in the marketplace. When Craig found out what we were doing, he offered us his building free of charge. This went on for many months. We were training the people how to hear God's voice and then to go out into the business world and reproduce what they had learned.

Our type of church ministry was different from the typical church and many people were not ready for such a drastic change. Since I was sure the Lord was leading us in this direction, I decided to follow his will instead of the peoples' will. Church tradition only causes people to fall into a rut and a routine and when the Lord wants to bring change to people's lives, with regards to doing things another way, there is much resistance and in many cases, people end up living their lives and dying there, never changing.

One service in particular, I clearly remember. During the service the Lord had asked me to announce to everyone that we would be going out every week into the streets of Calgary to start a ministry to the homeless people and that he wanted everyone from the church involved on a regular basis. At the time, there were some 3,000 homeless people in the city who would become our focus. Along with the new change came instructions and even these instructions were not the traditional way of doing ministry. We were not to bring Bibles with us or preach to them; we were simply to go to them and demonstrate God's love for them. None of us had been trained to do this type of ministry, but we soon found out it didn't require training; it only required having his compassion flowing out of us to them. We were simply to become channels of God's love for them.

One evening a few people decided to make some sandwiches and go downtown to see if they could find these homeless people and where they hung out. It didn't take long to find them. Several were gathered at Olympic Plaza and before long some approached our people and asked if we had anything to eat. That was the beginning of our ministry to the poor and homeless. The sandwiches disappeared in no time and soon there was a group of them gathered around us. Not knowing we actually needed a city permit to do this, we simply showed up every week and continued feeding them.

Soon we received a phone call from the city wanting to meet with us. The gentleman in charge of issuing the permits told us he was watching us from the window of his office every week, since he worked late almost every night. City Hall was next to the Olympic Plaza where we had been meeting. He said, "I heard from some of the homeless people who you were and what you were doing so I took it upon myself to issue in the name of your church, The Lighthouse, a yearly permit. Because of the community work you are doing and the needs you are meeting in this city, we will cover the cost of the permit as long as you decide to continue." This work continued for six years, growing by leaps and bounds every year.

We were seeing miracles happen every week but the greatest miracles were happening in our own hearts. It was like we had received a part of the Lord's heart for the homeless and his compassion flowed automatically through us to them. We were all growing in his unconditional love. The ministry started to expand and we were now not only meeting their hunger needs but were finding jobs for those who were able and willing to work. We then found them accommodations instead of sleeping on the streets in the summer months and in shelters in the winter months. They were slowly coming back to a normal lifestyle and off the streets of Calgary.

Many of them began to volunteer their time to come and help us. This was a great help to us, and since they had lived on the streets themselves for years, they knew most of the people who were in dire need of assistance and brought them to us. Then the Lord instructed us to speak to local businesses and get them involved in helping meet our ever growing expenses. This proved to be very successful. Three to four times a year we would put on massive barbecue evenings. Often more than a thousand people would show up. Because we needed help putting on such events, we started asking other churches to get involved, and always had enough people to help and cater.

We had professional barbecues donated for the event and with only two or three of these massive barbecues we could cook food for a thousand people in a matter of hours. All of the food was of restaurant quality. We would have steak and mashed potatoes with at least two vegetables. Desserts were also donated, pies of every kind you can imagine, ice cream, fresh rolls and butter. In the fall we would have large corn boils with hamburgers and hot dogs, always ending the evening with lots of dessert and coffee.

It was a special time for everyone involved and becoming more popular each year. Many new homeless people were showing up to the point where we would serve up to 500 sandwiches every week, along with coffee and hot chocolate. Desserts were always available and in great demand. We personally prepared and picked up all this food, but everyone did their part, alternating shifts, and thoroughly enjoyed what they were doing. We never heard any complaining from anyone. The Lord had changed our hearts.

On one of our weekly visits to Olympic Plaza, which was always held on a Monday evening, the weather was not cooperating at all. It had been snowing all day. Fortunately, before our meeting it had stopped but the temperature had dropped down to -35° C. With the wind chill factor it was close to -50° C. We all called each other that day to discuss whether we should go or not. Most of us came to the conclusion that it would be a waste of our time since no one in his or her right mind would show up on such a cold evening. As we were debating on whether to go or not, I heard the voice of the Lord loudly and clearly: "Go!"

One word, but that was enough for us to do exactly that. We took less sandwiches, desserts, and hot drinks and headed for downtown. As we drove there, we agreed that if no one showed up, we would simply take the food to one of the shelters.

As we drove there it was so cold outside that it was a challenge to keep the windows defrosted. At times we had to stop the vehicle, go outside and scrape the windshield to see where we were going. It was one of the coldest evenings we had ever experienced. When we arrived at our destination, we could hardly believe our eyes. There were at least fifty homeless people waiting for us in this sub-zero temperature. They looked like penguins from afar as they continually slapped their bodies with their arms, trying to keep warm. Why they had showed up on such a cold night was a mystery. I asked them, "What in the world are you doing here in this weather?"

The answer I heard rings in my ears to this day. One of the guys spoke up and said, "We knew you would come, and we didn't want you to come for nothing, so here we are."

Only hours before we had all been debating whether to show up or not. Their presence here was proof enough to us that they all appreciated what we were doing for them. That made our day. It was so cold that night that we couldn't continue serving hot chocolate because the spout kept freezing up on us. So in a very short time, all the hot drinks had disappeared as well as all the desserts and sandwiches. We had more than enough food, so they stuffed their coats with the extras and headed for shelter.

As we packed up containers we couldn't stress enough how extremely glad we were that we had showed up that wintery night. What would they have thought had we not showed up?

During those six years large churches came to do videos about us and our work in the city. Other churches wanted to join us on Monday evenings but I strongly urged them to start their own work on another evening of the week. That way the homeless would receive help more than just once a week. They agreed to do it. I offered to help get them started if they so desired but nothing actually ever transpired of it.

After six years of ministering to the homeless, another church started the same type of work, not far from the Plaza. We were very happy about that. We felt the Lord was now moving us as a church to meet other needs in other places. In those years we saw many salvations and deliverances right before our eyes. We would do simple things at the Lord's instructions, like kneel down and tie the shoe laces of a drunk, and then see him cry uncontrollably with this simple act and he would give his life to the Lord right there on the spot. Others would be set free from demons as they passed by. They would throw themselves on their knees and cry out to God for help. Unfortunately, our time there was not all positive. We saw many die from drug overdose and alcohol. Drunks would often pass out in back alleys during the night and be found the next day frozen to death.

We made many friends in those years and when anyone died it was like losing a loved one. We had become like family. It became a big part of our life and we will never forget what the Lord did for these dear homeless people.

TWENTY-FOUR

Going Back to Fix the Past

I would like to go back in time to when I was only twelve years old. One of my grandmothers lived in our home with us for years. Both of my grandfathers had died before I was born. The strange thing about this grandmother was that she went around all day, every day, praying with what she called a rosary. It was made of wood and painted black. All the beads on it were so worn out you could hardly see the black paint any more. She also spent much of her time in her room upstairs.

One day, just before I was to get ready to go to bed, I heard her call my name. I went upstairs to see what she wanted and she was sitting on the side of her bed, rosary in hand. She showed me the cross on the rosary with Jesus crucified on it. His form was being held to this rosary with small nails. The two nails holding his hands had fallen out somewhere and He was left dangling by his feet.

My grandmother handed me the rosary and asked me if there was any way I could fix it. I took it downstairs to my mom and asked her if she had any black thread. I took out the last nail from His feet and decided to tie His feet and hands back to the cross with the thread. It took me only ten minutes to fix it and I brought it back to my grandmother. When I handed it back to her, she was thrilled. She smiled up at me and said, "Isn't that nice? They crucified Him and drove nails in his hands and feet, but this is much better. Now you have simply tied Him to the cross."

As she kept on talking about Jesus, I suddenly remembered our teacher, who was a nun, had given us an assignment for our religion class. (All through school I was either taught by my mother, who was a teacher for thirty-five years, or by nuns.) This nun had given us two whole months to finish this project and it would count for half of our grade that semester. I suddenly realized I had completely forgotten about it until my grandmother started talking to me about Jesus. Then my assignment suddenly came to mind. I asked her what date of the month it was and panicked, because I only had one week left.

Knowing that my grandmother was very religious, I thought I would share my predicament with her to see if she had any ideas. After she listened to my situation, she simply smiled and said, "Follow me." She took me to a spare bedroom in the house and opened the closet door. She pointed to the ceiling and I could see there was a trap door in it. A well-secured ladder on the wall led to the door. She suggested I climb up and open the door into the attic. I had not known about this door before or that we even had an attic in the house. As I climbed up the ladder and lifted the door, I said, "Hey, it stinks up here."

She said, "The door hasn't been opened for years. You just follow my instructions when you get inside." My eyes started scanning the whole area and I couldn't believe how much stuff was up there. I saw three spinning wheels, old kerosene lamps, two scrub boards, antique picture frames with actual pictures in them, old trunks and seemingly a million dead flies lying everywhere on the floor. It felt like a scary place to be so I wanted out of there as soon as possible.

Grandmother said, "Do you see an old trunk in the corner with brass hinges and leather straps around it?"

I directed my eyes toward the different corners and spotted it and answered, "Yes I see it."

She said, "Be careful that you walk only on the cross beams to get there, otherwise you'll end up going through the floor, which is the ceiling down here." I followed her instructions carefully and finally made it to the antique trunk, which looked like a huge treasure chest.

She shouted up to me, "Take off the straps and open the cover and you will see a rolled-up piece of cardboard tied with a blue ribbon sitting right on the top. Bring it back with you and make sure you close up the trunk again."

Before long I was back down the ladder, cardboard in hand and gave it to my grandmother. She answered, "Good, now let's get to work on your project."

She brought me back to her room and started taking off the blue ribbon from this piece of rolled-up cardboard. As she unrolled it, she once again smiled and turned the cardboard around for me to see. There on this three feet by two feet piece of cardboard was a beautiful coloured picture of Jesus, with His nail-scarred hands pointing down towards a young boy who was kneeling in front of him on the ground. I had never seen such vivid colours in my life and thought it was the most beautiful picture in the world. The caption below the picture said in bright coloured letters, "Many are called, but few are chosen."

The whole episode just before that, when I was tying Jesus to her rosary with thread, had triggered her memory about this picture that had been sitting there in that old trunk for years and years. She assured me it would work very well for my project and told me that the next day I should go to the barn and try to find some old boards to frame it. I was excited about how good it would look with a frame around it.

I was a happy guy and my love for my grandmother had suddenly gone up a couple of notches. She wasn't so strange after all. She had gotten me out of a serious problem and possibly a failing mark in Religion. That had been an excellent day and I went to bed in peace about the whole thing. When I awoke the next morning, I realized it was Sunday and we all went off to church. I was glad we always attended early Mass. That would give me more time when we returned to find the wood and hopefully finish my project.

When we returned from Mass, I found some beautiful old dried-out wood and with a little help from my mother was able to put the frame together. What we had been given two months to do had been completed in two days with only a couple of hours' work. I couldn't believe my eyes and looked at the picture almost every day. After I handed in my project and brought it back home, she took it to her room for safekeeping and hung it on the wall. It meant a lot to her. I knew she was glad to have it with her again. I scored a 90% grade on my project and it boosted my overall grades for that semester. We were both very happy. Everything had turned out for the best and it all started by tying Jesus to her rosary.

I tell this story because it demonstrates how the Lord works so kindly in our lives. About thirty years later Jesus reminded me of this event. I could relive it as though it had happened yesterday. Joane and I were about to enter into our own ministry as pastors of The Lighthouse. I didn't think I was qualified enough, even though we had both attended Bible school for four years. It's one thing to have knowledge, it's another thing to have experience.

As I was seeking the Lord about my concerns, he somehow brought me back to that story when I was twelve years old. That picture didn't really mean much to me then, other than having a nice picture for my project, but now things were very different. He reminded me of the words on that picture and how they made an impression on me even at such a young age.

I then heard him say in my spirit, loudly and clearly the words on the picture, "Many are called, but few are chosen." He added, "Know that I have chosen you." For some unknown reason, I suddenly started to cry uncontrollably. By the time I finished weeping, I knew everything was going to be all right. My God was in complete control once again. He had preserved my life all those years when I was running away from him until that day. I was now realizing he had always been in control of my life so that I would fulfil the destiny he had planned for my life. He had truly chosen me and not the other way around.

Because of that revelation, I completely committed my life to the work of the ministry and determined to do absolutely anything he asked of me. He and I are a team for life. I was also so thankful he had given me an understanding wife and ministry partner. With both of us wanting to do his will, we were a three-fold cord that the Bible says cannot easily be broken. He gave us a promise from the Book of 2 Chronicles that we hold on to whenever we are sent on a new mission with him: "The eyes of the Lord are searching everywhere throughout the earth, looking to strengthen those whose hearts are fully committed to him." We have given ourselves, our time, and everything else to the Lord and to the plan he has for our lives. It has been an exciting journey and we wouldn't have it any other way. We love this life of being completely yielded to his ways and his path for us.

Several years after I was born again, the Full Gospel Businessmen's Fellowship area representative approached me at one of their meetings and asked me if I would be interested in being their main speaker in different meetings in Western Canada. These meeting were being held all across Canada for the purpose of giving people an opportunity to learn more about Jesus and his saving power. Over the years I had given a few short testimonies in their meetings and they were thrilled at what the Lord was doing in my life. I considered it an honour and a privilege to be able to glorify the Lord for all the amazing things he had done for me, so I accepted.

My first weekend trip was to be their main speaker in Regina, Moose Jaw and Assiniboine in Saskatchewan. The meetings would begin on a Friday night in Regina. All my travel expenses would be paid and I would receive an honorarium each time I spoke. The Regina meeting was at a local hotel with about eighty people in attendance. The first thing they did when I arrived was give me my honorarium of $350.00. Everyone was served supper; then the actual meeting was under way.

The arrangement for the meeting seemed like a wedding reception, with a head table at the front of the room. The main speaker and the local organizers of the Full Gospel Businessmen's Chapter sat there, along with a few other people who had been chosen to share a five-minute testimony before the main speaker. As I was listening to the second speaker sharing what the Lord had done in his life, the Lord spoke to me and said, "When you go up next to share, I want you to ask the crowd how many of them are born again."

It sounded like a strange request, but I had learned not to question what the Lord asked me to do. Soon I was introduced as the main speaker and as I listened to their introduction, I wondered where they had received all this information about me. I was surprised that they knew so much about me. When I came up to the mic, I looked at the crowd and asked them, "How many here at this meeting know the Lord personally and are born again?"

All hands went up and the Lord spoke to me again: "I want you to go to the President of the Chapter and tell him you will not be giving your testimony tonight, but since everyone in attendance is born again, ask more of them to give five-minute testimonies about themselves."

The President was shocked but it wasn't appropriate for him to argue with me. He said that I should do what I had come to do and that was give my testimony. I could see he was embarrassed by the whole thing and I went back to my seat as he announced to the people that I would not be giving my testimony that night. Most of the people moaned and groaned at that announcement but quickly stopped when he said he would be calling people up to give short testimonies. Many probably thought they could likely be called up to testify so they changed their attitude and waited to see what would happen next.

It was quite the experience sitting there throughout the rest of the evening listening to all the different testimonies. I could plainly see that the Lord was working in all of their lives and that made my evening. Just before the last person came up to share, the Lord spoke to me a third time. He said, "I want you to take your honorarium cheque out of your coat pocket, sign the back of it and give it back to the president at the end of this meeting. As you hand it to him tell him he's to use the complete $350.00 to buy tickets for their next monthly meeting and make sure they get into the hands of people who are not born again." I obeyed the Lord's instructions and was on my way.

I could see that the President was not too happy. I left that hotel and started driving to my next meeting in Moose Jaw. I couldn't wait to see what the Lord had in mind for that city.

The next morning in Moose Jaw, we were having a breakfast meeting at another local hotel. Again there was a good crowd gathered and after the meeting was over many had given their hearts to the Lord and were born again. I noticed that the President of that Chapter had been looking at me throughout the whole breakfast and it wasn't until he spoke to me privately, just before I was to go up and speak, that I understood what was going on. As he handed me my honorarium cheque, he said, "I heard what happened at the meeting in Regina last night."

Then I knew the reason he was keeping an eye on me. He was concerned about what I might do. I chuckled to myself and thought, *When the Lord does something different, the news travels fast.* However, I had no specific instructions from the Lord for this meeting, so everything went as planned. The President seemed relieved.

My last stop was Assiniboine, a place I had never visited before. One thing I did hear about that town which excited me was that there was a French population there. I hoped I'd be able to speak my native language with them. When I arrived there, it seemed like there was electricity in the air. I couldn't quite put my finger on what it was, but I knew the Lord had something planned for that area and I would be privileged to be a part of it. I had a few spare hours to myself before the meeting was scheduled to start so I spent them visiting different businesses in town. I was so glad I did. I met a lot of French-speaking people. They seemed to be so friendly compared to the other two places I had just visited. I couldn't wait for the meeting to start. I personally invited several French people I'd met in town who assured me they would be there. I knew there would be ample room because we were meeting at a Community Centre, which could hold at least 300 people.

The meeting finally was underway. About ten minutes into my testimony, I noticed a person coming in the back door and sitting along the wall where chairs had been stacked. I thought my eyes were playing tricks on me, but I was sure I saw a Roman collar around his neck. Could a Catholic priest actually be attending this meeting? Because of my dealings as a young boy at seminary with Catholic priests, I was a little nervous about giving my testimony, but the part of my testimony about the seminary had already been shared before he came in so that gave me some peace, and I continued.

When it came time for me to invite people to come down to the front and give their hearts to the Lord and be born again, to my utter amazement, this small Catholic priest was the first one to make a move. He came and stood right in front of me. Soon half of the people at the meeting were standing there with him. I had never seen such hunger from people to receive Jesus as their Lord and Saviour. After I prayed with all of them, I offered to pray for them to receive the Baptism of the Holy Spirit. Again, this priest was the first one to lift his hand. I prayed with him and within minutes he was praying in a heavenly language, in tongues. I could see that was something new for the people there and found out later that they had never heard about Christians speaking in other tongues, nor that it was a free gift from Jesus for every believer.

After the meeting was officially over, I stayed a few more hours and did some teaching on the subject of tongues. Many others were also baptized in the Holy Spirit and spoke in tongues. That turned out to be the best meeting I'd ever been in. To witness the power of the Lord in people's lives gave me overwhelming joy.

What had touched me the most in Assiniboine was the fact that a Catholic priest had been born again and filled with the Holy Spirit, with the evidence of speaking in other tongues. It had confirmed to me what I had suspected all along and that was that many Catholic priests were really not born again. When you are born again you are changed from what you are into a new person, a transformation that cannot be denied. I remembered when I was a newly born again Christian in Calgary how the Lord had me go visit many Catholic priests in different communities and ask them point blank if they were born again. The reception I received was hostile and I would rather not say what answers I received. My questions were, "Why are Catholic believers, who have been born again during the Charismatic Movement, still meeting in the basements of their churches and not in the main sanctuary on Sunday? Why doesn't the priest himself attend these meetings every week? Why do you never hear them talking about salvation?"

Those were questions that I had no answers to when I was growing up in the Catholic faith. I wanted to know where their beliefs came from. They were definitely not all from the Bible I was reading. Nowhere in my Bible did it say I couldn't eat meat on Friday. Nowhere in my Bible did it say I had to confess my sins to a priest. Nowhere did it say I had to spend time in Purgatory for my sins before I could enter heaven. Nowhere did it say there were different classifications for sin (according to the Catholic Church there were venial sins and mortal sins). Nowhere did it say we were not to read the Bible because we wouldn't understand it and that any questions we had were to be directed to the parish priest and he would decide what was best for us. But we were taught all of that. Now that I was able to read the Bible for myself, I found many things we had been taught were simply traditions handed down for hundreds of years.

A particular verse in the Bible answered those questions concerning what I had been taught. It said, "You shall know the truth and the truth will set you free." I have been free ever since I was born again and can plainly see today why so many people are still caught up in mere religion. People will never be truly free until they accept the Bible as the truth and the only truth. If they don't, they will simply be living and believing the traditions of men. The Bible is the roadmap for our lives that God gave us for our time here on earth. If we deviate from this map, and decide to go our own way, we will only get lost and suffer consequences.

I have met many born again Catholic priests in my travels, most of them being the fruit of the Charismatic Movement of the 1960s and 70s. Many still minister in the Catholic Church. With the epidemic of pedophilia happening in the Catholic Church all around the world, the Lord will have to intervene supernaturally in that arena. He loves sinners but will only tolerate the sin for so long. He is a merciful God and gives every one of them many opportunities to repent of their actions. Their response determines the outcome of their lives. We must love them, like the Lord did even though he hated sin. If we don't, how can we be used of the Lord to help them, if we only condemn them?

That was an important revelation, which would prove to be very helpful to me later in life. I had judged my dad and condemned him because of his actions towards our whole family. He was an alcoholic and was the main reason I left home at an early age. His addiction caused him to be two different people, one person when he was sober and a completely different type when he was drunk—like Dr. Jekyll and Mr. Hyde.

Unfortunately, he was more drunk than sober. This became very puzzling to me as a young boy. How could the same loving father be such a monster, for a lack of a better word, when he was drunk? It was like I was living at home with two different fathers. Whenever he drank, I would make a point of disappearing, usually to the barn with the animals. I would stay there for hours until he either went to bed or fell asleep in the kitchen. When I couldn't hear his voice any more, I came in the back door of the house and quietly crept to my bedroom, finally able to sleep.

When drunk, he would scream at my mother. We kids also got our fair share but when he continuously belittled my mother it was more than I could take. That is when I would disappear. Sometimes it went on well past midnight and would continue until he passed out. That was very hard on me, especially since I had to get up early the next morning to do the barn chores. I would often fall asleep in class from lack of sleep the night before. It was starting to take its toll on me. I always wondered what I could do to change the situation. The solutions I dreamed up were not positive and I remember at one point I was afraid what I might do to my dad if that continued. I was afraid I would do something I would regret the rest of my life, so I decided that one day I would leave home, as soon as the opportunity arose. In the meantime, I would continue enduring what we were all going through and see if I could somehow console my mother before my departure. She continually defended my dad's actions and his cruel words by telling us it was the alcohol that was making him act that way and that deep inside he truly loved us.

We knew that but it didn't change our feelings towards him when he drank. I then realized the saying, "Sticks and stones may break my bones but words will never hurt me" was one of the biggest lies I had ever heard. Words are very powerful and can affect you the rest of your life. I became living proof of that.

About thirty years after my departure from home, my father's words often still echoed in my ears. Joane and I were at one of our get-togethers one evening at our pastor's home when the subject of fathers was brought up. The pastor shared how his dad had been such an inspiration and blessing in his life. Suddenly all the pain and anger I had been harbouring for years exploded in front of everyone. I even surprised myself. I said angrily, "You want to know something? If my father died today, I wouldn't even go to his funeral!"

In my heart, I knew that was not right and that I definitely needed healing in that area of my life. People were taken aback by my statement but no one pressed the subject further. I wasn't in any frame of mind to say any more about it. After leaving the house, while driving back home, Joane said she was really surprised at what I'd said but I didn't want to talk about it. She said I should seek the Lord and let him heal the deep hurts I had towards my dad. I knew one day I would have to do that but I just couldn't right then and there. It would take time. The hurts were deep and still very real, even thirty years later.

After that, I kept asking the Lord somehow to bring healing to my heart. I talked to him about it for weeks because I was determined to get to the bottom of the situation, now that it had surfaced in my life. I knew that what the Lord reveals, he heals and I was anxious to get to the root of it before my dad died. He was getting on in years and wasn't well, according to my mother.

One morning while I was praying the Lord told me he was going to send me back to my home to pray for my dad. He even showed me how it would happen. I had a mental picture of my dad outside splitting wood next to the farmhouse. I knew that I was to walk up to him and put my hand on his shoulder. That was the first time the Lord had showed me, like a video clip, what I would do. I didn't even know when I would be going.

A month or so later, I sensed it was the right time to book my airfare. In the thirty days before leaving, the Lord began showing me all the hurts my dad had gone through when he was growing up as a young man and the things that had pushed him to drinking. My heart started to change towards him. I had almost memorized what I was going to tell him and what I was going to say as I prayed for him, laying my hand on his shoulder. I would ask for forgiveness for my part and was hoping that somehow he would do the same. I had rehearsed my time with him so many times, it felt like a done deal. I now was very comfortable about doing what the Lord had showed me. At first, just the thought of touching him was a challenge but the Lord worked to massage my heart and I became eager to see him. That was a miracle. I had never dreamed I would ever go to see him again.

Finally I boarded the plane for Nova Scotia with excitement in my heart. I rented a car at the Halifax Airport and drove two and a half hours before I reached our old farmhouse. It was the longest two and half hour trip I had ever driven. As I drove down the long driveway towards the house, many mixed emotions and old memories surfaced. I turned the corner around the barn and saw the house. Just outside of it was my dad, splitting wood for the upcoming winter months. I came out of the car and headed towards him. He stopped working, looked at me and was the first to speak. He said, "You're here to see your mother."

I replied, "No dad, I'm here to see you," and continued walking right up to him and put my hand on his right shoulder, ready to pray. Before I could get one word out of my mouth, he started to weep. Then it hit me too and there we stood, both crying our hearts out. The minute my hand had touched his shoulder, the Lord supernaturally brought healing to both of us. Not one word was spoken and I hugged my dad for the very first time.

Finally my mother came out, wondering why I had not come into the house yet. She had heard the car arrive but no one had come in. She was glad to see me but she was even more thrilled to see my dad and me embracing each other. When she got close to us, she could see that we were both weeping and wondered what was wrong and what bad news I was bringing home. We both tried to explain what had happened but it didn't seem to make much sense to her. As a matter of fact, it wasn't making much sense to either of us. We continued to talk and weep for the longest time and then my mother realized we were weeping tears of joy.

I stayed for three days and in those three days my father followed me around everywhere and bombarded me with hundreds of questions. He was trying to catch up on all the years we had not spoken to each other. We stayed up late every evening and just sat at the kitchen table, playing cards and talking. We both had forgiven each other and it seemed like the best three days of my life. Our relationship had been completely restored after all those years. The Lord had worked it all out. I also noticed in my time there that my dad hardly drank any more. He only had a few beers. What a change from before.

That special time will always remain in my memory. Three months later the doctors found my dad's body full of cancer and gave him little time to live. When I found out, I boarded another flight to Halifax to see him once again. He was in the hospital, thirty miles from the farmhouse, so I drove directly there. But he died one hour before my arrival and I was devastated. I had shared the Lord with him on my last visit, but he had not made any commitment to accept the Lord. Was this the last time I would see him? After the funeral, my oldest brother shared something with me that brought me great joy. In my dad's wallet, he kept a laminated copy of the sinner's prayer and just before dying, he had told my brother that he would get on his knees every morning and pray this prayer. He didn't realize he only had to do it once. That assured me that one day I would see him again and we would spend eternity together in heaven. It was the happiest funeral I had ever attended. How I look forward to being together again.

TWENTY-FIVE

Driving on God's Fuel with an Empty Tank

The following year, a very good friend of mine was losing his wife to cancer. She had always had a desire to visit the Maritime Provinces and when she began growing weaker every day, she asked her husband if he would fulfil her dream and take her to visit the Maritimes. He called me up and asked me out for lunch and told me the story. He had never gone to the Maritimes himself and since I was from that area, he wanted to know the best places to visit with his wife. As I explained where to go and where not to go, I could see he was becoming frustrated with the whole thing. I said, "Are you all right?"

He replied, "I really don't want the headache, trying to figure out what to visit when I'm there. I'm going to have enough on my hands just caring for my wife. She's at the point where even walking is a big challenge for her. Would you consider coming with us, if I paid for you and your wife to come?"

How could I say no? We agreed we would leave in a few weeks and I offered to organize the whole trip. From Calgary we would fly to Montréal and from there we would each rent a motorhome and visit the Maritime Provinces, with the exception of Newfoundland. We would be gone for a total of fourteen days. My younger brother lived close to Montréal and he had a friend who could give us a very good deal on two motorhomes. Everything was falling into place.

When we arrived in Montréal, the two motorhomes were waiting for us, ready to go. We started out that same afternoon and were on our way. My friend's wife had a smile from ear to ear. It was a marvellous trip. The motorhomes had been a great idea, since she was having trouble walking. She could spend most of her time inside sightseeing from the comfort of her motorhome.

We were able to visit all the areas we had talked about before we had left Calgary but several days before our return to Montréal, I encountered a big problem. We had stopped at Peggy's Cove in Nova Scotia for a lobster supper and after eating, we all returned to our vehicles. Our plan was to cross mainland Nova Scotia and catch the ferry to New Brunswick, which would save us at least four hours of travelling. We planned to take our time that evening, since the ferry was not scheduled to leave before 5:00 the next morning. Then the unexpected happened.

After travelling for about an hour, I noticed my gas gauge was very, very close to the empty mark. My friend's motorhome was much larger than mine and had two gas tanks; mine had only one. Since my friend didn't need any gas, I had forgotten to fill up after leaving the restaurant. I was leading the way, so I stopped on the side of the road to let him know my predicament. Being from the Maritimes, I also knew there were no service stations open after 6:00 p.m. He got out of his motorhome to see what was happening and I told him that we would miss the ferry since there would be no service station open until later tomorrow morning. He asked me how much gas I had left and I said it was basically on empty.

He said, "Let's keep driving until we get to the next village. If we make it we can turn into a service station, if you see one there. You probably still have enough gas to do that. I have an idea about what we can do once we get there. We both got back into our motorhomes and continued driving. I kept glancing at my gas gauge, as though watching it would somehow change its reading. But it just kept going lower and lower. It had gone as far down as it could.

I started wondering what my friend's idea was. Was he planning to steal some gas from a station? If he did, I wanted nothing to do with it. Within ten to fifteen minutes we entered a little village and sure enough, right there sat a gas station. I pulled into the parking lot with enough room behind me for my friend to pull in. I waited for him to come out, anxious to hear what his plan was. I couldn't figure out how we had ever gotten this far, when it was clear the gas tank was completely empty.

On my way, I had been praying for the wisdom of God. I knew the Lord always had a solution. This would be a good time to tap into his wisdom and allow him to get us out of this predicament. All I was getting from the Lord was, "Just keep driving." I guess the Lord didn't realize it took gasoline to be able to drive. Either that or he had a plan for when we stopped at the next service station.

I couldn't wait to hear my friend's brilliant idea and when he told me what he was going to do, it made a lot of sense. We might just make the ferry yet. He knew he still had one of his gas tanks full of gas, so we could siphon half of the gas from his motorhome into mine and be on our merry way. I wondered why I hadn't thought about that; it made so much sense. He took out a water hose from his motorhome and cut off a piece about eight feet long. There was only one problem: the hose wouldn't go down the gas tank more than a foot and a half. We looked under the motorhome and saw that the pipe leading to the gas tank was S-shaped. It was designed that way to stop people from doing exactly what we were trying to do.

My friend was not fazed there because he had another brilliant idea. He said, "Let's jack up one side of my motorhome high enough for the gas to bypass the S-shaped pipe and then we will be able to siphon it out." We must have tried for a whole hour to jack the motorhome up high, but neither of our jacks went high enough and we had to admit defeat. We talked about staying at the service station overnight to get gas the next morning, but it was time for my brilliant idea, which my friend thought was the worst idea he had ever heard and actually laughed at me when I told him about it.

I told him how the Lord had said, "Just keep driving." I was positive that since we had made it this far on empty, why not see how far we could still go? It did sound like a strange suggestion to him but we had nothing to lose and could always sleep on the side of the road if I ran out of gas (should the Lord's wisdom not work). I may have misunderstood what he actually said; yet I was convinced I had heard correctly.

We got back into our respective motorhomes and, lo and behold, my motorhome started. The gas gauge still showed empty. Now the warning light was on. We got back on the road and drove for hours. I constantly glanced at the gas gauge as if it would supernaturally start going up towards the full mark. It was not making any sense. We were almost at the ferry and my gas tank was bone dry. I was so excited to see what the Lord was doing and anxious to share it with Joane but she was fast asleep in the back of the motorhome, so I just kept thanking and praising the Lord as I drove.

I knew I was witnessing a miracle, but unfortunately I had to experience it alone. I wondered what was going through my friend's mind as he continued to follow me. It would have been interesting to hear his thoughts. But I didn't have to wait long. In less than an hour we arrived at the ferry terminal—supernaturally fast. The whole wharf area was in total darkness. The only lights we could see were coming from the ferry, which had already arrived from New Brunswick, but all its vehicles were still on board.

Immediately after we came out of our motorhomes, my friend said, "I knew there was another gas tank in your motorhome. I'm so glad you found it, otherwise we would have missed this ferry."

I explained to him there was no second gas tank and that I had been driving for hours on a red warning light and an empty gas tank. I told him we would talk about the whole episode once we were on the ferry. Right now we had another problem, since even though we had made it on time, the ferry was not going anywhere. We should go into the office to see what was happening. As we entered the office, we were told the power had been out for hours and no one knew when it would be restored or what had caused the problem. We bought our tickets for the crossing, the attendant reminding us there was no guarantee we would be leaving any time soon.

Knowing that the Lord had gotten us there on time with no gasoline, it didn't make sense that the ferry then would not sail. As we stepped back out into the parking lot, I stopped and faced my friend and said, "If the Lord can get me here with no gasoline he can also restore the power so we can go on our way as planned."

We joined hands and started praying that the Lord would intervene on our behalf and restore the power needed for the terminal. We had not even finished praying when suddenly all the lights came on. We looked at each other and said a loud, "Amen!"

Thirty minutes later the ferry was unloaded and it was our turn to board. Again the thought crossed my mind, *Will my motorhome start once more?* We had just witnessed two miracles and here I was again, my mind flooding with unbelief, the one thing that stops you from seeing and experiencing miracles. It was obvious at this point that the Lord was operating on his faith, not mine. We drove over to the ferry, waiting in line to board. Joy began to overwhelm me and I experienced total peace. We were definitely running on the Lord's fuel.

On the ferry crossing, we had time to share each the thoughts we'd be thinking throughout the night. We laughed, cried and experienced many different emotions as we talked. People next to us were scratching their heads as they listened in on our conversation. God was glorified and seeds were sown in their hearts. Before we knew it, it was time to disembark. The ferry had arrived at the New Brunswick dock. This time I had no doubt my motorhome would start and as we drove off the ferry, I was again thanking the Lord for his goodness and faithfulness.

Once off the ferry, we passed three service stations before we found one that was open. We filled up my tank and it took 100 gallons of gas. The "Lord's tank" was nowhere to be found. As we continued on our trip, I couldn't help but wonder how far we could have gone on the "Lord's tank," instead of putting gas in my tank but then realized that the Lord helps us when we are helpless but expects us to do our part when we are able.

Not long after we had arrived back to Calgary from our Maritime trip, my friend's wife died, but even years later and God is still being glorified through this story. What God does in our lives never dies, so we continue to share stories of his goodness with others.

TWENTY-SIX

Angelic Interventions

I mentioned earlier in my book about an angel of the Lord who appeared to me and opened a warehouse door for which I had no key. I have had similar angelic interventions since then.

One time it was a matter of life or death for our whole family. We were living on an acreage situated on a country road between Airdrie and Crossfield, Alberta. It took almost an hour to drive to Calgary from our place. Many of the roads were country roads, some of them gravel. We moved there because we wanted the children to experience country living, where they could have their own horse, dog, cats, etc. They could live in nature instead of in the city life. We also moved there because we were able to rent a 4000-square-foot farmhouse for $500.00 a month. The owner actually originally asked double that amount, but we were able to secure it for that price by a supernatural intervention of the Lord, another story.

We lived about thirty miles from the church we attended in Calgary and had to travel that distance three times a week, twice on Sunday for morning and evening services, as well as on Wednesday for an evening service. My wife and I were quite involved in the church and the children could hardly wait to get there each time we attended. One particular Sunday morning it was snowing quite heavily during the service, so we decided to skip having lunch in Calgary and go directly home. The roads were getting slippery but we made it home with no mishaps. When it came time to go to the evening service, it was very windy and as much as a foot of snow had drifted into our driveway. Visibility was extremely poor because of the wind, so Joane and I didn't want to risk going out into what had now become a raging blizzard.

We told the kids of our decision and they both started to cry. Sunday evening was their favourite service. After several attempts at trying to make them understand why, we realized that nothing was working. We reluctantly agreed to go check out the road conditions. If they were OK we would go, but if they were not, we told the kids we would have to turn around and come back home. So we all got into our car and headed down the road. As expected, visibility was terrible so we decided to turn around and head back. The country road was so narrow we had great difficulty turning around. The snow was blinding and at times we had to stop in order to see anything in front of us. I had been in drifting snow before, but because of the open fields on both sides of the road, the gale force winds were rendering our visibility to zero.

I started to panic because I realized we were probably the only crazy people on the road and what if we were stranded in the middle of nowhere, four miles from our house? To make things worse, we only had a quarter of a tank of gasoline. I tried to do a U-turn in the middle of the road and suddenly the car began sliding down an embankment into a deep ditch. My fear had become a reality. Here we were at the bottom of a ditch with snow up to the hood of the car. We all looked at each other. No one said a word as we sat and wondered what to do.

One by one, we each started to admit that it was our fault and if we had just stayed home this would have never happened. Of course, talking about it could not change the predicament we were in. I thought of leaving the car in the ditch with everyone in it and trying to go find help at one of the farmhouses along the road. But because of the drifting snow, the lack of visibility and the bitter cold, I decided instead to stay in the car.

We started to pray for wisdom to know what to do. We had calmed down enough to do that. As we were praying, some words came up from my spirit. I was hesitant to share them, since they didn't make any sense. I heard, "Put the car in reverse and back up as far as you can." I didn't tell anyone, but continued praying along with everyone else.

When we had finished praying, I put the car in reverse to follow the instructions in my spirit. Everyone said in unison, "What are you doing?"

I replied, "I'm just going to back up as far as I can." To everyone's amazement, including mine, the car started to go backwards. We must have backed up about twenty feet. I could see the snow piling up on the top of the trunk. When the car wouldn't go any further, I put it into drive and cranked my wheels towards the roadway. We all watched in awe as the car started to climb up the embankment until it was in the middle of the road. We stared at each other with our mouths open, realizing we had just witnessed a miracle. We even looked back to see if someone had pushed us out of the ditch, but no one was there.

All the way back to our house we tried to reason what had happened but we knew we'd had an angelic encounter. The next day the storm was over and as I drove to work, I saw where our car had been sitting in the ditch. It was impossible that we had ever been able to get out of there. It could never have happened without supernatural help. "With God nothing is impossible."

Not long after that experience, Joane had her own personal encounter with an angel. We were struggling with finances to the extent that all we could afford was an old car for her to drive the children to the many activities they were enrolled in. One evening she told me she was not comfortable in this old vehicle, never knowing whether it would make it or die in the middle of the road. I had to agree the car was not very reliable and promised I would see if I could find a more reliable one.

The very next day she was taking the children to one of their many activities. While driving, thoughts of the car breaking down flooded her mind. She tried to dismiss them when suddenly she saw a huge angel sitting on the roof of her car. It completely startled her, since she was looking straight ahead at the road as she drove, yet she could plainly see this massive angel sitting on the roof. Immediately total peace swept over her and the Lord gave her the assurance that nothing would ever go wrong with the car. As a matter of fact, she had trouble letting go of it once we were able to buy another vehicle.

Another time, I was finishing the electrical work at a house. An electrician had driven me to the job site and said he would pick me up at 4:00 PM when I should have the job completed. My boss knew I was fast at finishing houses, so every time there was a house to finish I would get the call.

Different tools are needed for different applications. For installing receptacles, a #6 screwdriver is needed. A flat blade screwdriver can work, but it takes longer to complete the task. I was working on a large two-storey house, which needed many receptacles and switches installed. I reached down into my pouch for my #6 screwdriver but it was not there. I emptied my pouch out completely to see if I had at least a stubby #6 Robinson screwdriver. I knew it would also work, even though it was not as good. The Robinson wasn't there either. I put all the screwdrivers slowly back into my pouch, one by one, taking one last look for my #6. Nothing. I decided I would just have to do the job using a flat blade. This really slowed my work down so I worked right through my lunch break, hoping to be able to finish by 4:00 p.m.

When the electrical work in a new house is done, there is nothing else in the house but carpeting so you can easily spot a screw or anything else on the floor as you scan the room. Nothing must be left on it. I completed my work and still had fifteen minutes to spare before my ride arrived so I quickly went through all of the rooms to make sure nothing had been left on the carpet. I saw nothing.

I sat down next to the door, relaxing from a long day's work. At 4:00 p.m. sharp the doorbell rang; the electrician had arrived to pick me up. I opened the door and started to explain my dilemma about not having a #6 screwdriver to do the job and how I had been concerned I wouldn't be able to finish before his arrival. When I told him, he laughed out loud and pointed to the middle of the room. "Is that the screwdriver you're missing?" he said.

I laughed, knowing he was trying to play a joke on me, but he repeated it again, still chuckling. I refused to look because I knew that was impossible and started to walk out. He again said, "Are you going to leave without that screwdriver?" To stop his dumb joke, I turned around and looked and, to my complete astonishment, there sat my #6 screwdriver in the middle of the carpet! Once he saw the look on my face, he realized I had told him the truth, but, like me, had no explanation about what had transpired. The screwdriver had literally appeared out of nowhere. To this day I wonder about this strange event and why it happened. Maybe some day the Lord will tell me.

Another mysterious episode happened while I was attending a church I had never been to before. Several other couples in attendance also witnessed it. Before the seminar started, the pastor's wife arrived with twelve red roses and randomly passed them out. I was one of the people who received a red rose. I was sitting next to the aisle on the front row and no one sat behind me. On the other side of the aisle were two couples, friends of mine who had come to the seminar. I placed my rose on top of my Bible in the aisle next to my chair.

Minutes later the speaker made his way to the pulpit. I reached down to get my Bible and, lo and behold, the rose had disappeared. I looked behind me to see if someone had picked it up, but no one was sitting behind me. I was perplexed and kept thinking about it so much that I wasn't able to focus on what the speaker was saying. The morning session finished and we all decided to go out for lunch at a nearby restaurant. The pastor's wife came up to the platform and announced she would collect all the roses and put them back in a vase so they wouldn't die while we were gone for lunch. Everyone brought her his or her rose, except for me, since mine was nowhere to be found. (I was hoping she would not count them or remember she had given me one. How could I explain what happened to it?) She collected eleven of the roses, put them in a vase and placed them next to the pulpit and we all left for lunch.

While sitting at the restaurant, I noticed the two couples who had sat across the aisle from me were also seated at my table. That caused me to think even more of what had transpired with the rose, to the extent that I had trouble selecting from the menu. Then I finally decided that the only way for these thoughts to stop would be to share it with the people at the table. I didn't know how they would react but I worked up enough courage and told them what had happened before the morning session. To my surprise, both couples said they had witnessed the same thing. One minute the rose was on my Bible; the next minute it was gone. Each one had been reluctant to share it because they were convinced their eyes were playing tricks on them.

Even though I had witnesses, there was still no explanation for what had happened. We finished our lunch with everyone trying to give an explanation. When we arrived back to the church, I went up to the vase of roses to count them and there were exactly twelve! An unexplained mystery, this time with four witnesses.

Since these two strange experiences, I have learned not to question the Lord about things. If he wants me to know why, he will explain them to me. Until then, I am satisfied knowing that his ways are better than our ways and we do not need an explanation for everything he does. We simply experience them and move on with our lives. A lot of things cannot be understood with the natural mind.

Ernie Fougere

TWENTY-SEVEN

The Lottery

One of the biggest financial blessings we ever received by hearing the voice of God happened after we had sold our estate home in order to use some of the equity to start up our own ministry, feeling that was how the Lord was directing us.

We had built our estate home, using a Christian contractor from Saskatchewan because he offered to build it at his cost, a big blessing from the Lord. When we first built it, we loved it so much, we wanted to spend the rest of our days in that home. We even had all our hands imprinted in concrete on the side of our driveway, including the dog's paw prints. Then God asked us to sell it.

We were in prophetic ministry, training people to hear the voice of God. We now needed another place to live and with the help of another Christian couple, we moved into a beautiful new condo.

We had gone to Regina for further teaching on hearing the voice of God, because the ministry under which we had been ordained was giving advanced training there. We would also be taught how to prophesy the word of the Lord to other people. This was new to us, but very exciting to see how the Lord works through ordinary people to bless others. After the training had come to an end, a well-known prophet from the United States came up to us and asked us if he could give Joane and me a word from the Lord. He said the Lord wanted us to know something, so of course we agreed.

The prophet said, "Since you have both been faithful in your obedience to me, by starting the ministry I asked you to start, I am going to bless you with a large house and the mortgage will never be a burden to you." That was all he said but it was music to our ears. A large house would definitely be more convenient for us than a small condo since we liked to have people over for food and fellowship. The condo restricted us from doing that; we hardly had enough room for our immediate family. Sometimes we felt like sardines in a can.

Often we had talked of our desire to have a larger house but our financial situation at the time prohibited it. We knew God loves to give us the desire of our hearts so we rested in that promise and decided just to exercise patience. We were learning that it is much better when things happen in his timing instead of ours and that in addition to having faith we needed to develop patience.

Several years after the seminar training in Regina, while still living in our small condo, we were asked by our church leaders to attend another Prophetic Training in Edmonton. This time Bishop Bill Hamon, the head of our organization, would personally be ministering to all the ministers under his leadership. He was a mature prophet, well known around the world for his accurate prophecies, not only to ordinary individuals, but even to world leaders. The invitation mentioned he would personally prophesy to all the ministers in attendance. People would be in attendance from all across Canada and we wanted to be part of that group. Since our financial situation was still not ideal, we made arrangements to stay at a friend's home.

A couple of months before the Edmonton seminar, it was work as usual day after day. One thing I always did upon my arrival at home from work was pick up our daily mail. One particular day, unbeknownst to me, my wife had gone to pick up the mail, something she never did. She went through it and noticed one of the flyers was for purchasing tickets to win a house through an Edmonton lottery, which they promote every year during their summer celebration called "Klondike Days." She immediately threw it in the garbage, knowing that was what I did every year when that junk mail came. She put the remainder of the mail on my office desk, knowing I would go into the office to see what came in. But after she had deposited the mail on my desk, for some reason she went back to the garbage can and took out the flyer for the lottery tickets and put it with the pile on my desk.

I thank God that my wife obeyed the nudge to go back to the garbage can to retrieve that flyer. But what transpired next was the biggest struggle I ever had in obeying the voice of God.

When I got home that day, I went to the mailbox, surprised that there was no mail, not even junk mail, which we received on a daily basis. As I opened the condo door, the first thing I said was, "I can't believe there was no mail in our mailbox today."

Joane told me why and I was puzzled as to why she had retrieved it that day. I went to my office to check out the mail. Sitting on top of the pile was the lottery ticket envelope, which I immediately threw into the garbage, ready to check out the rest of the mail. But before I could pick up the next envelope, I heard the Lord say, "Take that envelope out of the garbage can and open it." I recognized it as the Lord speaking but I really didn't want to obey because of my religious beliefs. I had been taught all my life that buying lottery tickets was a sin. I felt it would be particularly wrong for me to do since I was a pastor.

I looked through the mail when again I heard the Lord say, "Take the envelope out of the garbage can, open it, and read it." Now my curiosity was ignited and I half-heartedly reached down into the garbage and retrieved the envelope. I opened it and there in bold letters on the front page were these words: "YOUR DREAM HOME. IT COULD BE YOURS."

As clearly as anything I had ever heard before, I heard the Lord say, "Since you were obedient and willing to sell your estate home in Evergreen Estates to start up my prophetic ministry, I am now going to give you this dream home."

I crumpled the paper and threw it back into the garbage. I thought, *What would people say if they knew that I, a pastor, had bought a lottery ticket and won a house?* Our religious beliefs can be so strong they can stop us from receiving the blessings God has for us.

I continued to open the rest of the mail and the whole time the thought kept hounding me to take the envelope out again and buy lottery tickets. This continued for twenty-four hours. Finally I decided to obey. I couldn't eat, sleep, or think straight. I kept thinking, "You better obey."

I had to do it, because the lack of food and sleep was starting to affect my work. When I got home the next day, I went directly to the garbage can and took out the controversial envelope for the umpteenth time. Since my financial situation was not very healthy, I decided to buy a $100.00 ticket. I would mail them a cheque and trust that God would provide the funds to cover the expense. That would buy me time before my cheque cleared my bank. As I was looking for the telephone number to order my ticket, I heard the Lord say, "I want you to buy the Family Pack."

I was astounded. Sure enough, there in the envelope was the Family Pack for $350.00. I almost passed out when I saw the amount. Why would the Lord want me to buy the Family Pack, when he could give me the same house with one $100.00 ticket? I was completely unwilling to purchase even one ticket because of my lack of finances at the time.

I told myself, *Don't try and understand the Lord; His thoughts are higher than yours.*

However, I said to the Lord, "How do you expect me to pay for these tickets? You know how much money I have in my bank account."

He said something that stirred up my traditional religious beliefs once again: "Put it on your credit card."

What? First he was asking me to gamble by buying these tickets, and now he was instructing me to pay for it by credit card? I was flabbergasted, but I knew I couldn't win against that clear voice, and if I didn't obey I would only go back to sleepless nights and more thoughts hounding my mind. Out came my credit card, and so I could get on with my life, I bought the Family Pack.

Once I did, I heard the Lord say, "I told you to buy the Family Pack because this home is for your entire family. You are now the owner of this beautiful dream home."

Suddenly, unmistakably, I KNEW THAT I KNEW THAT I KNEW that dream home was mine to enjoy with my family. I would have to wait another two months until the draw. I wanted to run out right then and tell the whole world about my dream home and the Lord's goodness.

I sat there at my desk, thinking how I could have missed the Lord's blessing had I not obeyed. In spite of all my excuses, resistance and religious beliefs for not buying the tickets that sounded so logical to me, the Lord continued to prompt me to obey his will. I was overwhelmed by his love for me and with how he could accomplish his will in my life in spite of me.

However, a thought came to mind that was very logical, *Why would the Lord give me a home in Edmonton, when I live in Calgary and just started a ministry in the city for Him?* I later found out why. He gave the Calgary dream home to another Christian.

I asked the Lord, *What about this so-called gambling with lottery tickets?*

I heard him say gently, "Gambling is luck and can lead to addiction. What I did was simply the means I chose in order to give you the home because of your obedience to me."

I must have rejoiced there alone in my office for twenty minutes for the Lord's unbelievable love for me and my family.

After hanging up the phone and realizing that I now owned a new dream home from the Lord, the first person I wanted to tell was of course Joane. I wanted to tell her of the struggle I went through before I actually bought the tickets. I was excited at what she would say and could hardly wait to see her reaction. I started running up the stairs to find her and let her know about the good news—no, the GOD News. Halfway up the stairs the Lord stopped me. He said, "You are to tell no one about what I have given you until you have officially been awarded the dream home."

I agreed, *I will tell no one, just my wife, because I tell her everything.*

Instantly his words came back, "No one, including your wife." Since his words hadn't fully sunk in, I continued running up the stairs to find Joane, when again this voice said only one word, "Zechariah." I stopped. I knew then that God was saying I was not to tell anyone, not even Joane. Zechariah had not believed the Lord when he told him his wife would become pregnant and he was struck dumb until his wife gave birth. I didn't want to be struck dumb for two months until the day the lottery was officially awarded, so I stopped in my tracks and never did climb the last few stairs.

Returning back down to my office, I sat at my desk wondering why I couldn't tell anyone. This time I had been smart enough to obey without questioning the Lord's wisdom. The next two months were the hardest two months I ever experienced alone, because I couldn't rejoice with all of my friends. It had to be between just God and me.

Several thoughts crossed my mind as to why he forbade me to tell anyone. Maybe if everyone knew about it before it actually happened, pride would fill my heart that I was able to hear his voice so clearly. I knew that the Bible says God resists the proud, so maybe in his mercy, he didn't want this to stop his blessing.

Joane and I went to Edmonton for the advanced seminar in hearing the voice of God with the prophet Bill Hamon of Christian International out of Santa Rosa Beach, Florida. As was planned months before, we stayed with friends at their beautiful home on a golf course. At the breakfast table the next morning they started sharing how God had intervened in their negotiations to acquire the mortgage they needed. God had given them supernatural favour with the bank, without which they would not be living in that home. We rejoiced with what the Lord had done for them. After breakfast we all got ready to go to the seminar and arrived in just a few minutes. The Lord had even given them a house only minutes from their church. As we entered the church building, Craig, our pastor friend from Calgary, greeted us. Joane immediately started to share with him how the Lord had supernaturally given favour to the couple we were staying with, in acquiring a beautiful home on a golf course.

When she had finished sharing the story, Craig looked at her and said, "Wouldn't it be exciting if Bishop Bill Hamon prophesied a new house for you in this seminar?" He said this because he knew we had given up our estate home to start a new ministry in Calgary. He also knew we were now living in a small condo.

Joane simply replied, "Yes, that would be nice." I chuckled at her statement. She didn't know what I knew and how accurate Craig actually was. We went through the morning session with the main speaker and just before it started, the person in charge of the training, a good friend of mine, came up to me and said, "Oh, by the way, I have asked the main speaker to end his session fifteen minutes earlier than scheduled. I want you to go up and share what the Lord has been speaking to you lately and encourage the people with your testimony."

This would have been the opportune moment to share about the house the Lord had given us, but I knew I couldn't say what was the strongest on my heart. I was so looking forward to the day we would finally be awarded that dream home so I could tell everyone about the goodness and blessings of the Lord. However, I did speak about what the Lord put on my heart and then it was time to go to a ministers' luncheon.

At the luncheon, Bill Hamon started prophesying to all the ministers in attendance. When he came up to us, he started prophesying for our church and ministry. Right in the middle of a sentence, right out of the blue, he blurted out, "And Lord, release that big house to them now."

I felt like jumping up and shouting, "This is a true prophet of the Lord; I already have that new house." But I could not say anything and I reasoned that if I had tried to say it, I would probably be struck dumb for my disobedience and wouldn't be able to say anything anyway. Craig looked over at us and smiled knowingly, because of what he had said to us before the meeting.

Those two months were a real test for me, a test I only passed by God's grace. After the luncheon was over, Joane reminded me of the prophecy we had received in Regina years ago at our first Advanced Prophetic Training: "The mortgage will never be a burden for you." Since the Lord had given us the lottery dream home, there would be no mortgage and therefore burden-free. I was so tempted to confirm to Joane how accurate that prophecy was, but once again I had to be tight-lipped. When the training was over, we went back to Calgary, back to work as usual.

A few weeks before the draw for the dream home at the Edmonton Klondike Days, Calgary holds its annual Stampede. At this event, there is also a dream home that is awarded to someone. When the ticket was drawn for the house, the person who won it was a person I knew very well, who belonged to the same Christian organization as we did. She was a single mom who was struggling financially at the time. Because of her financial situation, it was obvious the Lord wanted to show his love and faithfulness to her. We all rejoiced with her and it was then I realized why the Lord didn't want to give me the dream home in Calgary. He had already decided to give it to her. Things were starting to make sense. I was very tempted to let her know the Lord was also about to give me one in Edmonton in a few weeks. I was really being tested in my obedience.

Klondike Days went into full swing. I had never attended that event once during the twenty-five years I had lived in Alberta so didn't know when the draw was supposed to take place. The date was on the tickets, but search as I did I couldn't find them. I must have hidden them somewhere so that Joane would not see them because if she did, I would need to come up with some serious answers as to why I had purchased lottery tickets. Because of the instructions the Lord had given me, I couldn't lie and I couldn't tell the truth, but that predicament never happened. I was only hoping that I would not be asked to prove my purchase and produce the winning ticket.

The evening of the draw for the dream home arrived, unbeknownst to me. I told the family I was going to bed early and didn't want to be disturbed. I was to preach the next morning at the Sunday service and wanted to get up early to go over my notes. Shortly after midnight, the phone rang and my son answered it right away so that the ringing would not wake me up. The person on the other end of the line began pressuring my son to let him talk to me. He said it was very important and that I would be glad he called. Since we had worked with homeless people in downtown Calgary for years, my son was convinced it was a homeless person who was in trouble with the law and he had given the police my name as a person to call. The person assured my son that he had very good news for me and my son finally agreed.

He came upstairs to my bedroom and knocked on my door. He said I had to take the call because it was very important and he couldn't get rid of the guy on the other end of the line. "It has to be important; I can't shake this guy."

By now Joane was awake along with my son's wife and they were all in our bedroom wanting to know what was going on at 12:15 a.m. I took the phone and went into the washroom to get some peace and quiet so I could hear clearly what was so important at this time of night, whatever it was that couldn't wait until the sun came up.

When I said hello, the person on the other end said, "Are you Ernie Fougere?"

I answered, "Yes I am. Could you please let me know what is so important at this time of night, that it couldn't wait until later?"

He replied, "Sir, you have just won the dream home at the Klondike Days and I need you to be here in Edmonton tomorrow morning at 9:30 a.m.

Although I was still half asleep, I blurted out, "Yes, I knew that two months ago."

He said, "What did you say? I must have misunderstood you."

I guess I was so excited finally to be able to tell someone after all these months of silence, he was the first one to know so I repeated, "I knew that two months ago."

He replied, "That is impossible; we just drew the ticket thirty minutes ago."

I said, "God told me two months ago that I had won that home."

He said, "God talks to you?"

I answered, "Yes, for as long as I can remember."

I heard him mutter, "Whatever!" Then he continued, "You need to be here tomorrow morning in Edmonton at 9:30 a.m.

The media will all be here and we want to make the official presentation to you of the gold key to the dream home."

I asked him a very simple question and he completely lost his cool. I said, "Do I have to be there in person?"

He raised his voice and started giving me a lecture. He said, "Sir, I have been doing this for years, awarding the home to the people who win, and when I give them the good news, they are all hysterical about it, but no, not you. You tell me God told you that you had won months ago, as if you think I'm crazy enough to believe such nonsense. Then I ask you to be here tomorrow morning for the presentation of the gold key and you ask me if you need to be here! Do you want this house or not? If you do, be here tomorrow morning at 9:30 AM sharp." Then he hung up on me.

I opened the door of the bathroom and everyone was looking at me, waiting to know what that was all about. Finally, finally, I would be able to let everyone know what had transpired between God and me the last two months. It took me thirty minutes to explain. Not a question was asked until I was finished telling them about hearing God's voice so clearly.

When I finally finished talking, no one seemed to believe me. They just sat and stared at me. I could finally talk about it and my family didn't even believe what I said! So I showed them the caller ID on the phone, which said, "The Klondike Days" and it finally sank in. We all shouted, laughed and rejoiced together for the longest time. My son's wife even called Australia to tell her parents the good news. The story had started to go around the world, just like the Lord had told me, "I will be glorified around the world as people hear this story."

Joane told me how she had taken that envelope with the lottery tickets and thrown it into the garbage can in the kitchen and then was compelled to take it out again and put it on the top of my mail in my office downstairs. I was reminded that that would never have happened had she not been obedient to go retrieve the letter from the garbage can and put it with my mail. What a lesson for all of us. We must obey the Holy Spirit, even when it doesn't make any sense.

What do we have to lose by being disobedient? The answer unfortunately is that we have every good thing to lose that the Lord wants to do for us. How many blessings have we missed from the Lord because we dismissed them when they didn't make sense to our natural minds? The good news is that it's never too late to start. A blessing from the Lord like this will change your life forever.

Ernie Fougere

TWENTY-EIGHT

The News of God's Goodness Spreads Worldwide

The whole family wanted to be with us in Edmonton to receive our prize, including the grandchildren. We all went to our separate rooms to see if we could catch a few hours' sleep before leaving. Needless to say, everyone was so excited few of us really slept well. The next morning I had to arrange for someone to do the Sunday Service for me since I couldn't be there. With that taken care of, we were on our way. The trip seemed to take forever and when we finally arrived we had to find out where the Klondike Days park was located. Everyone in town seemed to know where it was so we had no problem finding the location. We got there five minutes early, parked our cars and walked to the Dream Home sitting in the middle of the parking lot.

Thousands of people had strolled through the house in the past two months, each hoping to be the lucky winner. As I walked toward it with my family beside me, I kept thinking how the Lord had led someone's hand to reach down into the barrel of thousands and thousands of tickets, specifically pick my ticket, so that I would receive the gold key to God's Dream Home for us, and that through this event, he would be glorified around the world for years to come. It was mind-boggling. What an awesome God.

We noticed there were five official sponsors, which represented the various prizes that had been won through the lottery—luxury cars and trucks, motorhomes, world tours, etc. They all wore different coloured blazers, depending on which prize they represented. One gentleman started walking towards me and I noticed he had a badge pinned to his jacket that said, "Dream Home." Was this the guy I had talked to only hours before who had hung up on me?

I soon found out. He reached out his hand to me and said, "Are you Ernie Fougere?"

I answered, "I sure am."

He said, "I have a few questions I would like answered. First of all, is it true you hear God and he speaks to you?"

I said, "That's right. I believe the Bible and I'm a pastor in Calgary. God says in the Bible that his sheep hear his voice. I'm his sheep so I hear his voice. Don't you?"

I received no reply. He quickly went to his second question, "Why did you ask if you had to be here in person?"

I said, "I'm a pastor and I should be officiating in church right now. Since I didn't get a straight answer from you, because you hung up on me, I was able to find someone to replace me. So here I am. Let's get on with the show."

He then apologized and stopped questioning me. He must have told everyone that God had spoken to me about the house because everyone kept asking me the same question: "I hear God speaks to you. Is that true?"

An Edmonton Sun newspaper reporter requested an interview with me because they too had heard about God speaking to me. There were other newspapers present but I wanted The Sun to do the interview, because I knew the reporter didn't believe in the same God I believed in. This would be an opportunity for my God to be glorified. I agreed to the interview, but under one condition: I wanted the complete interview to be taped and the article to say exactly what I shared, word for word, not an interpretation of what I said. He agreed and immediately went to his vehicle to fetch his recorder.

When he came back, we agreed we would do the interview in the living room of our new Dream Home, with my family in attendance. They would be witnesses of the things I said. The interview went on for about fifteen minutes and he was so intrigued by what I was saying, he had very few questions to ask. After it was over, he leaned towards me and said, "Could I have your phone number in Calgary? If I ever get the chance to go there, I would like to have coffee with you. I want to know more about your God."

I have not heard from him since, but I know that day as he interviewed me, he got an earful about the loving God that I serve. Maybe all his questions were answered by some other Christian. The Lord is the one who draws people to himself. The seed was planted so I have the assurance it's being watered by someone. The Lord makes sure that seed never dies.

After the interview I toured my new home and as I walked outside I met one of the officials who had numerous questions about hearing God. As I shared my experiences in hearing the voice of God, he started to weep, trying desperately to hide his tears.

All the necessary paperwork and red tape was finalized for taking possession of our new Dream Home. Once it was moved into its permanent location in one of the estate areas of Edmonton, I would be contacted to come and inspect it to make sure it had not been damaged in the move. Then the final papers would be signed. The house would finally be mine, mortgage-free, worth close to four hundred thousand dollars.

To reinforce his assurance that this home was truly meant for us, God arranged for the centrepiece on the mantel of the fireplace in the living room to be a huge fern plant. Our surname, Fougere, means "fern" in French. Joane and I are both of French descent, and we found out that the contractor and sub-contractors who helped build this house were all French. The house was moved onto a street with a French name, and the person we eventually sold the home to was a French lady. Every piece of artwork had to do with places and buildings in France, all in French. The Lord loves details, even what we desire in decorating our homes. He did all that for us.

We finally sold our Dream Home and were able to take all the decorations and things the Lord had put in it. The Lord had another wonderful surprise for us after that. We were able to build our own dream home in a location we had always loved in Calgary. We could design our own place and have it custom built exactly to our taste and in the location we wanted. Our heavenly Father wanted to give us the desires of our hearts. The Klondike Days Dream Home we sold was a bungalow. The one we built was a two-storey home with a walk-out basement on a natural pond. This was the only natural pond in Calgary. We had always desired to build near a body of water that was not man-made. There was only one problem—all the lots had already been sold. However, we found out again that what is impossible for man is possible with God. More about that later. Let's get back to Calgary from Edmonton first.

After leaving Klondike Days, we went out for dinner together as a family and talked for hours about the importance of hearing God's voice and giving him glory for what he had done. We arrived back in Calgary late that evening and with all the excitement we had experienced that day and the lack of sleep the night before, we were all ready for a nice, long sleep.

But our sleep was cut short when the phone rang at 6:00 a.m. I was startled and annoyed by its ring and hurried to answer it before it woke everyone. As I answered the phone, the voice on the other end said, "I read the bold print in the Edmonton Sun newspaper this morning, and it says that God gave you, a pastor, a new house. I immediately called the newspaper in Edmonton to get your phone number and they were gracious enough to give it to me. We are a Christian radio station in Calgary called Shine FM, and we would like you to testify and tell your story on our early morning show. The greatest amount of listeners are tuned in to that show at 8:00 a.m., which will give you plenty of time to get here."

I asked them if I could give my story to them later that day, then they could tape it and air it whenever they wanted to. I said I was very tired because I'd only had a few hours' sleep when they called. I could tell they were disappointed with my decision but reluctantly accepted it. They agreed to call me later to set up a time to meet to do the recording.

I hung up the phone and climbed back into bed to get some much-needed sleep. My head had barely hit the pillow when Joane asked, "Who was that on the phone at this time of the morning?"

I said, "It was just a Christian radio station, who wanted me to tell my story live on their early morning show about the house the Lord gave us in Edmonton. But I told them I was too tired."

Joane jumped out of bed and said, "Get dressed; we are going! The Lord said he would be glorified through this Dream Home, so we need to do our part. Get dressed."

I could not argue with her logic, so groggily got dressed. We grabbed something to eat and rushed out the door to drive to the Shine FM radio station—half asleep, I might add. We then realized we had no idea where it was located. All we knew was that it was somewhere downtown so we continued to drive in that direction. When we arrived downtown we asked people where the station was located. No one seemed to know, which told me they probably had never heard of it, let alone listened to it. We finally found someone who knew what street it was on, but not the address. Of course it was on one of the longest streets downtown.

We rushed towards it, since it was getting closer and closer to 8:00 a.m. We only had fifteen minutes to find it but suddenly, there it was in front of us. We found a parking spot and rushed into the station. With barely seven minutes left before the show started, we ran up the stairs instead of taking the elevator.

We reached the third floor. The walls were all glass so we could see into the studio and the people in it with headphones on their heads, but their backs were to us so they couldn't see us. On the entrance door was a combination security lock. We banged on it but no one could hear us. It was almost 8:00 a.m. What was I to do?

I heard the Lord say, "Turn the handle on the door." I did and it opened.

Within a minute we were standing in front of the studio door, which was open, looking at three people. When they saw us, they almost fainted and the expression on their faces was incredulous. One of them came rushing out to us to find out how we had gotten in and what we were doing here. I said," I'm the pastor who won the Dream Home."

Within seconds I was fitted with a microphone, sat down on a stool and the announcer whispered, "You're on the air." He introduced me live to his radio audience and for the next fifteen minutes I was able to glorify my Father to the city of Calgary. They did not even ask me any questions; they were all so caught up with my story.

After my testimony was over, two of the three people in the studio brought us into the kitchen to offer us coffee. Their first question was, "How did you get into our office?"

I told them the Lord had told me simply to turn the door knob and it opened. One of them said, "That's impossible, you need to use the combination to get in, because the door automatically locks when it closes."

I said, "Sorry, I don't have an answer for that," even though I knew the Lord had opened it, but wasn't sure if they were ready for that explanation. I remembered my experience with the angel at the warehouse and how the Lord had told me afterwards, "I am the Master Key. I can open any door."

They were probably not ready for that story either, so like Mary the mother of Jesus did in the Bible, I just "pondered these things in my heart" and glorified him for his goodness and faithfulness. As we drank coffee with them they had so many questions. Suddenly, the Lord gave me a prophetic word for them. The word was conditional and today most of that word has come to pass because of their obedience. One day I will go back and visit them and give them a copy of this book so that their faith can go to a higher level, because their faith pleased God.

I was now ready to go back home to bed. So much had happened in the last twenty-four hours but joy filled my heart because the Lord was continuing to be glorified. *A good sleep would surely help*, I thought.

When I got home, I never did get back to my bed because by then many people had heard the broadcast and somehow had my telephone number, so the phone started to ring continually. Not only that, the newspaper was in everyone's hands. Other newspapers were also sharing my story. Most of the phone calls were positive and many rejoiced with us, wanting more details about my hearing the voice of God.

One church called me to offer me their services of deliverance for what they thought was my addiction to gambling. I graciously refused, not wanting to try and reason with them, since I could tell they were deep in traditional and religious beliefs. I simply thanked them for caring and calling.

One couple actually came to my home to let me know that the Dream Home was not of God, since God is against gambling. After spending time with them explaining the whole story, they became convinced it was indeed God. Some are willing to change their way of thinking, some are not, but we must accept all our Christian brothers, even those who disagree with us.

The Dream Home in Edmonton sold. Now we were ready for the Lord to find us the desire of our hearts in Calgary, where he had placed us years ago. We put all the Klondike Dream Home French theme furnishings in storage before selling the house, since we believed they were all hand-picked for us by the Lord, and we wanted them to be part of our new home in Calgary.

As mentioned earlier, we had always wanted to build a home on a natural pond where we could enjoy all the wildlife that would inhabit it and be able to have a beautiful view of the water. We found out there was only one such location in Calgary; all the other lakes and ponds were manmade. We went to visit the area and found out it was going to be developed that year, with two phases to the project. The first phase had already been offered on the market and within days all fourteen sites had been bought by individuals or reserved by a builder, with a down payment to secure them. We were very disappointed.

The second phase was not scheduled to be built for a few years, since the developer wanted to sit on the remaining lots, anticipating they would double in value. Nevertheless, we found out who the Phase One builders were. There were four. We decided to go and see what type of houses they would be building on the fourteen lots to give us an idea what we wanted in our own home.

Weeks before going to see this new neighbourhood, the Lord had given me a dream of what our master suite would look like. The next morning I explained it to Joane in detail. It had a three-way fireplace, a sitting room, steam shower and a Jacuzzi. It would take up forty percent of the upper floor. When I described it to her, we were both excited and couldn't wait for the day we would actually be living in it.

We looked through the four show homes of the builders who would be building homes on the natural pond. When we entered the first one, we were awed at how beautifully it was built. It was truly an estate home. The second show home was equally as beautiful and I wondered if the builders were each trying to outdo each other. As we went upstairs, both of our jaws dropped as we entered the master bedroom. It was exactly like the one I had seen in my dream. Right there we both agreed that this was to be the builder for our home. The only problem was that all fourteen lots had been sold and Phase Two wouldn't start for several years. We needed a home now. We could compromise and build elsewhere or we could believe the Lord for a miracle. We chose the latter.

When we inquired about the lots that had been reserved by contractors with a security deposit, we found out that one of the builders had only two days to commit to building on his lot or he would lose the lot. That was told to us confidentially by the builder we had chosen. What he said next caused our hearts to leap with joy. He said, "This builder owes me a big favour because I did one for him months ago. He promised me if he didn't use the lot, because his customer couldn't come up with the down payment, I would be the first to know and the first to have an option on it."

At that moment we both knew God had opened the door for us to have that lot, which was the most ideal location on the pond. He said to us, "You'll have to wait forty-eight hours to find out if I get it and if I'm lucky enough to get it then you can buy it right away. But you need to use us as your builder."

After having seen the master bedroom, we already knew they would be our builder. We didn't have to wait forty-eight hours to find out if that lot was ours, like the builder had to. We already knew the Lord had arranged everything for us. Sure enough, two days later we got a phone call to let us know the lot was ours and all they needed was our down payment to secure it, since there would be a waiting list ready to buy it if we did not take it.

The Lord had done so much for us already to get that lot. There was one more thing he would have to do. We didn't have the $30,000.00 deposit needed to secure the property. The sale of our house in Edmonton and all the documents needing to be signed were not yet finalized, so we had not received any money yet. It could still take a week to get the money. We went back to the builder and told him our predicament and the whole story on how the Lord had given us the Klondike Dream Home in Edmonton but that no money had changed hands yet.

After hearing our story, he said, "As the builder of your new home, we will make the down payment for you so the lot is secured. When your funds are released, you can simply pay us then and we will start the process of building you your new dream home on the pond."

I realized that God always finishes what he starts. He wants us to stay in faith and keep believing even while doubts and unbelief bombard our mind. He is constantly working on our behalf.

To make a long story short, our beautiful home was built on the pond and we enjoyed the geese, ducks, loons and muskrats for several years. A time would come when God would once again ask us to release this home to continue our journey with him to other peoples and places.

TWENTY-NINE

A Life-Dream Fulfilled—in Lights

In 2007, the Lord slowly began speaking to me about starting up a new business. We had been ministering to the poor and street people in downtown Calgary for nearly six years and we sensed that season was coming to an end. During that time others had started doing the same thing to the point where we knew they could continue the work. Many of them had worked with us and now they wanted to start their own outreach, which was encouraging for us.

Every time the Lord has had me start a new business, he's always had a purpose. We are not responsible to make things succeed. Our business will thrive because the Lord cannot fail—if we follow his directives and are obedient to his promptings.

I was sensing this time he wanted me to reach out to the wealthy people of the city, which made me nervous. I had no idea how to reach people who thought they didn't need the Lord, since they relied on what they possessed, not on God. This was new territory for me but these people were as much God's people as anyone else. They needed the same thing as the poor and the homeless needed, whether they realized it or not—to experience the love of God firsthand. God needed a messenger and this new business was the tool he chose for me to reach out to them. It would also be the way he would enable me to fulfil the desire of my heart.

Both my son and daughter are very gifted in the arts. They are artists and skilled in music. My daughter went all the way to the Royal Conservatory's Grade Ten with her piano skills and is talented in photography as well. My son is recognized as a clothing designer. I had always dreamed of being an artist as well, to express myself in paintings, but I lacked the skills. I always wondered where my children inherited their ability to do what I'd always wanted to do. They surely didn't inherit it from me.

The Lord gave me the desire of my heart, though, through this new business. He told me that he would teach me how to "paint" people's expensive landscapes—with lights. Wealthy people spend thousands upon thousands of dollars on trees, walkways, patios, water features, and flowers. They are only able to enjoy their landscaping during the daylight, but with my lighting they would be able to enjoy it any time of the day or night, all four seasons of the year. Not only that, they could use the lighting for security purposes.

I had much to learn but I knew I had a good teacher. I was very excited to start, even though I didn't really know how. I had no potential customers and no source for lighting products. Although I had been in lighting before with my electrical business and energy-saving products, this was brand new territory and I would have to learn everything about low voltage lighting, transformers and 12-volt systems. I was willing to do anything to become an artist and was sure the Lord would help me find customers. I waited on him for further guidance. Soon he began to let me see his plan for starting the new business.

My son-in-law had a very successful business in building water features for wealthy customers. The water features were quite expensive so they would only be purchased by those who had a lot of money, such as people who could afford large landscaping plans for their estate homes and acreages.

My business began by doing underwater low-voltage lighting for customers that my son-in-law had contracts with. He wanted me to run underground power to the pumps that would operate the water features. After the contract for the water feature was finished, it would become the central focus of their back yards and the remaining landscaping with trees and shrubs would be planted afterwards. When people saw the underwater lighting in their fountains and ponds, they wanted to know if it was possible for me to do lighting for the rest of their landscaping, including all the trees. That is how it all began.

Little by little, other landscapers saw my work and wanted to know if I would be interested in incorporating my lighting with their jobs. I gave them unit prices for the light fixtures, transformers and wire and they would include my lighting in their package deal to the customers.

Ever since 2007, I have worked mostly as a sub-contractor to large landscaping companies and things could not be better. If I had tried to figure out on my own how it could all work while I'm away, I could have never done it, since I didn't even know where to start. Like the electrical business the Lord had given me years before, he was once again bringing me all the customers without my having to look for them.

I continued my artistic "paintings" with the lights, and the Lord continued to give me witty ideas on unique ways of lighting people's yards. I am continually improving each year. I now receive calls on a regular basis from new customers, because they have seen my work at their friends' homes and want the same thing for themselves. I know this is the Lord's doing and I am very grateful for it. The Lord is the best and only salesman a person ever needs. Our part is to use those sales to touch people's lives with his love because so many people out there need to know how much he loves them.

I don't know how long I will continue doing this landscape lighting business, but one thing I do know, I'm loving every minute of it. As long as the Lord wants me to continue painting people's back yards with my lights and touching people's hearts with his love for them, I will be available and willing to do his work.

I also know that whenever he decides this business is over, he will have other projects for me. When he finds someone willing to do his work with him, there is no lack of projects available. In the meantime, as I await my next assignment, I savour and appreciate every moment of every day. Who knows what the future holds? Only my God.

THIRTY

My Introduction to Creative Miracles

I would like to share my first experience with a creative miracle that the Lord allowed me to witness first hand. The difference between a regular miracle and a creative miracle is that you actually see the creative miracle with your natural eyes. Nothing is there and suddenly something appears.

One morning I received a call from a builder who had heard about the work I did and wanted me to go to his acreage as soon as possible to do some lighting before the weekend. He was going to have a huge barbecue at his acreage for customers and friends. Cost was not an issue. The question was whether I could do it and have it finished for the weekend. I had only three days but, most importantly, I needed stock to do the job and delivery on my product usually took a week.

I told him I would have a look at what he needed and get back to him that day. First of all, I would have to go on site to see what was required for the job. After surveying his property and taking stock of which fixtures were needed to do the work, I went back into the city to see what I had in supply. To my delight, I found I had everything that was needed. I called and told him the good news. He immediately gave me the OK to proceed with the job.

I got all the stock together and prepped all the fixtures that afternoon so I could start the job the next morning. This client was one of the biggest builders in Calgary and I knew it would be great advertising for me when his guests saw the lighting I installed on his property.

I got an early start the next morning. When I arrived, the customer was still at home and he greeted me. In his hands he held a blueprint. He said, "I want you to have this so you know exactly where every underground pipe is located, should you have to go under any of the many concrete sidewalks throughout the property. It will save you a lot of time and me a lot of money for your labour." He chuckled and handed me the blueprint.

"If you open it up, I'll show you an area where a four-inch pipe was not put in. As you can see, most of the trees on the other side of the walkway are starting to die because of that one mistake. I've been wanting to dig up the walkway to insert a pipe, but I haven't gotten around to it. It would be great to have those trees lit up, but that will have to wait until I get this work done; but you can do everything else. Every white four-inch pipe location is shown on this blueprint. I personally supervised the work myself so it's really my fault that this one area was missed. I'm gone for the day, so I'll see you when I get back later today. The blueprint is very clear and you shouldn't have any questions. If you happen to need to speak to me, here is my cell phone number." We shook hands and he left for work. I walked towards my service van to start. I knew it would be a whole day affair, but his blueprint would save me valuable time.

Sure enough, the pipe locations were very accurate on the blueprint. As I dug underground to locate them, I found they were either only inches away from the measurements or exactly where shown on the print. It certainly did make my work so much easier.

Toward the end of the day, I had finished all my work, with the exception of that one area where no white pipe had been installed. Suddenly, I heard very clearly in my spirit, "Do that area as well. There is a way to do it."

I went to look at the area that had not been done. The walkway ran from the house to a large building where many vehicles were being stored. The length of the walkway was approximately 200 feet long. I calculated what it would take to get power from the storage building over to the area that needed to be lit, but because of the distance, it would not work for my low voltage lighting.

Then I heard the Lord say, "There is a way across the walkway which is not shown on the blueprint."

Since it was 200 feet in length, there was no way I was going to dig 200 feet to see what was there to get across. I thought, *Maybe there is a hollow area where the gravel didn't fill in and I could possibly fish my wire through that one small place.* I surveyed the both sides of the walkway to see if I could spot anything. I saw nothing, so knew my options wouldn't work. I thought, *With God all things are possible and if he spoke to me about it, that means he has a solution for the problem I'm facing; otherwise why should he say anything?* Then another thought came to me, *Why doesn't he tell me where that area is on the walkway?*

I sat there on the walkway waiting to get more direction and information. The Lord seemed silent. I got up and started walking down the walkway towards the house praying in tongues. When we pray in tongues we are praying God's perfect will and praying about things we don't know. I needed to hear from him or I could be there for hours. After I walked the length of the walkway up to the house, I turned around and started walking back towards the storage barn, continuing to pray in tongues. When I was about thirty feet from the barn, I heard the Spirit of the Lord say, "Right here."

I picked up a small pebble and placed it at the exact location the Lord indicated and continued praying in my prayer language as I walked back towards the house. I turned around again and headed back towards the barn. At approximately the same place I heard the Lord again and sure enough it was about one foot from where I'd placed the pebble. I continue my prayer walk again and this time the Lord stopped me in between the first two places. I decided there must be something there, but what was it? I certainly could not find it on the blueprint as I looked at it for the umpteenth time.

I went over to where I had left my shovel, came back and started to dig. I went down about one foot deep and nothing was there. I went to the other side of the walkway and did the same thing, with the same results. Then I heard the devil say, "This praying in tongues doesn't work. Pack up your things and go home. You're wasting your time."

I knew instantly, without a shadow of a doubt, there was something the devil didn't want me to find. I sat down once again on the walkway and started praising the Lord for his goodness and faithfulness. As I was doing this, I heard in my spirit, "Dig six inches over."

I picked up my shovel to dig. I didn't know in which direction to dig, right or left, so I started to the right and within five minutes I hit something. There was a two-inch black pipe sticking out! I started digging on the other side of the walkway and, sure enough, the other end was there.

I jumped up and started dancing on the walkway, rejoicing and thanking God. I did this for several minutes. Then I looked towards the house and noticed the owner's daughter standing on the walkway, staring at me. All that time I'd thought I was alone on his property. When she saw me looking at her she immediately went back inside the house, undoubtedly wondering who this nut case was dancing alone on the walkway.

When I got over that, I said to the Lord, "What if I had gone six inches in the other direction?"

He answered, "Why don't you try that?"

I thought for sure, I had misunderstood him, but I said to myself, *Why not? It will only take five minutes so what do I have to lose?*

I dug six inches in the opposite direction and hit a second two-inch black pipe. Now, I was not only surprised but confused. Why two pipes? I only needed one for my wires. As I exposed both pipes, to see which one was the easiest to fish my wire through, the Lord spoke to me again, "One pipe for you and your wires and one pipe for him and his much-needed irrigation. I have blessed both of you." The Lord had supernaturally installed two black pipes to bless both of us.

As I was finishing up and picking up my tools, my customer was arriving home from work and walked over towards the walkway near the barn. He asked, "How did it go?"

I said, "Better than expected. I found two extra pipes on your property, one for my wires to light up your dying trees and one for you to run your irrigation to them."

He said, "If they are not on the blueprint, then they do not exist."

I answered "They do now. I took the liberty to mark them on the blueprint with my Sharpie pen, so you can know their location."

He said, "Let me see." When he saw the location, he looked at me and said, "I wonder if somehow I missed marking them on the print...but I doubt it."

I said, "By the way they are not four-inch white pipes like everywhere else; they are black and only two-inch in diameter. They are two-inch plumbing pipes, not four-inch irrigation pipes, but they will work just as well as the others."

"That's not possible, since I would not have allowed those pipes to be put in. How did you ever install those pipes?"

I let him know again that they were already there and as he was writing me a cheque for the job he kept saying, "That is a real mystery."

I said, "No, that is a real miracle."

He replied, "You might be right there after all because there were never any pipes installed there, and even if there had been, I would have only installed one white four-inch irrigation pipe. As I was leaving, he said, "I need to talk to the guy that installed my pipes and get some clarification."

I said, "Let me know if you find out anything." I knew I would not hear back from him about it because the Lord had done a creative miracle. Weeks later, the gentleman asked me if I would have coffee with him. He wanted to know how I had located those two pipes. I told him the whole story about the Lord showing me.

Then he said," Oh! That explains why my daughter was shocked to see you talking and dancing alone for the longest time. By the way she was starting to get concerned when you kept walking back and forth—it seemed to her like forever. I've heard lots of stories in my day, but this one takes the cake. Next time I call you to come over and do work for me, we need to talk more." I gladly agreed.

My drive home took almost an hour. The devil constantly tried to bombard me with doubt and unbelief. He kept telling me the pipes had always been there, yet the customer had assured me they were never installed at all. This creative miracle was new to me and the devil knew that so he tried everything in his power to negate what had happened and what the Lord had done. However, because I chose to stay on the Lord's side and chose to believe him and ignore the devil's lies, soon the devil tired of harassing me.

God allowed me to experience a second creative miracle shortly afterwards. This would help to strengthen my faith in creative miracles as well as prove to me that the devil was nothing but a liar and to beware of his lies when you experience God's goodness in your life.

Monday morning. A new week was starting. As I drove down the road, I wondered what experiences I would have with the Lord this coming week. I always expected the Lord to do new things and he never disappointed me. Whether he did them for me or for others through me, it didn't matter. I was always excited to see what he would do, working to show himself mighty on people's behalf. There is never a dull moment in serving the Lord, when you let him be involved in everything you do. What we can do without him is very limited, but what we can do with him is unlimited. Never leave home without him; he's your everything.

As I was driving down the road to my first job, my service van suddenly stalled. It was all I could do to steer it to the side, out of the way of the traffic following behind me. When I was safely off the road, I tried to see if it would start again, but to no avail. I checked my gas gauge and I still had half a tank, so I knew it wasn't a lack of fuel. I tried several times but always with the same results. I knew it was something serious and since the van could only be diagnosed by computer, I decided to call CAA and because I am a member and towing would be free.

I called them and one of their tow trucks was delivering a vehicle in my community, only a few kilometres away. They told me this was my lucky day and that they would have someone there within fifteen minutes. I had used them before and never had been serviced in under an hour. They are always very busy, but this time was different and I was glad for that, since I had a lot of work to do. The sooner I got to my regular mechanic the better and hopefully he would rectify the problem in a short period of time. As promised, the tow truck arrived within fifteen minutes and we were on our way to the garage. Upon arrival, I told them about my heavy workload that day and asked if they could take a quick peek at my vehicle to see what was wrong. They agreed, much to my relief, because I had no appointment with them and they were always booked days in advance. I knew that the Lord was involved in all of this. The tow truck had been minutes away from where I was located; the garage immediately agreed to look at the van upon arrival.

The tow truck backed my van into the garage next to the diagnostic machine and I was asked to wait in the waiting room until they found out what was wrong. They assured me it would not take long to get the results. Within twenty minutes they asked to see me in the garage. They told me the gas pump was finished and pointed to the diagnostic machine. I would need a new pump installed. I asked them how long it would take and how much it would cost. The cost would be important, because I had just spent a huge amount of money on a large order of materials for my upcoming jobs. They told me they would be able to get a new pump within the hour but it would take most of the day to install it since the fuel pump was located inside the gas tank. I had never heard of this before and thought they were mistaken but that turned out to be the exact location, according to the service manual. Then they said the cost would be approximately $1200.00.

At that moment, I heard the Lord say, "Ask them where the van keys are and start the vehicle." I did and they told me the keys were in the ignition.

I asked, "Could you please close the hood?" Then I heard myself say, "I'm going to start the van and go to work. I have a lot of work to do today."

Two of the mechanics standing there burst into laughter, and said, "Sir, you're not going anywhere because this van won't start without a new fuel pump."

They could see that I was ignoring their comment and walking over to the driver's side of the van and they continued sneering at my remark. I entered the van, turned the key that was in the ignition and immediately the van started. I was almost as surprised as they were but knew that my obedience to the Lord caused that van to start. Their snickering suddenly ceased as they jumped away from the front of the vehicle. I asked them how much I owed them for the diagnosis and they replied, "Nothing. We'll see you back here in a few minutes; you're only running on the gas left in your gas line and carburetor."

I drove out of the garage and went to work, rejoicing the whole way. Three years later my new gas pump, installed by the Lord, kept on working perfectly. That creative miracle caused my faith to jump by leaps and bounds and now whenever I get into impossible situations, the Lord reminds me of it.

I have been back to that mechanic for oil changes and different things like wiper blades. The first time I went back for service, they asked me who had put in a new fuel pump. They remembered the day I drove off with a defective fuel pump. I simply told them, "No, it's running fine." They are probably still scratching their heads trying to figure out that mystery. Some day, if the Lord prompts me to do so, I will tell them the story behind it all. They are probably not ready to hear the truth yet.

THIRTY-ONE

Sell All and Go to Asia

In January 2010, I was in Australia and the Lord spoke to me very clearly. It seems the more important the word is, the more distinctly my spirit picks it up. I had no doubt he was asking me to do something out of the ordinary, something I had never done before. He wanted to make sure I knew he was the one giving me the instructions.

After he told me what to do, I knew it would be the greatest challenge I had ever faced. It involved Joane as much as it did me; she would have to agree to it. I had no idea how Joane would react and I didn't really want to be the one to tell her. It's one thing when the Lord speaks to you about something that concerns you personally; it is a completely different thing when your wife is as much a part of it as you are. How can you ever convey to her what the Lord said and make it as real to her as it was to you?

So I made a deal with the Lord: "You are going to have to tell Joane yourself. I have no idea where to start and knowing my wife all of these years the way that I do, it might not turn out well if I tell her what you told me."

The Lord had said, "I want you to sell the home you have built on the natural pond, the one I gave both of you, as well as all the furniture in it. That will free you to go wherever I ask and stay as long as I need you to stay. You cannot have anything that will tie you down to one place. I want you to be free to go, without being concerned about anything you leave behind. I told you years ago I would have you walk the walk of Abraham. Didn't I take care of all his needs? I will do the same for you, so you don't ever need to be concerned about anything. I will go before you and prepare the way for you."

That sounded reassuring, but still I was firm that he had to let Joane know. In mid-February, we were on vacation. Every morning, Joane and I would walk along the oceanfront to a cafe, approximately five kilometres from the condo in which we stayed. One particular morning, as usual, we chatted about various things as we sipped our coffee and watched the waves roll in to shore.

Suddenly, out of the blue, Joane asked me, "Has the Lord spoken to you about a major change that is about to happen in our lives?"

At first I was a little perplexed at the question, then remembered what the Lord had told me about six weeks ago concerning selling our beautiful home on the pond in Calgary. I wondered, *Has the Lord spoken to her about it as well?*

I said, "Now that you mention it, he told me we would be selling our home and all the furnishings in it. I sense it will happen sooner than later. What do you think about that, and how do you feel about it?"

Since she didn't answer me right away, I kept on talking and told her in detail what the Lord had told me and the assurances he had given me if I obeyed. What came out of her mouth next convinced me the Lord had already spoken to her and it wouldn't be nearly as much of a challenge as I had thought. She said, "I guess when we go back to Calgary, we'd best get cracking and start the process of selling everything we have so we can be free to do his will." I was so relieved that God had prepared her heart before this conversation took place. Now it would simply be a matter of doing what he asked when we got back.

With the Lord in charge, the process went smoothly and once all the furnishings were sold or given away, the house sold. We had fulfilled our part of his request much easier than we had expected. The year before selling the house, at the Lord's instructions, we had left Canada for five months and gone to Asia. There we worked with children at risk, children caught up in the sex trade in both Thailand and Cambodia. After our time in Asia, we went to visit family in Australia and New Zealand. We had been gone for five months and both saw what a financial burden a house can be when you are gone for a long period of time. The logistics of snow removal, insurance, and having someone check the house on a regular basis were very costly. Now we could see why not having a home any longer would give us the freedom to go wherever the Lord sent us. We could stay any place for as long as he needed us there.

We have now worked with the children at risk in Asia since 2009. Every time we go, the ministry we do is different but God continues to direct every step of our way. Even though our assignment there changes each year, we know God helps make those precious orphans become his leaders of tomorrow. When we are back in Canada, we seek financial support from friends, family and customers to meet the needs of the various projects. Also, in the summer in Calgary, I work at my seasonal business six months of the year and this income enables us to pay all expenses incurred when we travel to Asia. All donations received go 100% towards the projects and desperate needs there.

We are presently working on supplying a solar-power system for an orphanage so they will have electricity. Things we take for granted in Canada, such as medical services, education, food, electricity and transportation are non-existent in many poor areas of the Asian nations. One person cannot fix all these problems, but every person who is more fortunate than they are can do something.

We have recently taken on another nation, Myanmar, formerly known as Burma. Their borders have recently been re-opened to foreigners and we were asked to spy out the land to see how the children were treated. The nation had been under military rule for decades, so many children had been forced to become soldiers at a very young age. Some experienced horrific things while fighting. We have now connected with various organizations from Canada, Thailand, Cambodia, Myanmar, Australia and New Zealand. We network together to bring hope to these children who literally have no hope without God. Many positive things are happening. Now many of the children are beginning to see a light at the end of the tunnel. They have hope for a new kind of life, one they never experienced before.

THIRTY-TWO

The Favour of God

One of the most important things we need from the Lord, which goes hand in hand with hearing his voice, is his favour. When we operate and live in the favour of God, we operate in his perfect will for our lives. Before I elaborate on my experience in walking in the favour of the Lord, I want to share with you a very important and exciting thing the Lord told me in 2012.

In 2012, God had me go back to Nova Scotia, the place where I was born, and taught me about his favour. First, I want to take you to a few weeks prior to this event. It all ties in together.

My very good friend, David, and I had gone fishing together for years in Duck Lake in Montana. We always went there because we were never disappointed with the results. We hadn't fished for years, but that summer we decided to go back and continue our adventures. The trout were anywhere from three to six pounds or more and just the fight they gave us when we hooked them was worth it all. We left early Saturday morning before the sun had risen and drove to Montana, anxious to relive the wonderful times we'd had together in the past.

When we got there we immediately put the boat into the water. We could see the white caps on the lake and rain starting to fall but that didn't deter our eagerness to get to our favourite spot where we always fished. As we were heading out, the waves were getting bigger and some of them even splashed over into the boat. But no, nothing was going to stop this fishing trip. We finally reached our favourite spot and put down the anchor, getting our rods ready for action. We immediately noticed that the boat was moving backward because its anchor was not able to hold it in place. Try as we might, nothing would work, so we had to admit defeat and head back to shore. The storm had had its way. We spent the rest of our day in the lodge, where we decided to stay for the night, so we could go out nice and early the next morning. We didn't catch any fish that first day but we were both convinced we would get our limit the next day, maybe even enough for lunch, before heading back home. When we went to bed it was raining and very windy. We prayed that the weather would clear up overnight so that we could get an early start in the morning.

As we woke up before dawn, we could see our prayers had been answered and now it was time to get down to business and accomplish what we had come to do. As the sun came up, we headed out to our favourite spot. This time the lake was so calm it almost looked like a mirror. In no time we had reached our destination. We were both excited because we could see the fish had already started swallowing up all the flies they could catch. We always caught our limit with flies and fly-fishing so my heart started to beat faster as we approached our catch. It was time to give them a taste of our flies. We knew exactly which flies always caught trout and we'd made sure we had an ample supply before we left home. We threw the anchor into the water and it securely attached to the bottom. We were ready for action.

In record time we both had our fishing lines in the water. We could even see the trout circling our boat. Their fins stuck out of the water as they swam by us, munching on all the flies in the water. For some unknown reason, they were not interested in our flies, ones we had successfully used for years. We then decided to see what kind of flies they were eating and even tried many different types that looked close to what they were devouring on the water. Nothing worked. After hours of fishing, we both knew it was useless to continue. The trout were so close to our boat, I could have taken my oar and killed one, which at one point I suggested, but David said that would not be legal. (I still haven't found that rule in the fishing guide.)

So we came home empty handed and disappointed. The outcome of that trip was puzzling to me for weeks. I had been so excited to fish once again, the sport I enjoy the most, but the results were baffling to me. Why would the Lord allow me to go fishing somewhere, where we had always been successful, and let me come home empty handed?

That brings me back to what happened between the Lord and me in 2012. While I was home in Calgary one morning, as I was getting ready for work, the Lord spoke to me and said, "I am bringing you into a season of fog. Without faith it is *impossible* to please me." He seemed to stress the word "impossible."

I knew it was the Lord; I also knew I didn't have a clue what he was talking about, except for the faith part. When that happens, I usually ask the Lord to elaborate a little so I know what he's talking about. He has always answered my request and clarified his words for me. About ten minutes later, I was in our washroom and it was as though the Lord took me back to Nova Scotia, where I relived my lobster fishing day trips on the ocean with my uncle. We would leave at 3:30 AM. We had 600 lobster traps to pull up before returning to shore with our catch around 10:30 AM.

What came back to memory was how the fog would roll in unexpectedly and by the time we were ready to head back into the harbour, we couldn't see twenty feet in front of our boat. I remembered being so afraid we would never find our way back home. My uncle would take out his compass and head in the general direction of the harbour. As he approached closer to shore he would point into the fog with his finger and show me the beam of the lighthouse cutting through the fog. That was his assurance that he was going in the right direction. We always made it into the harbour safely, even though we had a narrow path to follow, because of rocks along the shoreline and at the mouth of the harbour. I was always amazed how he was able to do that every time, without incident. As I relived that lobster fishing trip, I thought the Lord was bringing me into a season of "fog," meaning I would have to rely on him completely without seeing where I was going, in order for me to do the things he had prepared for me. Now I would have to wait for the details.

Several weeks later, while checking my emails early in the morning, I saw I had received one from my American supplier from whom I bought all my products for my seasonal business. It read that I had been their "Diamond Elite Distributor" in Alberta for five consecutive years. I thought, *Whatever does "Diamond Elite" mean?* They said I would also be officially made a member of their President's Club, which would give me free products and other perks every year. Because of this, they were inviting me to spend three days at their head office in Cleveland, Ohio, all expenses paid.

They also wanted to know if I would like to go on a one-day fishing trip on one of the Great Lakes. If I did, they would arrange it. There were only seventeen of us invited to their head office in Cleveland. They suspected the others would probably want to go golfing, but they would arrange a fishing trip for me if I wanted to go. Immediately, I knew the Lord was involved so I said yes to their invitation. The Lord knew how disappointed I had been after my fishing trip in Duck Lake and I was sure this was the way he planned to surprise me.

I was eager to go because of the fishing trip. Any fishing trip the Lord organized would be great. I answered them and said I wanted to go fishing and not golfing. Within a week I received my airline e-ticket and the confirmation that four other men and I were booked for a fishing trip on Lake Erie. Attached to the e-mail was a form to use for every expense I would incur for this trip including airport parking, gasoline, taxi, coffee, etc. All I had to do was attach the receipts and claim my expenses after my return home. I would be leaving the following month and I was very excited. Whatever else happened would be secondary in importance to the organized fishing trip. The day of departure finally arrived and off I flew to Cleveland, Ohio.

Upon my arrival, someone met me with my name in bold print on a placard. I was taken to my hotel in a luxury vehicle and given ten minutes to change and join everyone at the bar in the hotel lobby for free food and drinks. An hour later, we were all boarding a luxury bus for the first of many surprise dinners in Cleveland. Our destination was about thirty minutes from the hotel and as we pulled into the parking lot I noticed a huge glass pyramid in front of us. We had arrived at the Cleveland Rock and Roll Museum and were ushered inside. There in the entrance they had set up a bar, a stage and tables with white tablecloths. They had arranged a buffet-type meal and, without exaggeration, everything you could desire was available at that buffet. I had seen many buffets but nothing like this one. I even noticed fresh oysters on ice, lobster, and caviar. What a feast!

The first hour would be free drinks and then dinner would start. During that hour a professional band had been hired for our entertainment. Of course, being a Rock and Roll Museum, that was the type of music they were playing. This museum usually opened to the public every night, but this particular evening it was a private function just for us. The company had hired and paid for the staff to stay that night so that they could answer any questions we had and show us around. There were many floors to this museum and many things to see. I was completely blown away with their hospitality towards us.

I remember going to the bar and ordering a glass of red wine and gave the black gentleman a tip. After I sat down at my table with the others I noticed something peculiar. Whenever the others at the table wanted another drink they would have to go back to the bar and get it, but for some reason, every time my glass was half full, the barman would leave the bar and come and serve me at my table. The others at the table found this strange. They asked me if I knew this barman and I said no. I then remembered I had given him a tip and that was probably why he was serving me and not them. This intrigued me so much that before the buffet started, I went up to him and asked him why he had been serving me and not the others. He said, "You're the only one that treats me like your equal and doesn't look down at me. You took the time to see how I was doing and you were genuinely interested in my life and what I did. You are different than all the others and therefore deserve better service." I was floored. I hadn't noticed that I had been different towards him than the others had been.

It was time for the buffet and usually people eat too much at a buffet, but I thought I would make an exception in this case and just try a little of all that was offered. It was a feast at its best. After dinner I spent hours seeing and hearing many things throughout the museum. It had been a fantastic evening. Around 11:00 p.m. we were asked to hop on the bus and return to the hotel. The next morning we would have to get up at 5:00 to board another luxury bus in order to go fishing. Four of us were going fishing along with one member of management. The others had opted for a day of golf. Why they had hired a large luxury bus for six people, including the driver, I don't know, but that is what they did. I had a problem falling asleep that evening, just thinking about the fishing trip the next day. Before I knew it, my wake-up call from the hotel rang. It was the first time in a long time that an alarm was music to my ears. I showered and dressed in record time and waited in the hotel lobby for everyone else that was coming to show up. They had prepared six hot individual breakfasts which we would eat on the bus. We found out it was an hour-long trip to the chartered fishing boat and we would have ample time to eat our food on the way there.

As we walked out of the lobby outside towards the bus, we noticed it was starting to rain and the wind was picking up. Several wailed, "Oh no!" as they headed towards the bus. I was instantly taken back to Duck Lake where the rain and wind had stopped my last fishing trip from being a success. I desperately tried to erase that picture from my memory but as we drove towards the chartered boat the weather got worse instead of better. I sat by the window and tried to enjoy the scenery on our way as daylight slowly came into view. I was looking at all the different high-rise buildings and their brightly-lit signs when suddenly this one sign really caught my attention. Up on top of a high rise building was a bright neon sign that read "FOGG."

The minute I saw the sign the Lord spoke to me and said, "When I told you some time ago I was bringing you into a season of the fog, this is what I meant. The word 'fog' you heard stands for the 'Favour Of God.' You are entering a new season of my favour where you will have to trust me 100%, no matter what the circumstances look like around you. In the same way your uncle trusted that lighthouse 100% to bring him to the harbour, I have allowed you to be on this trip in Cleveland to experience firsthand my favour (FOG) for you. You will experience my favour throughout the whole trip. Your first test will be this fishing trip."

At that point, I knew he had brought me here to bless me and it would be up to me whether I would experience his favour or not. I would have to trust him, my lighthouse, 100% and not go by what I heard or saw before me. I knew I was in for a surprise and couldn't wait to see what he was going to do for me.

I reflected back on the night before at the Rock and Roll Museum and realized that the service I had received from the waiter was the beginning of God's favour on this trip.

We arrived at the dock and fog had set in. It was hard even to see the boat anchored there. The rain had subsided somewhat but the wind had picked up. The captain and his helper were waiting for our arrival. As we stepped off the bus, the first thing that came out of the captain's mouth was, "Guys, it doesn't look good for fishing today at all." Everyone gathered together to discuss the situation but no one could agree on what should be done. I remembered what the Lord had told me on the bus so I left the group and climbed aboard the fishing boat. As each of the men continued to give their opinions, I shouted back at them from the boat. "Hey guys, let's go fishing. That's what we came here for, isn't it?"

The captain looked back at me, as well as the others. He walked up to me and said. "I can tell you are not from here. When we have this kind of weather here, we don't usually go out fishing. It's too dangerous."

I said to him, "How long does it take to get out to our fishing spot?"

He replied, "About thirty-five minutes."

So I said to him, "For your information, I have fished most of my life. I was born right on the ocean in Nova Scotia, and like everywhere else, the weather can change in a hurry. So, why don't we start going out and if it doesn't get better or starts to get worse, we can always turn around and come back. I know we are to go out fishing and I know things will be OK. You'll see."

The captain snapped back at me, "The rest of us have no assurance, but you think things will be OK."

I answered, "Oh yes, I do. The Lord told me we would go fishing today and have a wonderful fishing trip, and I choose to believe him."

He sneered at what I said, walked back to the others and said sarcastically, "Let's do what this avid fisherman from Canada says and start out to our fishing spot. If the weather doesn't improve we can always turn around and come back to shore. What do you say? I won't mention something else that guy said that didn't make any sense. You can ask him yourself. What do you think, guys?"

Everyone agreed, got on board and seemed happy with the decision. I couldn't wait to see what the Lord was about to do to show himself mighty on our behalf.

The fog was so bad upon departure that the captain had his helper stand on the front of the boat to help give him directions. We hadn't left the shore more than ten minutes when the rain completely stopped, the wind dropped down to a gentle breeze and the clouds parted. There for everyone to see, the sun showed its face. The captain looked back at me and said, "You need to come with us on all our fishing trips. You're our good luck charm, my friend."

I replied for everyone to hear, "No, it has nothing to do with me; it has to do with what I told you about the Lord, before we left shore. It's because of him."

He quickly changed the subject and started to give everyone instructions on how the fishing would proceed and how we would all have turns taking in the fish that were on the line. We would fish using outriggers, with six lines on either side of the boat. I had never fished like this before and couldn't wait to see how it would work out. Before I knew it, we had reached our destination, and the captain looked at me and said, "Hey, you from Canada, for your information, we are going to be fishing about 100 yards from the Canadian border right over there."

I didn't realize there was a border on Lake Erie and yelled back to him, "That's great. Then I'll call the fish over to our side of the border and that way we can catch our limit."

To my surprise he said, "It worked with the weather; maybe it will work with the fish as well." He laughed and started setting up the twelve lines on both outriggers. I had to give him credit. The way he managed it worked really well because none of our lines became tangled. All the fishing poles were in their separate sleeves on each side of the boat, each line attached to the outrigger about six feet apart. Whenever a fish would bite, he yanked the pole out of its sleeve, gave it a jerk to make sure the fish was still on and then handed it to the next person, everyone taking his turn. It was the best setup I had ever seen and I had been on a lot of fishing trips.

It wasn't long before the fish started to bite, but unfortunately, we were not catching the fish we wanted, so the captain said, "Don't worry, we will just start fishing at a different depth." No sooner said than we were at another depth, and within minutes were starting to catch the fish we had gone out there to catch. We were so busy, taking our turns in line that within three hours we had to stop fishing because we had reached our limit. Even as they were pulling in all the lines, fish kept biting and when the lines were all in we had five fish over our limit. The captain called another fishing boat over and gave them the five fish. They were shocked that we had caught our limit in less than three hours. They had never seen that before.

Everyone was happy and on our way back, the captain looked at me and said, "Are you sure you're not looking for another job? We'll hire you today."

The Lord had showed himself mighty on my behalf as promised. It hit me like a ton of bricks that whenever you walk in the favour of God, everyone with you benefits from it, even though the Lord did it for you. God is so good. On the entire trip back to shore, the only thing that was talked about was the sudden change of weather and the miraculous catch of fish. God was being glorified.

When we reached the shore, the miraculous catch was taken out of the boat, some 250 pounds of beautiful fresh fish. There were three men there to clean the fish, filet it and pack it in five-pound bags. We decided to share our catch with all seventeen people who had been invited to the headquarters in Cleveland. Everyone received a portion of the catch whether they had fished or not. It was vacuumed-sealed and instantly put on dry ice and shipped to everyone's destination, so that when they arrived home the next day, it would be waiting for them at the airport. I had never experienced such favour. I have all the pictures of this fishing trip, including the fog at the dock, the rain and wind, the skies clearing up on our way out to fish, the miraculous catch of fish, all 250 pounds. I sit and reflect on the goodness of God as I look at these pictures over and over again so I don't forget I'm living and walking in his season of FOG (the Favour of God).

We returned to our hotel in the afternoon to rest from our fishing trip. That evening as we visited and got to know everyone, we were told to board another luxury bus that would take all of us to our second surprise dinner. We were to be in the lobby ready to leave at 6:00 a.m. sharp. No one was late and we all boarded the bus. Within half an hour we were at our destination and when the bus parked, we noticed we were in front of a dinner theatre. There was a sign on the front of the building advertising a famous comedian from the USA. He would be performing there on the weekend, and anyone wanting to see his show needed to get tickets as soon as possible. It was a Tuesday evening so we all wondered who was playing tonight. When we entered the building we found out that the dinner theatres are only held on weekends. We were brought to our tables and served drinks and entrees. At my table the men kept talking about this comedian who would be there that weekend and everyone was wondering if there were any tickets left so they sent someone off to go find out. This comedian was famous in the USA and in great demand. Personally, I had never heard of him before and still don't remember his name.

When the gentleman arrived back to our table, he told us there were some tickets left but not many choice seats. Most people at the table said they could not attend anyway because they were returning home. A few at the other tables decided to stay the extra days to catch his show on the weekend.

I said to myself, *This guy must be really popular,* and wondered why I had never heard of him before in Canada.

Before I was able to ask any more questions, a man from management went up to a mic on a stage. He asked how everyone had enjoyed their time so far and of course everyone clapped. Then he announced something that shocked us all. He said, "We just want to let you know that a famous comedian who is at the dinner theatre this weekend is here with us tonight. We have flown him here early so that he could be with us and do his show. We have put him up in a hotel for three nights so he could entertain us tonight at this private dinner."

The crowd went wild. Everyone seemed to know him but me. Suddenly he appeared on the stage and began his act. As a comedian, he got the audience involved, which made it much more entertaining. I must say, he put on a spectacular show and everyone was thrilled with his performance, even me. He went on for about ninety minutes with another fifteen minutes of encores. One of these days I should find out what his name was.

We had a wonderful steak dinner with all the trimmings during the show and after a long day of fishing and getting up at the crack of dawn, I was ready for bed. It was back into the bus and back to our hotel. The next morning would also be an early wake-up call. We would be meeting all of the management team in the hotel conference room—engineers, product managers and sales managers would be present to introduce all their new products coming out the following year. They would also answer any of the questions we might have regarding the future of the company and new products soon to be on the market.

They would also address the problems we were encountering in the field with their products. I was really looking forward to that meeting so I decided to go to bed the minute the bus arrived at the hotel, which I did.

That would be our last day in Cleveland, and after the morning meetings we would once again board the bus, only with our luggage, and proceed to their head office for lunch. There we would meet the CEO, President and Vice-President. On the way to the head office, we found out they had 506 employees working there, which meant it must be a pretty big place, since we were told the warehouse alone was the size of one and a half football fields. I couldn't wait to see their operation.

On the way we also found out they had two other offices in the U.S., as well as a manufacturing plant in China. Quite impressive. Within a few minutes of receiving all this information, we arrived at their premises. Their sign was the give-away. The bus pulled up right in the front of the main walkway leading to the front entrance. To our surprise, a red carpet had been laid down on the entire walkway. There to meet us at the bus were six employees who asked us to follow them into the building. The seventeen of us followed them into the main entrance.

Upon entering the reception area, another group of employees waited for us with smiles on their faces as they welcomed us by clapping continuously. We noticed that the red carpet continued to a large double door where we were directed to enter. As the doors opened we saw a wide corridor going throughout the building, which must have been at least 200 feet in length. On both sides of the carpet hundreds of employees clapped as we entered and continued down the red carpet. It was an overwhelming feeling and tears started to well up in my eyes. On both walls on either side of the carpet I saw they had made huge banners of our names and company names and in bold print, it said "Thank You, Thank You" several times. "We appreciate the business you give us. Thank You."

I had never been so honoured in all my life and I was so thankful to the Lord for his favour.

Even though everyone present was benefiting from the company's generosity, hospitality and honour, there was no doubt in my mind that the Lord had done all of this to show me his favour and to fulfil his word to me, when he told me on my first bus ride, "I have you on this trip to Cleveland to demonstrate my favour to you."

We had a wonderful lunch in their massive cafeteria and all the big brass were sitting at a long table that was set up especially to honour us. A visit to their impressive warehouse before heading back home was the icing on the cake. Their complete warehouse operation was computerized and robots picked up the orders that came in. The aisles were hundreds of feet long and about 65 feet high. Stock was delivered daily by semi-trucks from their plant in China as it arrived by ship. This would be a trip to live in my memory for years to come.

That day as I arrived back into Calgary, as promised, at the airport was the fresh fish I had caught the day before. It was almost like a fantasy, but I knew in my heart who had orchestrated it all, just for little old me. What an expression of God's love for me. What an experience of his supernatural favour. Within ten days, I had also been reimbursed all of the expenses I had incurred.

I wondered how long I would continue experiencing the FOG as I returned back to my daily work in Calgary. I continued to complete my lighting contracts, knowing that before long, we would once again be leaving for overseas to work with children. I had pondered the favour of God and wondered if I would continue to experience it.

I got my answer. I was now working ten to twelve hours a day, six days a week in order to get all my work done before leaving for five months. By the time we were approaching our departure, I was completely exhausted and really needed a rest before arriving in Asia, so we decided we would take a two-week cruise to Hawaii and board a plane for Asia from Los Angeles when we arrived back. We would be well rested by then.

A day before our departure from Calgary for our cruise, I received a call from one of my customers who said she needed me to check her lighting system before she left for her holidays. She had been a good customer for years so I decided I would quickly check things out for her before she left. Upon arrival at her estate, she informed me that she had a condo on the beach in Maui, Hawaii and she was going there for a few months. I told her we were going on a cruise and would be visiting all the islands and would be in Maui for a day in about a week from now. She said, "Why don't you come and spend the day with me at my condo?"

I told her our friends would be with us and that there would be four of us on the cruise. She said, "Bring them along as well if you wish."

God's favour further enabled us to get a room on the cruise ship with a balcony for approximately forty percent less than the regular price. In December, with Christmas holidays around the corner, cruises were not usually discounted. We knew God was graciously giving us not only a much-needed rest before leaving to do his work in Asia but other miracles as well.

My customer had a taxi waiting for us at the cruise ship upon our arrival. She lived on the other side of the island of Maui so it took us an hour to get to her place. She had all the chairs, food and paddleboards waiting for us and had planned our entire day. We all had a wonderful time together. The taxi took us back to the cruise ship at the end of the day and we were off to our next island that night.

After a wonderful cruise we arrived in Los Angeles well rested and ready to go to Australia, New Zealand, and Asia. God's favour continued to accompany us through the whole journey.

I had been looking at starting an online business with a product line I had seen at the World Trade Show in Hong Kong. I had met a gentleman and his wife at the show who had started the same online business in Australia where he lived. In the three days we were there, we became good friends. He and his wife invited Joane and me to visit them at their home in Cairns, near the Great Barrier Reef, during our stay in Australia. We did and during our stay there, he showed me how he had set up his business online. He said he would help me do the same in Canada. I would be able to buy directly from the manufacturer in China as he did. We left Australia and headed to Asia to work with the children at risk.

During the time we were there helping with the children, little did I know that my friend from Cairns was busy setting up a complete Canadian website for me, free of charge. It would take another six chapters to share all the things God did in those five months and still does up to this day. Maybe it will have to be in another book in the future. For now, we are experiencing, on a daily basis, God's loving favour. We simply listen for his voice and obey his directives.

THIRTY-THREE

Secrets to Hearing God's Voice

I want to answer one of the most frequent questions I receive from people who hear my testimony about my walk with God over all these years. They say, "Why do I not hear the voice of God the way you seem to?"

That question puzzled me for years since I had never struggled in that area, even before I gave my life to him—although I didn't know it was he who was speaking.

I would like to share a few key things I have learned. Have you ever asked someone you know quite well to do something for you, but they always seem to be too busy with their own things? After asking them again and again at different times to help you and their answer is always the same, you stop asking them. On the other hand, you have friends who are always willing to do something for you. They make time and go out of their way to help you. When you have such people in your life, whom do you call when you need help? Of course you call the available friends, because you know they will be there for you.

We have a couple such as this in our lives. Not everyone is as blessed. Let's take that same example and see how it concerns hearing the voice of God.

Did you know it's possible to have a quiet time with the Lord every morning and still not be available to him? When you are truly available for someone, you are available for him all the time. We should allow the Lord to re-order our time any way he wants.

If you are always available for him, you will always be at the right place at the right time.

I don't know if you ever noticed this, but Jesus was never in a hurry. He never needed more time, because he was available for his Father's desires, not his. All his time belonged to the Father. The Lord helped me understand this about time, and I still remember when he asked me not to wear a watch—for over five years. It took me that long to break the habit of owning and controlling my own time. It was a hard lesson to learn, but I'm glad I finally passed the test of "time." True friends make themselves available. Jesus doesn't want us to be servants, but friends. There are different levels of friendships, just as there are different levels of availability.

For instance, not all your friends have your personal cell phone number. Our home number is listed in the phone directory but we let people know what hours we are available. Then there are a few close friends that have the freedom to call us any time of day. The deeper the friendship, the more our availability to them. I believe the Lord is most available to those that are most available to him.

In true friendships, availability is a two-way street. If we desire a deeper relationship and friendship with the Lord, it is important for us to cultivate (it doesn't happen automatically) a state of mind where we view our time as God's time, which means we are totally available to him 24/7. Some of the ways he chooses to test our availability can be annoying. He can ask something of us at the most inopportune, most inconvenient time. Has your availability ever been tested in the middle of the night, when you are sound asleep? Has he asked you to stop doing what you are doing, at your busiest time of the day, and do something for him? Has he ever asked you to go somewhere for him, when you were going in a completely different direction?

With his disciples, when Jesus called and appointed them, he made it very clear to them that their first commitment was not their ministry for him, but rather their availability to him (Mark 3:13-15). I am convinced, through personal experience, availability to the Lord is the first prerequisite for hearing His voice. James 4:8 says, "Draw near to the Lord and he will draw near to you." In other words, make yourself available to him at all times and he will make himself available to you at all times.

Second, it is one thing to be available to the Lord, but another thing to be willing to do what he desires. The chances of hearing God's voice are increased for those who are willing to do whatever he asks. One of the reasons Jesus heard his Father's voice better than anyone else was his utter obedience to this principle. Jesus said, "By myself I can do nothing; I judge only as I hear, and my judgement is just, for I seek not to please myself" (in other words, do my own will) "but the will of him who sent me" (John 5:30).

God looks on the heart, and when he sees that we are truly willing to do whatever he asks, our chances of hearing from him are increased. Why would he speak to us if he knew we would not do what he asks? Jesus said, "I have come to do your will, O God" (Hebrews 10:7). When you get to the point in your life where you want to do only his will, no matter what anyone else says— yes, even if it means the disapproval of friends and family members—you will be able to hear him clearly tell you his will.

Believe me, it is not easy sometimes, because often it contradicts what we want and what other people think. Jesus' obedience to the Father's voice led him to much rejection during his ministry. It won't be any different for you, but your reward is great! You will be hearing the voice of the one you love the most and the one you want to please the most. It takes faith to accomplish but the simple question to answer honestly is,

"Would you rather please God or man?" We have been given a free will to choose.

Finally, I want to elaborate on the third important requisite in helping you to hear the voice of God and that is humility. James 4:6 says, "The Lord resists the proud, but gives grace (his strength and abilities) to the humble." The opposite of humility is pride and we all struggle with it, whether we like to admit it or not. What we do with it determines the outcome. The more the Lord works in and through you, allowing you to receive more and more of his revelation and power, the more vulnerable you are to pride trying to come into your life. How you see yourself will determine whether you are operating in pride or humility.

While studying at Rhema Bible Training Centre in Tulsa, Oklahoma, I remember the first sermon I had to preach. Everyone had to prepare a sermon and deliver it in class. This sermon dealt with humility. My three point sermon (as we were taught) was this: 1) Apart from him I can do nothing; 2) Apart from him I am nobody; and 3) Apart from him I know nothing. But the conclusion was that in him and through him I can do all things. I am more than a conqueror. I have access to his wisdom and knowledge. When I know that truth, it will set me free.

The best definition I have found in the Bible for humility is what God said to King Saul in 1 Samuel 15:17: "You once were small in your own eyes." That was Samuel's rebuke to Saul. Being small in your own eyes doesn't mean you think you are worthless or that you have no abilities, but rather you have a profound distrust of your own abilities and goodness. You realize that when you operate in God's grace you operate in his strength and ability. Your abilities are limited, his are unlimited. We can tap into his abilities, whenever we are willing to cooperate with Him.

I have said many, many times and still continue to say it today: if you are not sure whether it was God speaking to you or some other voice, including your own mind, there is a plumb line, there is a foolproof way of knowing.

If you can do it on your own, then you don't need him to do it. If you don't want to do it, it's because you don't think he can do it through you. When the Lord speaks to you, you always need his help to accomplish it. Humble people know, without a shadow of a doubt, that neither their physical strength (Prov.21: 31) nor their intelligence (Prov.16: 9) or so-called "luck" (Prov. 16:23) gets the job done. Instead it is the Lord who always determines the outcome.

Humble people put their confidence in the Holy Spirit to speak to them, not in their ability to hear. They put their confidence in the Lord's ability to lead them, not in their ability to follow.

Humble people are willing to associate with and serve people in low positions. They enjoy associating with the lowly. A sobering verse in the Bible sums it up beautifully. Psalm 138:6 says, "Though the Lord is on high, he looks upon the lowly, but the proud he knows from afar."

In other words, God wants to be intimate with the humble, but he keeps the arrogant at a distance. I reiterate: one of the key elements to hearing the voice of God is humility. Humility is the pathway to intimacy (a one-on-one relationship with the Lord) but arrogance and pride lead to a spiritual desert in our lives.

Jesus rebuked the sins of men while on earth and the greatest rebukes he made was not against the openly sinful, but to the hypocrites and spiritually proud. Unfortunately today, that is still prevalent in the church. We reward proud leaders, laugh at arrogant humour and look down at those outside our religious circle. Churches lack supernatural revelation and power because of their pride. If we are ever going to hear God's voice, we have no choice but to embrace humility. If we ever decide to make ourselves completely available to the Lord, are willing to do whatever he asks us to do and if we set our hearts to pursue humility seriously, he will speak to us. We will definitely hear his voice.

The outcome is his responsibility not ours. My advice is simply to listen for God's voice and obey his directives. Our only responsibility after hearing his voice is to obey him. He will do the rest.

We all hear voices. The question is: "Which one are you listening to?" cre

Yawn Schare Sept 13 to 23
Eph 4 - 16   Sept 13/2015
This week is First fruits
Asking God for Advance
year of Visitations the Moment
Break Through and Anglic angels

43432810R00169

Made in the USA
Charleston, SC
28 June 2015